For the Patchogue-Medford
Library,
And its Director, Judy
Gibbard,

with Admiration.

Jeffrey Potter

June, 1991

DISASTER BY OIL

Oil Spills:
Why They Happen
What They Do
How We Can End Them

JEFFREY POTTER

(Long Island author)

Copyright © 1973 by *Jeffrey Potter*

The Macmillan Company
866 Third Avenue, New York, N.Y. 10022
Collier-Macmillan Canada Ltd., Toronto, Ontario

Library of Congress Catalog Card Number: 72-85183

First Printing

Printed in the United States of America

FOR

R. H. HORATIO POTTER

CONTENTS

ACKNOWLEDGMENTS

To list all those who have helped make this work possible would deny them suitable recognition. I extend to them my sincere appreciation and the hope that they will find justification herein for their cooperation and trust.

It has meant much to share with them concern for the future of all of us and for those who come after us.

East Hampton, N.Y.

JEFFREY POTTER

PREFACE

Oil and water have been meeting for as long as each has been, but they still don't mix. They do work together, though—oil soothes water, saving many a stricken vessel, and water supports oil, keeping the sea floor from becoming deep in the stuff.

There are those who claim that time and tide can cure even the biggest oil spills, and they like to point out that in spite of the pollution caused by uncounted oil tanker and drilling platform disasters, the sea is still there. As to the other major cause of marine oil pollution—the ever-present oil slick—these old-timers say that ships' engineers have always discharged bilge water and tank washings over the side, pumpmen have always overflowed cargo and blown lines, and platforms have always had blowouts and fractured well casings, yet we are still here.

Most of us hear what these views are really saying—death cures all—and we know that not much has been learned about the effects of marine pollution accumulation. But we can make a good guess: unless a way is found to keep oil and water apart, or when they do get together of separating them as effectively as baby oil removes crude oil from our feet and from the feathers of birds, the sea may not be there, or we here. For oil pollution can still all that lives above, on, in and under the sea.

In spite of warnings that we can't demand more oil to serve us without expecting more to threaten us, many experts believe that we can have our oil and control it too. Consumers can find the will, but it will cost them money; producers can find the means, but it will cost them privilege. Is it worth it? Yes, for we can still be here, and the sea can still be there.

DISASTER BY OIL

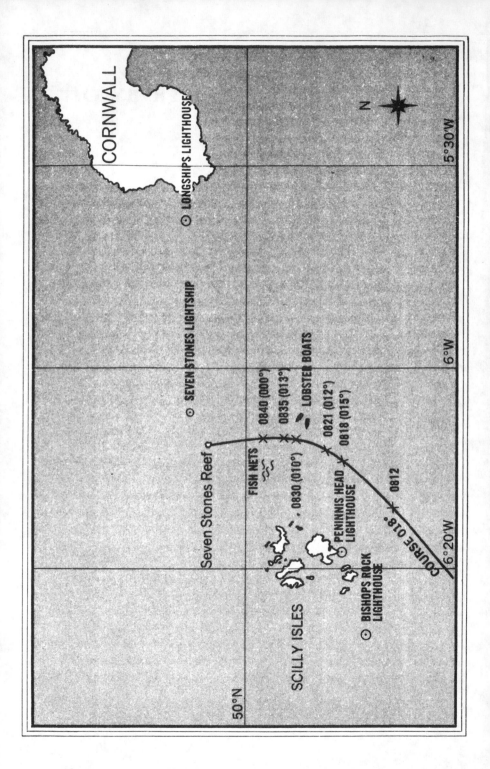

"STANDING INTO DANGER"

The S.S. Torrey Canyon *Stranding*

CAPTAINS WHO LOSE their ships, according to a legend from the days of sail, are tried by an admiralty court at the bottom of the sea. The jury in these submerged halls of justice is composed of seamen called from watery graves, and the bench, graced by the latest late cabin boy, sentences the guilty master to a hulk on a far, dead sea. His cargo is the memory of those whose lives he lost, for wind he has the curses of their next of kin, and his landfall is never.

Such a court today might be less interested in fixing the blame for loss of life at sea than for loss of the sea's life, but either concern would warrant its trying a case known as the *Torrey Canyon* stranding. On March 18, 1967, the S.S. (Screw Steamer) *Torrey Canyon*, a supertanker, became one of the more than 250 wrecks that have been claimed by the Scilly Isles,

1

21 miles off Cornwall's Lands End. On a clear morning just before eight and in a moderate sea with light wind, she drove herself at full service speed on Pollard Rock, largest of the Seven Stones Shoal. So unbelievable was this stranding, more than a quarter of an hour passed before the crew of a nearby lightship thought to warn her off. Then they fired rockets and signaled by flag and lamp: YOU ARE STANDING INTO DANGER.

Those aboard the *Torrey Canyon* knew that whatever had caused the shuddering crash that knocked some off their feet, it wasn't an explosion, a fear that swims with tankers as pilot fish with sharks. They also knew that their cargo of 119,000 tons of Kuwait crude oil was spewing from her wrecked tanks, but they didn't know that this black gelatinous discharge from the bowels of the earth, already working itself downwind with the lazy confidence of death, was to change the ways of oil tankers and a lot of other things too. Before it was done, a couple of seldom used words—ecology and environment—became clichés, another—pollution—became a topic for kindergartners, and the world had begun to wonder how much of our living space is to become dying space. For she was a sea killer, the *Torrey Canyon*, and she would be known for it by all who find meaning in the sands, the rocks and the crash of surf.

"She was only a ship, the *Torrey*," says an able-bodied seaman who served on her, "not the demon they make her out ashore."

If not a demon, monster will do. And as with monsters, everything about her was big. She was named for one of the world's biggest oil-producing fields, and this California tract was itself named for a New York physician, John Torrey, who was also a geologist, U.S. assayer, mineralogist, chemist and botanist. Since he died in 1875, he was saved from knowing his name was borne by a vessel that caused so much ecological damage that the final bill isn't in and never will be, there being no way to price the items of loss or to count them. The *Torrey Canyon* was the thirteenth biggest vessel in the world (a rating as disturbing to the superstitious mariner as her master's having been in mourning and in command for just a year and a day), she was the biggest ship ever lost, carried the most cargo ever lost, caused the most environmental damage, and was the cause of both the biggest oil spill in history and the most expensive to clean up and explain away. She was owned by a Liberian corporation with a Bermuda address which there is reason to believe was controlled by a California oil producer, financed by a New York investment house, American-built, Japanese-enlarged (through a technique known as "jumboizing"), Italian-manned, British-chartered, and was carrying a Middle East cargo to a Welsh port.

When launched by the Newport News Shipbuilding and Dry Dock Corporation in 1959 for the Barracuda Tanker Corporation, the owner of record if not ultimate fact, she was a single-screw, twin-steam, turbine-drive tanker of about 67,000 tons deadweight. Known as DWT, deadweight tonnage is the measure in tons of 2,240 pounds of all that a vessel is designed to carry, including her equipment, ballast, bunkers (fuel, a holdover from the coal-burning days), stores, cargo and crew. She measured (without going into overall dimensions, summer waterline or draft calculations) 810 feet long, 104 feet wide (beam) and 46 feet deep. Fully loaded with 470,000 barrels of oil, her service speed was 17 knots (1 knot equals 1.32 land miles), she cost $17,418,000, and she was a credit to her designers, builders and owners.

Lloyd's Register of British and Foreign Shipping, the oldest and foremost maritime classification society (now separate from but in frequent contact with the underwriting Lloyd's), saw to it that she met their highest standards. A resident Lloyd's surveyor, who inspected her construction daily, was satisfied with her.

"If the yard made any mistakes with the *Torrey Canyon*," he says, "they were honest ones. I can certify to that."

Lloyd's highest classification was granted her again after being jumboized, and if the society rated foreign-licensed masters as they do vessels, the *Torrey Canyon's* captain would have received the equivalent of his command's rating. Captain Pastrengo Rugiati was proud both of his ship and of his employers, which he identified less as Barracuda Tanker than as Union Oil Company of California. While Union's officers maintain that Barracuda is a separate entity, the trade sees them as one and Captain Rugiati was hired by the Consulich Company of Genoa, Union's shipping agents, in 1963.

Born at Elba in 1911, the son of a noncommissioned officer in the Carabinieri who became a steel mill foreman, Captain Rugiati's introduction to a disciplined life of service began with youthful membership in the Young Fascist League. After training for the Italian Navy, he saw service on a dreadnought, and then, transferring to the Merchant Marine, he served on a cargo vessel. During the Abyssinian War he held a second mate's berth on a transport, and becoming a favorite of the master, was presented with the latter's silver maneuvering whistle on signing off. It must have felt at home in the *Torrey Canyon* disaster, for the transport's master had had it with him when his vessel, too, was claimed by the Scillies.

Although Captain Rugiati received his master's license in 1936, it was over fifteen years before he earned command. In World War II, he served as a sublieutenant on a submarine, later seeing service on a destroyer. His first command was a Liberty ship, a tired one, and with the exception of sailing as chief officer on the liner *Homeric*, he held command from then on. Included were a couple of U.S.-built T-2 tankers, 16,000-DWT vessels which earned a name for themselves in World War II, and a modern 32,000-DWT tanker. On joining Union Oil, he was given a sister ship of the *Torrey Canyon*, the *Lake Poularde*, of Liberian registry. Captain Rugiati's Italian certificate qualified him for a Liberian master's license, and he sailed the Persian Gulf–Los Angeles run for fifteen months. Before going on leave, he delivered the *Lake Poularde* to Japan for jumboizing. By the time he rejoined her, he had benefited from a lengthy leave and she had gained a capacity almost double that at her first launching. After another ten months on the *Lake Poularde*, Captain Rugiati took over the *Torrey Canyon*, which by then had also been jumboized in Japan. It was March 16, 1966, and they were to be together until her end as a ship and his as a master.

Captain Rugiati's record as a master on Italian vessels had only two marks against it, minor collisions when maneuvering under pilot control. His record with Union was faultless, and while the *Torrey Canyon* had grounded in Los Angeles when newly jumboized, that was before he took over. Known for the respect his crews held him in, Captain Rugiati's landfalls were on schedule and his commands were well maintained. As his reputation grew with Union, he could look forward to the possibility of becoming senior master and retirement on a substantial pension.

"The *Torrey Canyon* was a fine, big ship when she left us," an executive of Newport News recalls. "The Japs made her more so, but it gets me the way we play with tankers these days, cutting them apart and slipping in a new forebody. A ship is more than that."

The way a ship develops a life of its own is a mystery, and that a part of one can also do it is even more strange. About 600 feet of the *Torrey Canyon*'s forebody—her bow and midsection but without deckhouse—was towed from Japan by the ocean tug *Jacob van Heemskerck*, of N. V. Bureau Wijsmuller, a Dutch towing and salvage firm and one that would have a line on the *Torrey Canyon* again. Tied up at an old Norfolk, Virginia, railroad pier while awaiting resale for possible attachment to a T-2 tanker stern section, the *Torrey Canyon*'s forebody lies next to that of the *Lake Poularde*. Their after ends, neatly incised, face the shore, and viewed head on, they look an able pair of vessels; their paint is still good, their names are still on the fine sheer of the bows, and with hove anchors they seem ready to clear for the open sea. You can feel life aboard the *Torrey Canyon*'s foresection, and it's not that of the roosting pigeons and perched gulls. Her mooring lines creak as she shifts with the tide, and the wind blows rust scale the length of her decks. It's as if that life is straining for another voyage, and it will remain with her until it's time for the boneyard. There it will give up, for a cutting torch is the great stiller of a ship's life.

Daniel K. Ludwig, of National Bulk Carriers, Inc., is often called the father of the jumbo. While the technique was not original with him, yards in which he has interests, especially in Japan, have done much to make it commonplace, and now vessels are even being returned for a second enlarging. His five Universe-class, 326,000-DWT mammoths, new and twin-screw, are under charter to Gulf Oil, but even these might be jumboized one day. Ludwig is a major figure in the tanker world, and some of its members have a way of looking over their shoulders when discussing him, as if fearful of being overheard. "Big money isn't measured in dollars, but in opportunities," said one, on being asked if Ludwig's holdings truly exceed a half-billion. "One thing I know—I don't want to be in his debt, ever."

The Japanese have been able to claim such a large share of the postwar shipbuilding market because they have the advantage of new yards in which mass-production methods can be used. Such is their efficiency that one of Ludwig's yards jumboizes tankers the size of the *Torrey Canyon* in four months, and it was here that Ludwig showed his competitors how to strengthen a ship's hull by stretching it, as once he led the industry in replacing the riveting of ship's plates by arc welding. He probably has gone with more long-term charters to banks to obtain funds to build tankers than any other operator, and certainly he has built more of the big ones. He is supposed to have said that what limits tanker size is ocean size, and that a tanker which could be operationally profitable is technically feasible.

"Ludwig is like one of his mammoths," says a competitor. "He's big, he's rugged and he works."

The thinking that led to jumboizing and the construction of mammoths began with the closing of the Suez Canal, which coincided with an increase in the European demand for crude oil. The operating costs of a 150,000-DWT tanker are not much greater than for a 75,000-tonner; crew size and maintenance are about the same, even if insurance and some basic costs do go up with size. An operator of a mammoth can move a ton of crude from the Persian Gulf to a British port for about $2.50 today, but so great is the shortage of long-haul tankers he can charge as much as $20. The ease with which the *Torney Canyon* grew from a 67,000-DWT tanker into a supertanker of almost double that capacity with a speed reduction of only about 1 knot seems a kind of magic. Her length was increased by only 165 feet and beam by 21, meaning that above the waterline she was nowhere near twice as big. Her growth was in her depth, which measured 69 feet after jumboizing, giving her a draft of 54 feet. (This is deep, but not as deep as that of the mammoths, which are limited by both the ports and dry docks they can use.) When the yard in Sasebo was through with her, she was only 57 feet shorter than the old *Queen Elizabeth*, which might have become a tanker herself instead of a tourist attraction had it been practical to convert her. The *Torrey Canyon's* new cargo capacity was enough to keep 50,000 cars runing a year, her 24-foot-diameter propeller and shaft horsepower of 25,000 could take as much as 4 miles to stop her from full speed if the watch engineer wasn't on standby, and her crew of thirty-seven was happy with their air-conditioned individual staterooms and all that her designers were able to think of by way of amenities. Her operators were happy too, even if she was too big for the Suez; indeed, it was her size and that of the mammoths which has made the Suez obsolete.

The *Torrey Canyon's* final voyage began with the taking on of 119,000 tons of Kuwait crude oil at Mina al Ahmadi on February 17. All was routine, including the fact that crew members were not allowed ashore, as is the custom at Persian Gulf oil ports unless there are medical or replacement reasons. The loading was done under the supervision of the chief officer, Silvano Bonfiglio, with a cadet and pumpman in attendance. Spills can happen easily by filling a tank too fast or severing a line, and on Captain Rugiati's commands they were a serious matter. It meant more than messing up a ship or polluting an anchorage—it meant an interruption of routine, and routine was the basis of his command philosophy.

The British Petroleum Company's senior master, Captain Charles Colbourne, of that company's flagship, the *British Argosy*, visted him the evening before sailing. They had a drink in Captain Rugiati's quarters, and several times during the hour they were together Captain Rugiati was consulted by one of his officers, prompting Captain Colbourne to observe later how conscientious his host was. They had never been to sea together, so it was impossible for Captain Colbourne to form an opinion of Captain Rugiati's seamanship, but he was impressed by the latter's attention to detail. It was clear that Captain Rugiati insisted on knowing everything to do with the running of his ship, and that all decisions of importance were his exclusively.

The *Torrey Canyon* sailed for Milford Haven on February 18; the Cape of Good Hope was rounded, then the Canary Islands were passed on March 14. A course of 18 degrees true was laid out to take her 5 miles west of the Scillies, position and course were checked March 17, and she steamed ahead at her service speed of 16½ knots on automatic pilot. Off the Scillies, which Captain Rugiati had passed when chief officer of the *Homeric*, he would set a course for the last leg of the voyage, 145 miles. Until then, the ship was run by routine, and that was the way he liked it—each hand tending his job and each element of his fine command performing as designed. He could look down from the wing of his bridge to the great length of foredeck stretching to the *Torrey Canyon*'s fo'c'sle head and know that every inch of her was his to command. At sea masters are not called gods for nothing, and many act it. It takes a big captain to remember that before he is a master he is a man, and this quality of Captain Rugiati's, together with the luxury of life aboard the *Torrey Canyon*, made for a happy ship. Being of Liberian registry, she didn't pay as well as U.S. flag vessels, but life aboard was an advance over that which her crew was used to ashore. The three changes of climate on the Persian Gulf–British Isles run were no problem due to her air-conditioning and heating systems. There was a modern laundry and a recreation room offering games, sound system and films twice a week. Watch standers had free run of the pantry and its ever-present espresso, cold cuts, foccaci, cheeses, baked goods and fruits. Lunch was a five-course meal with antipasto, soup, pasta, fish, or perhaps, fogato allo veneziana, a sweet, and dinner was even more impressive. Wine and beer were limited only by the steward's judgment of the capacity of crew members, but the officers, who messed separately, were permitted spirits. They had their own hours at the swimming pool with its piped-in music, and a rather more luxurious recreation room. Their quarters were even larger and better appointed, the chief officer and engineer having office-sitting rooms, and the master a commodious four-room suite.

As with the ship, Captain Rugiati's day was governed by

routine. Usually he was awakened at 7 A.M., and after washing and dressing, would go to the bridge. As a good master, he would try for a feel of his ship while checking the course in the wheelhouse—was she being pushed too hard, working in a seaway, or not hard enough? He could tell much from the "Good morning" of the watch too—the mood of the crew is important. After reading log entries in the chart room, checking the barometer and the weather, he would go below to his quarters for a continental breakfast, while the steward made the bed and cleaned up. He would put in some desk work, a master today being also an executive, then have conferences with department heads, and being the stickler for detail that he was, these took a while. After lunch, he would go to the bridge to chat with the watch and the cadets, then conduct ship's inspection. Much of this was concerned with ' maintenance projects, nominally the responsibility of the chief officer, and at sea it is never ending—rust chipping, painting, gear overhauls and cargo pump and valve servicing. After inspection, it was Captain Rugiati's custom to have a nap before returning to the bridge. There he would go over work for the next day, then put in more desk work. As the ship neared port, there was an accumulation of this—lists of stores to be taken on, repair parts, crew changes, payroll sheets and so forth.

There was always some kind of entertainment after dinner, often Ping Pong, of which Captain Rugiati was fond, but on this last night at sea, he stayed up late working on his port papers. Six crewmen were due to sign off for vacation, and because of some uncertainty as to which day they would be discharged, he made up a choice of payroll slips. The unknown here was due to the ship's draft and the predicted tides; a signal had been received from the British Petroleum agents in Pembroke asking for the figures on draft and trim, and it was apparent that if the *Torrey Canyon* didn't make port by 03:00 hours the next day, there wouldn't be enough water for another five days. Also, there was a sag amidships of 2 inches, which meant that cargo would have to be pumped from the forward tanks to the after ones to correct it. Every day counts on supertankers, for they pay their way only when working, and a day lost for a ship is a day of which owners may remind a master. For Captain Rugiati, there would be another reason to remember a lost day—it would be a break in routine.

His desk work finished at last, he went to the bridge. There his second officer, Pierpaolo Fontana, and he chatted until 02:00, when after writing night orders for the chief officer, who had the four-to-eight watch, Captain Rugiati pinned them to the chart room board above the table. They called for his being awakened at 06:00, or sooner if the Scillies were picked up on radar. Then, his duties for the eighty-sixth day of voyage accomplished, the master of the *Torrey Canyon* went below to turn in. His final rest aboard was a good one and it should have been—the voyage was routine.

Chief Officer Bonfiglio called the master Saturday morning as ordered, reporting only that the Scillies' Bishop Rock had not appeared on radar. On being asked, he said it should be picked up about 07:00 hours, and the master told him to call him then, if the islands weren't sighted earlier. The log showed that at 05:00 the Raytheon set had not picked them up, in spite of its 40-mile scan, and offered only the lubber's line (the ship's heading). Wind was reported light northwesterly with haze, and the seas as 5 feet. The master's phone rang again at 06:35, Bonfiglio reporting that he had the Scillies on radar at 24-mile range. The message brought the first rupture of routine, as the Scillies were off the port and not the starboard bow as planned. This put the ship east of them instead of west, and while Captain Rugiati was satisfied that she had been set off by the current, he was not satisfied with the next break in routine. Bonfiglio reported that he had changed course about five minutes earlier to 06 degrees, a heading lining them up with Bishop Rock light and exactly half enough of a course change to leave the Scillies to starboard. The master's anger in asking his Chief Officer who had told him to change course surprised the latter, and the surprise was reinforced by the curtness with which he was ordered to return to the original course of 18 degrees.

Captain Rugiati did ask if that course would clear the Scillies before ordering the change, and said that he planned to pass the Scillies to the east. It was an odd decision, since there was more sea room to the west, and Bonfiglio asked him to repeat the order. Captain Rugiati did, adding that he would be on the bridge shortly, but almost a half-hour passed before his appearance. That much we know, just as we know the ship had an hour and a half before reaching the Scillies, but we don't know what Captain Rugiati was thinking in the time it took him to appear on the bridge—was he wondering if Bonfiglio had plotted their position on his radar contact with the Scillies (he hadn't), or was he wondering what drove his chief officer to make a course change without orders? Conceivably, he might have been running over Bonfiglio's history. Then thirty-six, this big man had over ten years at sea, had been third officer in 1959 and chief officer for a year, held both Italian and Liberian master's licenses and was always sure of himself—for his master's liking even too sure, perhaps. He had very little in common with Second Officer Fontana, who was small, wiry, quick and always ready for a joke, and he had even less with the third officer, Alfonso Coccio, who was able and conscientious enough, but lacking in experience. Or could Captain Rugiati have been considering his anger? While he was every inch the professional officer, he was gregarious and had earned the loyalty of his crews by such gestures as having his commands' whistles blown and a party given each time a crew member had an addition to his family. Of course, as with other skippers, he made the good weather and the bad aboard, and, as also with them, he might not have been a stranger to frequent changes of mood and sudden anger at the end of a long voyage.

The two early morning ruptures of routine were the first links in a chain of circumstances and decisions that would end by destroying the *Torrey Canyon*. If Captain Rugiati's anger endured, it could be seen as the agent that forged the links together. On the bridge, where he had no lighthearted greetings for the watch, he checked the course (18 degrees on automatic pilot), found the speed just under 16 knots, visibility 12 miles, wind northwesterly at about 25 miles per hour, temperature 50 degrees and current moving at roughly a mile an hour on a bearing of 130 degrees. He saw the Scillies' outline on radar, and by the lubber's line it was clear that they would be free of them. The chief officer plotted Bishop Rock on the chart at 07:09 hours by radar observation with a bearing of 345 degrees, watched by the master.

Captain Rugiati then paced the bridge wing, where this stocky man in his late fifties with erect posture and heavy shoulders had only his anger for company. He wore winter-weight salt-and-pepper trousers which were held up by a broad black belt under wide loops, a dark blue windbreaker was zippered to the top and tucked into the trousers, and a black beret was pulled down square to the broad forehead. A resolute man with his alert, expressive face, he wasn't about to discuss the course change with his chief officer even if it was his watch, nor was he about to offer a reason for passing eastward of the Scillies. He felt he needed to save time to make the tide at Milford Haven, but as was later made clear, both the need and that the easterly passage would be shorter were questionable. Just as questionable was Captain Rugiati's failure to discuss the matter with his chief officer.

The latter took a compass bearing on Bishop Rock light-house, now visible from the bridge, and confirmed it by radar at 07:45. He took another, checking the distance by radar, at 07:56 when his relief, Third Officer Alfonso Coccio, reported to the bridge. Coccio, a short, stocky man, had spent much time the previous day plotting the course the ship was expected to take, familiarizing himself with the landmarks he would be using for bearings. He was surprised to find the course had been changed, and saw that his work had been for nothing. The chief officer established the ship's position for him by taking a cross bearing on Bishop's Rock and Peninnis Head light on St. Mary's Island, then checking the distance by radar. Their position was 5 miles southeast of the light, course was still 18 degrees on automatic steering, tide was just about high and the current was running as before. Finding all in order except that the fathometer wasn't operating, Coccio took over the watch. The cadet left the bridge at 08:10 with Bonfiglio, who had planned to start the cargo transfer, but had yet to receive the master's approval. While he felt it could be done in the present sea condition safely enough, Captain Rugiati was to say later that he preferred more protected waters.

Third Officer Coccio must have felt uneasy on assuming the

watch; the captain's distant manner was as surprising as the course, and it would be almost an hour before Coccio would discover on which side of the Seven Stones they were to pass. It was information that the watch officer should have, and the relieving helmsman, Scotto di Scotto, knew even less. On automatic steering, the helmsman serves largely as lookout and performer of chores—he had already been sent for ash trays, and soon he would go after sandpaper. He had received his seaman's book at sixteen, and had been an able-bodied seaman for almost twenty years, the previous two months having been served aboard the *Torrey Canyon*. He would spend most of his watch as lookout on the starboard wing of the bridge, crossing occasionally to the port side.

The ship's position was plotted at o8:12 by Coccio. Peninnis Head light was 4½ miles off the port bow, and he took another fix at o8:18. Their speed was 15¾ knots—about a half-mile a minute, which seems a lot for so large a vessel in waters with shoals a mere half-hour ahead. Captain Rugiati observed the plot, then as Coccio checked the radar, now on 8-mile range, another link was forged in the chain—two blips showed up on the screen. Coccio hurried out to the starboard wing and identified them with binoculars as lobster boats. He reported them off the starboard bow, adding that their course would cut across that of the *Torrey Canyon*. Captain Rugiati said that he knew about them, and this increased Coccio's uncertainty. It had been reflected in the difficulty he had experienced in getting fixes, and it was made worse by the helmsman adding a new element—confusion. He reported not two but three lobstermen bearing down on them, and this new link in the chain was soon joined by one of the master's making.

After a long look at the chart, he decided to swing left in order to pass between the Scillies and the Seven Stones, a decision made in spite of contrary instructions in the *Channel Pilot*. As it turned out, there was no copy aboard, even though this wasn't the first time the ship had been in those waters. The channel chosen is 6 miles wide, but the one bounded by the Stones and Lands End has a 12-mile width. Had Captain Rugiati used it, such an oblique approach would have been unnecessary, both wind and tide would not have been setting the ship to starboard when he wanted to come port, and the expected position of the lobstermen would not have forced a very pinched turn. Nevertheless, the decision once made was adhered to, and Captain Rugiati set the course at 15 degrees, operating the controls himself.

The Sperry steering control is mounted on a console in the wheelhouse. To the right of the ship's wheel on this console is a selector lever with three positions—aft, by which the ship is steered automatically by gyro on a preset course; center, manual, in which the wheel is used as in conventional steering; and forward, which is called "control." This is a seldom used auxiliary system in which a lever on the left side of the console directs the steering. Only officers moved the selector lever on this ship, and when it was in automatic position, as it usually was except in maneuvering, the maximum course change was 3 degrees at a time. For a larger change, the lever was put in manual position and the wheel was used until the desired heading was reached.

A few minutes later, the master set the course at 12 degrees. Third Officer Coccio took a bearing on St. Martin's Island and Peninnis Head lighthouse at 08:25, later admitting that both it and his next two fixes might have been inaccurate. Captain Rugiati had a look at the chart, and at about 08:30 gave another course alteration. This brought them to a heading of 10 degrees, and it also brought them into a cluster of buoy-marked fish nets, a couple of which were severed. He wanted to come farther left, but was prevented by the presence of still more nets. His frustration was increased by Coccio's reporting a lobsterman crossing their course from starboard. Rugiati responded by putting the selector lever into manual, then with the wheel setting a course of 13 degrees, he put the lever back in automatic position.

Coccio plotted their position at 08:38 by radar and cross bearings. It showed them to be about midchannel between the Scillies and the Stones, but he was not sure of landmark identification. He was ordered to use the lightship instead of the Scillies for bearings, and this order was a new link in the chain. They were not sure of their actual position, and this in a situation of little sea room, traffic, fish nets, and with shoals ahead.

Had the fathometer been working, it could have been helpful, but along with the loran and one of the radar sets on this well-maintained vessel, it was out. It may have been the sense of the growing peril for his ship that rattled Captain Rugiati to the extent that he neglected to reduce speed, or have her steered manually by the helmsman in case of a needed major course change. At 08:40 Coccio established their position as being a mere 2.8 miles from South Stone, and yet he still didn't know the master's intentions. He did know that the two lobstermen were now off their port bow, which he reported. Captain Rugiati promptly put the selector lever in manual and changed course by wheel to due north, then returned the lever to automatic position, At this point the crews of both lobstermen, which turned out to be French—*Mater Christi* and *Cité d'Arvor*—hoisted warning flags and began shouting and waving. But while they could see officers running about on the bridge of the *Torrey Canyon*, there was nothing to indicate that their warnings had registered, for the great vessel continued to steam ahead. (Captain Rugiati was later to claim that there was a third fishing vessel to starboard.) The *Torrey* was as committed to the course chosen by her master as she was to her doom.

A couple of Seven Stones lightship crewmen had seen the *Torrey Canyon* before 08:30, but except for being surprised by the direction from which she approached, gave no thought to her situation. The lightship's master reported all well by radio, and at 08:40, after looking at her, he returned below. At about this same time Coccio was trying for another fix, but by the time he had run into the chart room to plot it, he had forgotten the bearing. He ran back to the starboard wing for a second bearing, and this time was able to plot it. It was 08:48, and the position showed them to be about 2¾ miles from the lightship and less than a mile from the nearest of the Seven Stones. He and Captain Rugiati, who had watched the plot, exchanged a look.

Captain Rugiati ran from the chart room, shouting to the helmsman, still on the starboard wing of the bridge, to come to the wheel and take her hard to port. Helmsman Scotto ran in from the bridge wing to find Captain Rugiati at the console, shouting for a course of 350 degrees, and another link was formed. Captain Rugiati left him to make the course change with the wheel, but neglected to put the lever in manual position. Next, he asked for another course—340 degrees, then 350—and hurried back to the chart room. Scotto took the wheel as ordered, while Third Officer Coccio on the port wing tried for a bearing on the Seven Stones light vessel. Things were happening fast on the *Torrey Canyon*'s bridge. Scotto called that she wasn't answering the helm, but neither the third officer nor the master heard him. The latter had just discovered by radar that they were even closer to the Stones than he had figured, and he shouted for another course change—to 320 degrees.

On his way to check on another danger—the position of the lobstermen to port—Captain Rugiati paused in the wheelhouse, having sensed something wrong. He had not been hearing the click of the gyro which accompanies a major course change, and although the helmsman was turning the wheel freely enough, neither the helm nor the rudder indicator confirmed the turn— the *Torrey Canyon* was still on a due north heading and time was running out. The captain's immediate reaction was that the helmsman must have blown a steering engine fuse by turning the wheel too fast, but all proved live. Next, he wondered if the steering engine could be out—both the *Torrey Canyon* and the *Lake Poularde* had had trouble with this system in the past. He hurriedly dialed what he thought was the engine room, but to his anger a steward in the officers' saloon answered, "Captain, are you ready for breakfast?"

Captain Rugiati was trying to redial when he noticed that the selector lever was in the control position, which meant not only that the wheel was disengaged, but that the ship could be steered only by the lever controlling the auxiliary system. He rushed to the console, put the selector lever in manual, then helped Scotto with the wheel. The rudder responded and the bow had just reached a heading of 350 degrees, according to the course recorder, when the *Torrey Canyon* struck with a shuddering crash. Then began her slow death, along with that of the creatures of the sea and air, many of the ways of the tanker world, and of truth. No one has admitted putting the lever in control position, yet someone must have. And that someone helped put the *Torrey Canyon* on Pollard Rock.

The time of the stranding is uncertain, as with so many elements of this disaster, but 08:50 has become generally accepted. The confusion was such that those who did register the time cannot agree among themselves, and all had better things to do than clock watch. An engineer was stunned to see water rushing in from the after pump room, the second officer rushed to the bridge in his pajamas to find only an eerie quiet, steward department members hurried to the open decks in fear of an explosion and the chief officer, who had been doing the rounds of work details, lost no time in getting to the bridge, the occupants of which he found in a condition close to shock. Without orders, he went to survey the ship's condition and his report was not encouraging—he estimated that she was hard on, probably forward near No. 1 cargo tank, a little aft at between No. 3 and No. 4, then still further aft between No. 5 and No. 6. They were spilling cargo, a lot of it, and he guessed that they were badly hurt.

There is doubt, too, as to when the engine room telegraph rang down its STOP, but it took a while. The master ordered full reverse without effect, and although the two lobstermen eased in to roll with the swell off the *Torrey Canyon's* starboard side, it was ten minutes before anyone thought to send a distress signal. When it was sent, it wasn't by the *Torrey Canyon* but one of the lobstermen, the *Mater Christi*—she contacted Lands End Radio to report that the great vessel had run aground on the Seven Stones. The *Mater's* skipper, M. Frollic, had first tried Radio Conquet, but as he hadn't declared an emergency he was told he would have to wait. It seems consistent with the odd apathy present immediately after the stranding, and while the event itself was almost unreal to M. Frollic, he knew that the *Torrey Canyon* was doomed from the time he and his crew, along with that of the other *langoustier*, had tried to warn her off. He guessed that the ship would need almost 4 miles to stop at such a speed, making it too late to avoid the Stones unless she veered off, and had she done that, her head reach (forward movement in a turn) would have more than taken up the clearance left—a 20-degree turn for her would have required almost a fifth of a mile. And when she struck with a hideous, ripping sound that lasted for several seconds, the black oil that gushed upward between her plates to fall into the sea was as hard to believe as were her deserted decks. Not a soul seemed aboard, and except for the sound of her engines still at service speed, all was still.

With M. Frollic's signing off Lands End Radio at 09:06, an automated alarm system, telephone and radio, was set in operation. It could alert all ships within Morse-receiving distance, as well as search and rescue controllers on the mainland. At least eight vessels responded, varying in distance from an hour's steaming to an unidentified ship over 500 miles out in the Atlantic (she was thanked, anyway). Eyes other than French had noticed the *Torrey Canyon*, even if her plight was not understood. The crew of a scheduled British European Airways (BEA) helicopter flight to the Scillie, were puzzled that such a large ship was on the wrong side of the Seven Stones light, and simultaneously they were aware of a strong smell of oil. Alarmed, they checked their instruments, then noticed a purple smudge growing on the port side of the ship. The smell was strong, although they were a good 5 miles from her, and they wondered if she had been lightening cargo to approach the light closer. Radio Scillies had no information, and on its return flight the helicopter went in for a look at her—she was down by the bows, losing a huge amount of oil, crewmen in lifejackets were lounging about on the stern, and the scene was strangely inactive.

Things were happening, though; the tide was falling, and since she had stranded at near high water, this was a plus. The tide would rise again, and with it would come a chance to have a try at getting her off. Cargo was being shifted to try to lighten her at points of contact (it was also being pumped over the side which, while it might help to solve *her* problem, certainly wasn't going to help the growing pollution), and a number of organizations were being alerted. One of the fastest reactions to the emergency was that of the Wijsmuller company's salvage tug, the *Utrecht*. In acknowledging the signal, she advised that she was getting under way from her station near Penzance. Without any lost motion, she was soon steaming at her maximum of 18 knots, and the good reason she had was not humanitarian so much as business.

Worldwide towing is Wijsmuller's regular diet, but marine salvage is a favorite delicacy. It's a risky calling, but if all goes well with a stranding the size of the *Torrey Canyon*, the salvager can pick up a million dollars or more. Under the normal procedure of a Lloyd's "no cure—no pay" contract, it better. This agreement provides that if the salvor fails in his effort, the owners and insurers need come up with no compensation. If he is successful, then an arbitration procedure takes over and makes a salvage award—in the eyes of admiralty lawyers a neat and tidy way of doing things. In practice, though, procuring a salvage agreement can lead to some pretty fancy navigating in which traditional rights of way can be forgotten. It used to be that the first vessel to get a line aboard the wreck had the job, and while it nc / depends on which salvor the master elects to sign with (at the owner or underwriter's bidding), it is still a competitive exercise; when a wreck is up for grabs, almost everyone gets away with something, even if it's only souvenirs.

Another organization had a fast reaction to the *Torrey Canyon*'s plight, too—St. Mary's Island lifeboat, the *Guy and Clare Hunter*. An able, self-bailing ocean rescue craft with ample power, she and her crew of eight were launched on the rails from her boathouse fifteen minutes after the call came in to their homes, and within an hour she had eased into the lee of the *Torrey Canyon*. Her skipper, Coxwain Lethbridge, was shouting up to Captain Rugiati on the bridge wing to ask if he wanted to abandon her with his crew. The captain answered that he would wait for tugs to try to get her off, and that there were no casualties. Lethbridge so reported by radio to St. Mary's Coast Guard, adding that the *Torrey Canyon* had begun to sag forward of the bridge. This was a bad sign, indicating that she might break her back, and the lifeboat crew began taking soundings. There was a good 80 feet of water on her port side, but to starboard the depth averaged only 40, and at some points amidships the reef was a mere 18 feet or less under the surface. Had Captain Rugiati been on a course even half his beam to port, Pollard Rock would have missed its chance; at most the *Torrey Canyon* would have lost a few barnacles, and Captain Rugiati would have gained a few gray hairs.

The role of the Seven Stones lightship that morning remains

obscure, except that her people were not about to believe the unbelievable. Filtering the claims and counterclaims as to who did what when, it seems likely that the *Torrey Canyon* had been hard on for almost twenty minutes before the lightship skipper had another look topside. His reaction was immediate and by the book; the JD flag was hoisted, rockets were fired, the Aldis lamp was flashed, the siren was blown and crew members are said to have waved shirts from her deck. This went on for some time, but the stationary monster of the sea which looked as if still under way made no reply. There wasn't much for her to say on being told she was standing into danger, except to answer that such was her danger already that some were certain she wouldn't survive it. Others were certain of something else—the thick black mass of escaping crude was 1 mile downtide and spreading.

The Royal Navy entered the picture early, dispatching a helicopter with the commanding officer of the Culdrose Air Station to have a look, and a commander at the Plymouth headquarters dispatched the destroyer *Barrosa*. He contacted the Board of Trade, Ministry of Defence and British Petroleum regarding pollution and detergent use, and that afternoon received permission to use additional Navy vessels but was cautioned not to spend more than £1,000 on the attempt. That might have seemed substantial at the moment, just as did ordering the minesweeper *Clarbeston* to the scene with 1,000 gallons of detergent and the naval tug *Sea Giant* with 3,500 gallons, but the *Torrey Canyon* carried a lot of crude oil— enough to teach a lot of people a lot about handling a lot of spill.

Captain Rugiati's "Mayday," eventually sent out at 09:10, was picked up by the Wijsmuller office in Holland, and no time was lost in contacting the *Torrey Canyon*'s California operating agent, Pacific Coast Transport, Inc. The news had already reached them, and as soon as Union Oil was alerted, the underwriters were advised. There was coverage of $16,500,000, and from now on all concerned were to try to make only the right moves—on the ownership, operating, governmental and intergovernmental level. This was not to be easy, for in view of the size of the problems, there weren't many precedents to go by.

"All we knew that Saturday morning," says one official of Her Majesty's government, "was that we faced a problem which would be as hard to dispose of as it was unexpected. There was precious little comfort in that."

At 10:55 Captain Rugiati canceled the distress signal, asking that the situation be treated instead as urgent, but if he had found some reassurance, he was the only one who had. Five minutes later a Royal Navy lieutenant was lowered to the *Torrey Canyon*'s deck from a helicopter for a survey of conditions, and Captain Rugiati escorted him to his suite. The comfort of the quarters impressed the lieutenant, and there he met the chief engineer, Michel Miccio. Later the master explained that he hadn't been feeling conversational, and so left his chief engineer to take the lieutenant over the ship. The lieutenant reported to Culdrose that the vessel was indeed in a bad way—over half her tanks were ruptured, she was discharging heavily, was aground amidships and pierced by a rock forward on the starboard side, the main pump room was already flooded, water was in the engine room and she was rolling and grinding heavily. This was the first hard news the shore had received, and it didn't encourage anyone.

The salvage tug *Utrecht* arrived at 12:35 with towing equipment, ground tackle, pumps, cutting and welding gear, rigs for diving and material for hard and soft patches. Her master, Hille Post, thirty-six, had the St. Mary's lifeboat ferry two salvors to the stricken vessel shortly after arrival. Their job was to have a look at the situation and to get the master's signature on the Lloyd's "no cure—no pay" agreement. Captain Rugiati took his time over that, studying the papers assiduously, and when word came at last that the agreement had Pacific Coast's approval, he signed and Wijsmuller was in business. That afternoon came the first indication that it was going to be a rough piece of business, though—Second Officer Fontana headed a work party to check the water level in the engine room, but the vapors were too thick and they didn't waste any time below. The *Utrecht* made several tries at passing a towing cable to pull the *Torrey Canyon* off at high water without success, then gave up as the wind rose and visibility became poor. An eerie night was spent by those aboard, as they listened to the grinding of the hull against the rocks and their fear of an explosion increased. Other than packing their suitcases, there wasn't much to be done except wait out the long night of fear. Boilers were shut down due to water and oil in the fireroom, and an 8-degree starboard list developed.

The weather on Sunday, March 19, didn't raise any spirits. The wind was northwesterly at 20 knots with gusts up to 35, the sea was kicking up and the forecast predicted worse to come. The ship not only was farther down by the bows, her list was now 10 degrees, and as the lifeboat reported to the Coast Guard, she did not look good. The Coast Guard advised Captain Rugiati to get the crew off, and soon after daylight the lifeboat eased alongside to take off fourteen of them. It took some skilled boat handling, but the crewmen made it, as did their very considerable amount of luggage. All felt that the ship was done for, and they were happy to be delivered with their belongings to Penzance by the Trinity ship, *Stella*. A black gang member was frank enough to tell the press that he had been frightened in the night, but had taken courage from his "brave captain."

Wijsmuller, recognizing the size of the problem, now decided to put their assistant operations manager, Captain Hans Stal, in charge as salvage master. His rise with the firm had been rapid; he was an experienced seafarer and inventive salvor, and had the invaluable talent of being able to drive his salvage crews and make them like it. In terms of support, he was well supplied—he had at his disposal the salvage tugs *Titan* and *Stentor*, a Portugese tug under charter, *Praia de Adraga*, and a DC-3 aircraft full of compressors, hoses, generators, cables and other salvage gear, in addition to divers and engineers. If the great ship could be salvaged, these were the men and this was the equipment to do it. The growing pollution problem, of course, belonged to others. These were short on technique, equipment and manpower, and although the spill now was about 10 miles long, working south from the Stones and east of the Scillies, it was merely the beginning.

The next attempt to pull the *Torrey Canyon* off involved four tugs, and while they were able to secure towing lines, itself a feat in the rising sea, the 5-inch cable from the *Utrecht* parted almost as soon as a strain was taken. Complicating the great ship's peril was her tendency to yaw as the swells rose, which was no help to her bottom plates or the mood of those aboard. She was working in the seas, working hard and against herself, and just before noon the lifeboat skipper contacted Captain Rugiati with the proposal that between the lack of success in floating her and the deteriorating weather, it would be well to get the rest of the crew off. Rugiati rejected the proposal, but shortly afterward had a change of mind. The crew, twenty-one with officers, were called together and given their choice of remaining aboard or leaving. To his disappointment, none of the officers volunteered to remain and only three of the unlicensed personnel did—two A.B.'s and a steward's mate. The last had known his captain in Elba, where their wives had gone to school together.

"How could I leave my Captain?" he asked, in a press interview.

Those who decided not to stay had no trouble in reaching their decision, but putting it into effect was something else. The seas were running 25 feet by now, and as much maneuvering skill was required of Coxwain Lethbridge on the lifeboat as timing on the part of those anxious to get off. Eight crewmen made the leap from the *Torrey Canyon's* oily decks to the *Hunter* safely, but the ninth misjudged the timing and fell between the vessels. Only some really fast reversing by Lethbridge saved him, and he was pulled aboard the *Hunter* well oiled, shaken and grateful. The next nine refused to jump, having seen enough, and later were lifted off by helicopter. Captain Rugiati admitted that staying aboard was beyond duty's call, but he saw it as loyalty to his employers. He had been hurt by the crew's disloyalty to him—in addition to the loss of his command, he felt he had to face loss of respect by those he had considered his sons.

That night Salvage Master Stal contacted his office with his report, and it was a grim survey. He had found that only four of the *Torrey Canyon's* eighteen cargo tanks were still intact, the bunker tanks (fuel) were also fractured, pump rooms and fo'c'sle stores were flooded, the ship was grinding hard and about 20 feet of rock had pierced the hull, holding it fast. Most salvors as experienced as he would have advised abandonment of the contract at this point, for while there was a lot to salvage and much money to be made if they succeeded, the chances of pulling it off were disappearing fast. The *Torrey Canyon* was no longer a good salvage bet, but in order to oblige the underwriters, more tries had to be made. And so plans were formed for new approaches to the problem, but their success wasn't being helped by the general air of discouragement which began to infect the salvage crew—they just weren't happy about their chances and, more important, their safety. All hands agreed that one way to get her off the ledge was to blow her off, and with the volatile mixture of vapors and air ever increasing, this could happen spontaneously—all it would take would be the right spark at the right time in the right place. And if the *Torrey Canyon* blew, those aboard would go with her.

The pollution report given to Britain's Navy Under Secretary, Maurice Foley, who arrived in Plymouth that night to head up the antipollution forces, was grimmer than he or others then realized. It was estimated that at least 20,000 tons of crude oil had been spilled, and the resulting slick extended over an area about 18 miles long and 4 miles wide. The wind, which had been pushing it south, now veered to the west and the Cornish coast found itself threatened. At a guess, Foley put the cleanup job at two weeks with an expenditure of one-half million pounds, which he was authorized to spend as long as it was understood the government's right of claim for liability and reimbursement wouldn't be affected. As it turned out, his view of the disaster was highly optimistic, but since he was the personal representative of the Prime Minister, Harold Wilson, even those who knew better weren't about to dispute him. And not many did know better, for they had no way to measure what they were up against—such a massive spill had never happened before. They had a lot to learn, beginning with the fact that the 5,000 gallons of detergent used was about as useful as "a tyke spitting in the ocean," as one hand put it. It was to take much more than that to break up the oil. It would also develop that the detergent ended up damaging the ecological balance even worse than the oil itself.

Monday brought fine weather, even if there was a sizable ground swell running, and Captain Stal was quick to make use of it. He put fifteen salvors aboard, together with portable generators, pumps and three big air compressors. Work was begun on sealing the deck openings preparatory to charging the tanks with air to expel oil and seawater in an effort to increase buoyancy. The charging didn't begin until later in the day, being an operation no one was looking forward to—pumping pressured air into spaces filled with volatile vapors is a dangerous business. It wouldn't have been done had there been a choice, but there just wasn't sufficient liquid-pumping capacity to empty the tanks and keep them dry.

The ship was visited by some seagoing V.I.P.'s during the day, who were experts instead of seagoing sidewalk superintendents, and among them was British Petroleum's Captain James King. He was put aboard by helicopter in the morning, and in the half-hour that was all he had aboard his mood of optimism changed. The stern area felt live enough, but he didn't like the heaviness of the forward areas, nor the mournful sound of the plates constantly grinding on the rocks. That the interior spaces were being flooded to such as extent worried him too— he suspected all the bulkheads must have shifted. In the afternoon, an admiralty salvage specialist, Peter Flett, came aboard with a couple of Union Oil officials. His survey not only told him that she didn't feel right, he was also pretty sure she never would. The Union men insisted, however, that she still offered a reasonable chance of salvage. They were concerned about the increasing pollution, and believing that the best way to stop it was to off-load the cargo, they urged the continuance of salvage efforts.

Captain King's report put Her Majesty's government in an awkward position. There were three possibilities of solving the pollution problem—off-loading on site into another tanker, which was impractical due to the exposed location, lack of pumping capacity and expectation that the hull would never hold up long enough; destruction of cargo by burning, which no one was optimistic about (though experiments and studies were to be made); and getting the mammoth vessel off with as much of her cargo as remained. The last was decided upon, in spite of strong views that she should be bombed at once, where is and as is. But before that step could be taken (and the problems involved were considerable), Union would have to waive her claim to the vessel, and this couldn't be done as long as the underwriter's contract had to be honored. Her Majesty's government couldn't condemn the vessel because she was in international waters, however close to home some of the British felt the Scillies to be, so salvage her it would have to be, come hell (which did) or high water (of which not enough came). Among those who saw small chance of success was the Wijsmuller firm—by the end of the week they were to suggest that Her Majesty's government join them in the salvage operation as a partner. A definite no was the response.

The wind and sea rose Monday night, and those aboard listened for hours to the ship grinding away on the rocks, while their nostrils were assaulted by the heavy stench of crude oil. The weather improved on Tuesday, and in the eyes of some so did the *Torrey Canyon's* condition. Her list decreased to about 5 degrees, and she began to feel lively. Her increasing buoyancy encouraged Captain Rugiati, but neither he nor Union Oil's Captain Povey, who was landed on the ship that morning, was happy about the marked increase of oil vapors, which seemed particularly heavy in the machinery spaces. Captain Stal wasn't either. A door below slammed loudly enough to remind Captain Rugiati of the danger of explosion, and he left Captain Povey in his quarters while he hurried out on deck to find out who had been so careless. He was just in time to see some of the engine room flying up through three decks, taking the swimming pool with it. A roar and blast of air from the massive explosion hit him as he crouched on the deck to avoid the flying shrapnel. Captain Stal didn't have time to—he was blown overboard, his spine cut by a piece of metal, and three other salvors were also blown over the side. All were rescued by tugs, and those salvors still aboard were taken off because of the fear of further explosions and fire. A doctor who was helicoptered

out to treat Captain Stal confirmed the gravity of his condition
—unconscious, he was suffering from a ruptured liver, broken
back, shock and much loss of blood. He died aboard the tug
Titan before she was able to make the shore, and the loss of
such a good and able leader took the heart out of the salvage
crew. They saw this latest tragedy as an omen, and the feeling
that the *Torrey Canyon* was doomed became increasingly widespread.

A survey party of salvors, consisting of Captain Stal's assistant
and the *Utrecht's* chief mate and chief engineer, returned to the
Torrey Canyon and found a good 25 feet of water in the engine
room, a large opening where the topside superstructure over
it had been and a buckled fire room bulkhead. The ship was
farther down by the stern, but they still thought that there was
a fifty-fifty chance of salvage success. On the basis of such an
estimate, Wijsmuller would have had a hard time getting out
of their contract and so it was decided to continue. Union's
Captain Povey, however, had a different view—he saw the
chances as very long indeed.

Although the weather was good on Wednesday, the only
progress, if it could be called that, was a statement by Her
Majesty's government that there was still a reasonable chance
of success, and that the operation would continue. Thursday
brought good weather again, but more decisions than work
were accomplished. It was decided for safety reasons to use
an inert gas—nitrogen—to pressurize the cargo tanks, and the
salvors thought to have a try at pumping plastic foam into the
ship, both to lighten her and to force out gas accumulations.
A Royal Navy helicopter landed parts for a gas generator
aboard, and its pilot found the salvage crew demoralized by
the loss of Captain Sfal and in no mood to assemble the generator without help. By Friday night, nitrogen was being
pumped into the *Torrey Canyon's* tanks, together with a covering of plastic foam, but the procedure was called off before
midnight. There wouldn't have been time to finish the job if
the expected spring tides were to be utilized; they would run
5 to 6 feet above normal, and although it was estimated that
at least one rock was more than that into the ship's bottom,

it was as good a chance as they would get. And so, with many fingers crossed, charging the tanks with compressed air was resumed on Saturday morning.

The ship was evacuated preparatory to a towing attempt shortly before high water, 05:42. Three tugs were hooked by cables to the *Torrey Canyon*'s port side in an effort to swing her toward the nearest deep water, and once a strain was taken, throttles were opened slowly and the pulling began. Eventually, and to the excitement of onlookers, the great ship started to move, but not for long and not to much advantage. She simply lay over on her port side, but in doing so her stern pivoted to starboard, leaving her in a more difficult towing position than she had been. The effort was given up after an hour, and the gloom was increased that night by deteriorating weather. Easter morning brought near gale winds and huge seas, but they moderated enough in the afternoon for another towing attempt to be made. Four tugs were used in this attempt, a pair forward and a pair aft, but before long a cable parted. The remaining pair kept pulling, and again movement was seen. This time, however, it was of a disastrous nature—the force of seas and towing combined was enough to slowly break the *Torrey Canyon*'s back, and bow and stern sections separated with a great rending of steel and gushing of oil. The stern settled deeper over the night, and on Monday the bow section began to break up into two pieces. The *Torrey Canyon* was done for now, but the salvors still felt they had a hope of getting the stern free and clear, thus having at least something to show for their days of hard work and high risk. They had to face a prohibition against towing whatever they salvaged into British waters, though, and by Monday night Wijsmuller gave up hope and the salvage contract was abandoned. The great ship and its cargo was now officially a total loss, and Union Oil gave notice of abandonment to the underwriters. It was all over as far as the ship was concerned, but what to do with the menace she had created now presented problems even larger than the salvage attempt itself. She was done for, the *Torrey Canyon*, but far from gone and never to be forgotten.

The people of two nations—England and France—reacted to the menace with fear, rage and wonder. An estimated 30,000 tons of crude (about a third of the cargo) had escaped to foul the sea by Thursday night, but because the wind was pretty much from the north, the shore was still free of oil. A fleet of vessels was doing its best to break up the massive slick over 250 miles square by spraying detergents and then churning up the mix with their propellors. It was slow, discouraging work, and although the feeling grew that there must be a better way of defeating this black enemy, no one came up with much in the way of improvement. It wasn't known then that the detergents would cause extensive ecological damage by destroying myriad and minute forms of sea life and growths, but it has since been suggested that they were more effective in this than they were in breaking up the oil. The principle on which the detergents were employed was that they would thin the oil, and then, by coating it with an oleophobic film, make it impossible for drops of oil to merge. This resulted in an emulsion of chocolate color (soon to be called mousse), which in time would be broken down by bacteria and dissipated by sun and wave action. After available stocks of detergents in the British Isles were consumed in the first weekend of the disaster, production was stepped up to 100,000 gallons a day—an impressive effort but nowhere near enough to do the job. The only comfort to be found was that the more oil that was broken up at sea, the less there would be to eventually find its way ashore.

But on Friday night, as the wind became southwestly, the south coast of Cornwall was assaulted with oily waves and black spray, and by Saturday morning many of its beaches and rocks were coated with the gelatinous, intractable stuff. The coast stank with it, and as the fear of the people turned to anger, Her Majesty's government demonstrated its concern by putting the Home Secretary in command, seconded by the Minister of Housing and Local Government. The latter flew to Cornwall to reassure office holders that the cost would be largely assumed by the government, and to further organize forces to combat the increasing menace. On Sunday, Prime Minister Wilson promised the country that whatever part of the *Torrey Canyon*, if any, were refloated, it would not be allowed into territorial water until it was oil-free. It was decided on Monday night in London that the oil remaining aboard the shattered vessel (thought to be at least half the original cargo), would be disposed of by burning in place. Experiments had been conducted on firing a similar grade of crude oil by the use of electrically-fused oxygen tiles, or oxygenated bricks, and about 95 percent success was claimed. If that should fail, the plan was that the ship would be fire-bombed by the Royal Navy. The intent was to set fire to the cargo rather than sink the ship, thus avoiding the possibility of a steady flow of oil from the hulk for years to come. It would be a tricky operation and one that would have to be done before the eyes of the world press; any slipups would be hard to conceal. The experts had to admit that they didn't know if the conflagration might be so immense that all life for miles around would be endangered, or whether firing the oil would simply increase its flow without igniting it. If the latter were the case, spill-rate control would be no better than it had been. A giant plastic boom, designed to contain the oil on the sea's surface for siphoning off, had failed to arrive at the scene due to rough weather. But even if it had been available, no one knew if it would be effective or for how long, for experience with booms had been limited to protected waters and much smaller areas. As with spilled milk, there wasn't much use in crying over it, but for most of those threatened there was little else to do.

The Royal Navy was taking no chances that the effects of their bombing might get out of hand. A half-dozen destroyers patrolled to warn shipping off, the Seven Stones light vessel was removed to safety, a helicopter stood by to evacuate those manning the Longships light and the public was ordered off the beaches (not that they obeyed). The initial contact with advance forces of the enemy—the oil around the wreck—was made Tuesday afternoon by helicopter. It was the first application of the oxygenated bricks, and it was literally a fizzle. Even the presence aboard the helicopter of their inventor didn't encourage them to do their job, and it was clear the *Torrey Canyon* was going to be tough to get rid of. Pollard Rock held her in its unshakable embrace and she held on to her cargo, letting it discharge only as fast as she chose.

Just before four on that fine Tuesday afternoon, a flight of eight Royal Navy Buccaneers went in on a dummy run at

7,500 feet, then wheeled to come back, all business at 500 m.p.h. The lead Buccaneer let go two 1,000-pound bombs, and while their water spouts impressed thousands of shore viewers, they were a clean miss. The following plane connected, though, and the stern of the *Torrey Canyon* burst into flames. Once the rest of the flight had done its work, smoke was rising to 3,000 feet and Prime Minister Wilson announced that he was well pleased with the Royal Navy's performance. Soon after a big flight of Royal Air Force Hunter fighters dropped wing tanks of jet fuel on the conflagration. This attack was followed by another Buccaneer bombing mission, and by the end of the afternoon a total of 18 tons of bombs and over 5,000 gallons of jet fuel had been turned on the enemy. Considering the dangerous nature of the cargo, this should have been enough to keep the fire going for days, but its duration was one of minutes. Just before dusk another helicopter application of fire bricks was tried in an attempt to reignite it, and although the oil gushing from a section of the hulk did catch for a bit, it wasn't long enough to do much good. By night, all was dark and the *Torrey Canyon* continued to spew its poison upon the sea. A dead ship, she still posed a very live threat.

The next day, Wednesday, the situation was surveyed early. All that anyone was sure about was that the hulk of the *Torrey Canyon* was still there, oil remained within her and the giant slick was growing steadily. It was not known how much oil was still to be disposed of, nor had anyone come up with a better way to do it than had been tried on the previous day. It was decided, therefore, to try more of the same, with napalm added for good measure (to the surprise of the British public, which had thought only the United States possessed the barbarous weapon). Fires were started, but once again the bricks fizzled. The Royal Navy pilots were as pleased with the number of hits they registered as they were frustrated by their lack of effectiveness. The operation was continued on Thursday, and again, while hits were numerous, fires were few. Before the day was out, officials came up with a reason that satisfied them, at least—there wasn't enough oil left in the hulk to burn. This claim was disputed by many, and more oil did appear in the area a few days later.

The bombing of the *Torrey Canyon* cost well over a half-million dollars, but just how effective it was remains open to question. The government maintained that at the start there were 40,000 tons of cargo still aboard, and that most of it was consumed by fire. Others, however, insist that the amount was half that, and that most of this escaped at an accelerated rate due to the bombing and thus added to Cornwall's pollution problem. Indeed, over the weeks to come, the wreck continued to break up and settle and it may have released small quantities of oil. Royal Navy divers in June found no more than a film of oil on the upper sections of cargo tanks. They also found that the after section was so badly mangled it barely resembled a ship, and yet they came across a few intact bed sheets. In spite of the Navy pilots' report of bombs that failed to explode, they found none. The assumption is that these unexploded bombs lie on the sea floor near what was once the *Torrey Canyon*, adding another element of danger to Pollard Rock and the wrecks it holds. And so, in spite of the fact that she is no more and her cargo is gone, the *Torrey Canyon* still poses a danger.

Two sure things are known about the *Torrey Canyon*'s cargo —it consisted of 119,000-plus tons of Kuwait crude oil, and in its disposition more mistakes were made than lessons learned. For instance, it was estimated that 30,000 tons of cargo were released the day of the stranding, Saturday, March 18, but no one will ever know how good the estimate was. Of that amount, it is known that some was dissipated by wind and wave action together with attack by detergents, as it worked its way southeast to end up on the Channel Isles and Brittany coast. Another 20,000 tons was spilled during the week, it is claimed, and a final 50,000 tons on the breaking of the *Torrey Canyon*'s back, Saturday, March 25. Westerly gale-force winds, eventually shifting to the north, drove the monstrous slicks toward France, but not before the Cornish coast was heavily fouled on the morning of March 25. A final 20,000 tons, by estimate, remained in the hulk for the bombing treatment.

Thickness of the slicks presents another series of guesses. Some claim that it was as heavy as a foot high adjacent to the wreck, others that there were miles of slicks of at least 6 inches. The estimates vary but do agree on the final film thickness before disappearance—4/100 of an inch. What made the attack by detergents futile was not thickness of the slicks, however, but area. The Royal Navy's fleet of forty-two vessels, reinforced for inshore work by innumerable smallcraft, were rigged with spraying booms and pumps, including high-pressure fire units to hose the surface in order to help emulsification. Almost 700,000 gallons of detergents of at least a dozen makes were used at sea, and it has been claimed that more oil would have come ashore had it not been thus broken up.

The shore operations were even larger, but no less difficult. Well over a million gallons of detergent were sprayed and poured and dumped on the beaches and cliffs. There was also active harbor and surf treatment. The assault on the spill utilized thousands of local volunteers, including the young, 1,400 British Army and Marines, a U.S. Air Force fire-fighting team, earthmovers, tank and dump trucks, flame throwers, forks, shovels and fill. Both straight crude and chocolate mousse were battled. The mousse, a water-and-oil emulsion, is probably formed by wave and wind action and is bound together by the asphaltic crude oil residues. Although detergents foam in water and can break down mousse, there is no proof that alone they can form it (in spite of the claims of the French, who blamed the mousse they encountered on British detergents). Where detergents were simply poured and dumped on the beaches, without being mixed with water, ensuing tides would create a deterged penetration of as much as 5 feet, and use of excessive amounts resulted in a structural breakdown of the beaches, turning them into quicksands. At least some of the oil stench was due to the interaction with detergent, and the latter had a caustic effect on both skin and rubber.

For all the back-breaking work, it was a losing battle and many despaired. As fast as beaches and harbors were cleaned, new tides brought new waves and new oil. As has been said, if all the oil which came ashore was merely the 20,000 tons claimed by the government, they were the biggest tons in history. And as has been asked, if flamethrowers and napalm do such a fine job on people, why don't they work on crude at sea? The answer seems to be that although both are mostly liquid, people do not douse flames with their own steam.

In Brittany, the *Torrey Canyon*'s cargo became known as *La Marée Noire*. It arrived on that shore early the morning of April 10 and kept on coming until the 28th. The cleanup operations continued through June, using in all 3,000 troops. The French were opposed to detergents, both for reasons of economy and because they believed the British had contributed to the already enormous problem by their use of 2,500,000 gallons of the stuff. They preferred a local product, *Craie de Champagne* (stearated chalk), to sink the sea of mousse, and in the Bay of Biscay an estimated 20,000 tons was sunk by a mere 3,000 tons of that weapon. None appears to have since surfaced, due in part to the fact that the mousse has a density close to that of seawater and is happy to remain in its bosom when put there.

The French also avoided using detergents because they were more concerned about their fishing industry than tourism, and therefore concentrated on oil removal instead of treatment. Thus they avoided the toxic effects of detergents, and their methods, both economical and efficient, demonstrated a willingness to try almost radically simple ways of solving a problem that had become even more complicated than it had been for the British. Most of the *Torrey Canyon*'s crude had become mousse by the time it reached the Brittany beaches, making it more difficult to collect than as a gelatinous crude. (Having criticized the British for not trying hard enough, the French now said that the crude would have been easier to cope with if left alone.) Sawdust was tried as a collecting agent at sea, where it was found to be too water-absorbent, but it worked well on the beaches, even helping to pick up oily sands in addition to the mousse. Straw worked better at sea, becoming the chief collection agent, and even fine brush was tried. Pumping of the mousse was also done, both at the tide edge by portable rigs, and at sea by a special scavenging vessel. Booms to protect inlets and coves were constructed, again by a simple method—burlap was used as an envelope to hold tightly packed straw, and while it was only efficient in still water, it worked well and was inexpensive to construct.

One problem the French faced was that the *Torrey Canyon's* crude oil was treated as a disaster so potentially serious that it came under their Plan Orsec, which was designed to permit localities to continue governmental operations even if the larger centers had been destroyed in a nuclear holocaust. The result was that Brittany officials were called upon to make decisions for which they did not have sufficient technical background, and except for incorrectly forecasting the near impossibility of a northeast wind at that time of year (which is what brought the oil to Brittany), Paris initially stayed out of the picture as much as possible. There was considerable disorganization at first, to say nothing of much local anger, but eventually the pride and ingenuity of the local people produced an efficient attack upon *La Marée Noire*.

The Côtes du Nord received the heaviest onslaught of the *Torrey Canyon's* cargo, and much of it was less mousse than crude. Oystermen worked hard to save their beds by removing them, but even so over 2,500 acres of oysters were considered lost. In addition to the hard-hit hoteliers, the fishing industry suffered a disaster, with sales off at least 40 percent in the Paris markets. Cleaning of the beaches went on for weeks, and the methods used included detergents as the battle continued. As had been the case in Cornwall, these efforts were not made any easier by the crowds of curious blocking the roads, and not many showed any interest in helping the embattled Bretons— they were there to look, not work. They could have been used, though, for in spite of the presence of troops and earthmoving equipment, the main effort in Brittany's cleanup consisted of backs, buckets and shovels. The job was done, some lessons were learned, but no one in Brittany was left feeling very happy about the *Torrey Canyon*, the British or Paris. It had been a bad time, and as all knew, it would not be the last *La Marée Noire*.

Definite figures on the losses affecting birds and creatures of the sea are as hard to come by, as are other statistics in this case, but estimates run as high as 30,000 seabirds. The coasts of southern England and Brittany are breeding grounds for many varieties of seabirds, among them guillemots, razorbills, shags, puffins and Great Northern divers. The spill coincided with their northerly migration, and although thousands of oil-soaked and helpless birds were picked up on the beaches for treatment, the survival rate was at best 1 percent. The deaths resulted from the birds' condition of shock, improper cleaning and handling, ingestion of oil, ingestion of toxic chemicals by preening, and pneumonia. Many of those which did not reach the beaches died of starvation and exhaustion, being unable to fly in the search for food. Others were prey to exposure, since the insulating ability of feathers is destroyed by oil accumulation. The only comfort in these deaths, if it is true, was suggested by a bird watcher of long experience: "At least, the poor blighters didn't know how it would end."

According to Britain's Plymouth Laboratory, man applied pollutant was far more damaging to the ecology than the accidental one and this view of the attack upon the spill by chemical agents finds increasing acceptance. Limpets and winkles kept scurrying about on oily surfaces, some life survived in oil-saturated rock pools, and beaches that had suffered minor oil pollution showed little evidence of deleterious effect to crustacea, mollusks, worms or anemones. Seaweeds and other littoral fauna and flora didn't seem much affected either, but as the detergents and dispersants washed ashore, the scene became one of disaster. Worms, rock pool life, crustacea, anemones and most sublittoral fauna and flora were found dead, and the effect on littoral life was as severe—bivalves, starfish and sea urchins were affected, crabs suffered severely and plankton did no better. Evidence of the effect on deep-water fish is sparse, one explanation being that as they sickened they were devoured by others. The effect on the latter can only be guessed at, but detergents and dispersants had a definite effect on the sea floor—grasses were killed and seaweed appeared in areas new to them.

The Plymouth Laboratory strongly recommended that in a future spill disaster the French practice be used. Their report points out that rocky areas left untreated returned to a near normal condition after a few months, and urges that inaccessible coves be left untreated. Straw and sawdust, together with mechanical oil collection, were recommended, as was the use of chalk to sink the oil at sea. This is a practice frowned upon by other authorities and among them is the National Audubon Society, which objects to the possibility of having the sea floor paved with asphalt. Aside from the fact that there is no guarantee that the sunken oil will stay at the bottom of the sea, there is no chance for the destructive bacterial action that takes place on the surface. Many observers were impressed by the slow but efficient dissolution of spill accumulation by oxidation and bacterial action, and it was found that the process could be accelerated by frequent churning through vessel propulsion at sea and on the beaches by plowing. Even without such action, rocky coves and untreated beaches returned to an approximation of their original condition eventually, leaving us with the thought that letting nature take its course is an example of when doing nothing is better than doing something.

Another aspect of the *Torrey Canyon* disaster soon made its appearance—money. To satisfy this largest single loss in maritime history, insurance underwriters had to come up with $16,000,000 for the hull loss. The British government calculated its cleanup and bombing costs as $8,500,000 and brought suit at Bermuda, the head office of Barracuda Tanker Corporation. The latter filed a court action in New York seeking to restrict damage claims and exoneration in U.S. courts, saying that it faced claims from the French government for almost as much and from British Petroleum Trading, Ltd., shipper of the cargo, for $1,500,000. Barracuda claimed that under British law a ship's owners' liability for property damage is limited to $67 a ton of the vessel's weight, roughly $3,500,000, and that U.S. practice limits the liability to the value of the ship and cargo, if delivered. Hull and cargo were a total loss (with the exception of a lifeboat appraised at under $50, presumably not taking into account its value as a souvenir), and thus the U.S. custom had much appeal. Nevertheless, a sister ship, the *Lake Poularde*, which had inadvisedly put into Singapore to pick up some cable, had a writ of attachment affixed to her mast and the sum of over $8,000,000 was posted to obtain her release. As she steamed from the harbor she was pursued by a launch with representatives of the French government on a similar errand. The *Lake Poularde* made it, though, and she stayed clear of Singapore until the case was closed.

While a lot of legal maneuvering was being conducted in

New York on behalf of Barracuda, the French, whose view of Britain's handling of the *Torrey Canyon* spill had not been improved by the British government's failure to notify them of the Singapore attachment in time for them to join it, had instructed their agents in foreign ports to keep a sharp eye out for either of the *Torrey Canyon*'s sister ships. It paid off as an April Fools' Day ploy with the attachment of the *Lake Poularde* in Rotterdam, resulting in the posting of a bond of better than $7,500,000 to obtain her freedom. France was now able to bring an action in the Netherlands separately from Britain, which was a further worry to Barracuda, and made their ship one for which two countries had developed a real attachment. Further, it appeared to convince Union Oil, which had at last accepted its responsibility as charterer of the *Torrey Canyon*, that both England and France were quite prepared to fight it out in court. Rather than face such protracted litigation, Union agreed to pay damages on November 11, 1968, in the amount of $7,200,000, to be divided equally between the two governments. While their claims amounted to almost twice as much, it was still a larger settlement than expected, and it provided an unusual feature—Union would pay a total of $60,000 additional to satisfy claimants not reimbursed otherwise, and the two governments would protect Union against private claims beyond such amount. It does seem a paradoxically minor note on which to end such a large case, and one wishes that the decimated wildlife could have been compensated too.

On another April Fools' Day, that of the previous year, the *Torrey Canyon*'s master had signed a formal statement bearing on the disaster. He noted in his large, clear hand that "where necessary, it was translated into italian [sic] for me." The wording is cautious, the signature is elaborate, and we are assured that all "the equipment on board was perfectly satisfactory, and that I had a very good and competent crew." This is a generous view, in the case of the equipment even overgenerous, as it neglects to mention malfunctions. In the case of the crew, it is in contrast to the statement's preceding paragraph: "but for the rudder not having answered to the turn to port, the accident would have been avoided" (a claim disputed by many). The paragraph continues, and one wonders if it is one of those trans-lated for Captain Rugiati: "I am perfectly sure that this was not due to any defect of the gyro pilot, which, as I said before, has always worked perfectly. It is possible that by mistake the helmsman, when taking the wheel, moved the lever from auto; matic to control position thinking to move it to the manual. It must be noted that when I moved the lever again back to the manual position and turned the wheel, the vessel answered immediately."

This is a curious statement in view of other testimony indicat-ing that Captain Rugiati was the last person to move the lever, that the chief officer stated, "It is my custom to move the lever personally," and that the third officer stated that a helms-man never touched the lever on his watches. Curious also is helmsman di Carlo's statement, which exceeds in generosity that of the master, even if it is short on punctuation: "Immediately after I had taken the wheel the Master told me to come to port and then to come on course 350 degs. and I turned the wheel hard to port. I realized however that the rudder did not answer and so advised the Master who meanwhile had gone in the chartroom. The Master rushed back to my right side and I saw him with his hand close to the selector moving his hand in a direction I am not able to remember since I was paying atten-tion to the compass." Not many A.B.'s have done as good a job of eyeing the compass and thus seeing to it that their captain's reputation didn't go down with his ship.

The Liberian Board of Investigation "In the Matter of the Stranding of the S.S. *Torrey Canyon*," held in Genoa, issued its findings on May 2, 1967, which were that the master alone was responsible for the casualty. The board pointed out that the decision to pass east of the Scilly Islands exposed the vessel to unnecessary risk, and that on being advised by the chief officer that their landfall put them to the east of their projected course, the master should have gone to the bridge, consulted with the chief officer and weighed the situation carefully be-fore making his decision on how he would pass the Scilly Islands. In addition to criticizing Captain Rugiati's naviga-tional decisions, the board found him negligent in permitting the steering to remain in automatic control, for failing to reduce speed in restricted waters and for never having established a routine for operation of the steering selector lever. Said the board of the stranding:

Inasmuch as the cause, as here found, was due to the negligence of the Master, it is the Board's opinion that the penalty be commensurate not only with the gravity of the casualty but with the degree of negligence which we consider to be of a high order.

We recommend therefore that License No 21127 issued by the Republic of Liberia to Pastrengo Rugiati, the master of the *Torrey Canyon*, be revoked.

The legendary court at the bottom of the sea would not question the board's finding of the cause of the *Torrey Canyon's* stranding, but it might have been troubled by the board's all-American composition. American shipping interests were well represented, the board members having been appointed by an American in New York who was deputy commissioner of Liberian Maritime Affairs. For chairman he chose a former vice president of Texaco, then appointed a member of a prestigious New York admiralty law firm who had written some of the legislation setting up Liberia as a major maritime power for American convenience (even if few of the vessels carrying her flag ever see their home port of record), and added one of his own assistants who had served as second mate on U.S. vessels. The hearing, which was open to neither press nor public, was attended by observers of two parties in interest, Great Britain and Union Oil, and it cleated both owner and charterer of any negligence.

The undersea court would wonder why the inquiry didn't penetrate to the whole truth of the disaster. And it would wonder why some of the following items were not explored:

The master's insistence on turning left when blocked by the lobstermen, instead of right where there was sea room.

The vessel's steering malfunctions.

Absence of a copy of the *Channel Pilot* and other sailing directions for Britain's waters.

The master's not retiring until going on 03:00 the morning of the stranding (affording him less than four hours of sleep with a busy day ahead).

His delayed appearance on the bridge after landfall notification.

The course recorder's clock being eighteen minutes slow.

Identity of person who put the steering selector lever in control position.

Reason control level wasn't employed when selector's position was realized (instead of returning the selector to hand control, then manning the wheel with helmsman).

Malfunction of 35-mile-range radar set, loran set and fathometer (these malfunctions being ignored by both master and board; indeed, both stated that all systems were in perfect working order).

Master's curious statement that he had decided while still in his cabin to pass east of the Scillies, as he had to make the tide at Milford Haven and needed to allow time to transfer cargo in quiet waters (then discussing the transfer at length with the chief officer on the bridge without reaching a decision).

Relationship of master and chief officer.

Master's physical and emotional condition.

Pressure of tide deadline upon master.

The undersea court might also fault the board for failing to call expert witnesses, or indeed any witnesses except four, all of whom had been on the bridge that morning. And the court might wonder not only why the Liberian inquiry was the only one, but also why a mere two days was devoted to fixing the cause of this greatest single maritime disaster. Also, it might wonder why the board, for all its courtesy in questioning Captain Rugiati, didn't bother to inform him of its findings. In addition, that court might wonder about compliance with the board's ways and his reluctance to offer a defense (except for implicating the helmsman). The court, if at a loss, might ask if he was as loyal a master in the hearing room as he had been on the bridge.

Being composed of seafarers, the court would be sorry to learn that the ex-master of the *Torrey Canyon* was in such physical condition after the inquiry that he was hospitalized, suffering from loss of weight, hypertension, pleurisy and a tubercular condition of one lung. He had a private room in a Genoa hospital, and although visitors were limited, a press photographer stalked him successfully. He snatched a shot of the patient in dressing gown trying to hide under a bed, and the world which had had a last look at the great ship awash with a broken back and spewing forth flame, smoke and oil now had a last look at her proud master in the huddled form of a shattered, frightened old man with a head strangely vulture-like, one whose days on the beach to come would never be free of the memory of his lost command.

It was no end for a shipmaster, for all that his ship brought such death to creatures of the sea, the shore and the sky. And it was no end for a man.

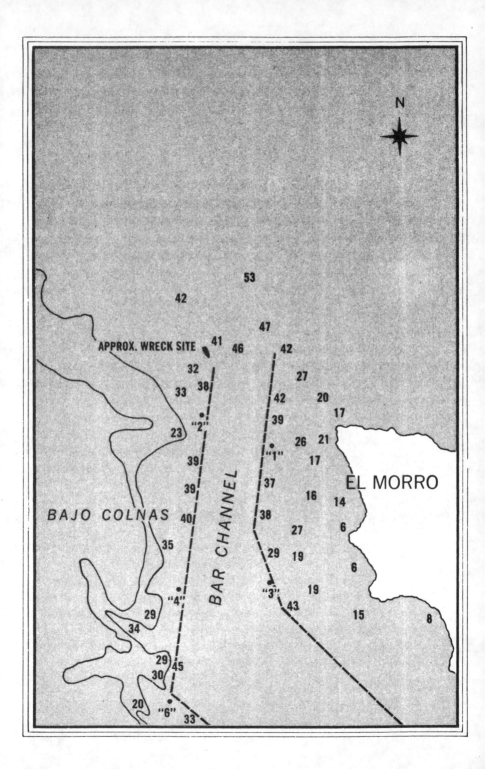

CHAPTER 2

"DOOMED!"

The S.S. Ocean Eagle Disaster

A COUPLE OF WEEKS before the anniversary of the *Torrey Canyon* disaster, the world leearned of a new oil pollution crisis. The S.S. *Ocean Eagle,* another modern, steam turbine tanker of Liberian registry, grounded at the entrance of the San Juan, Puerto Rico, harbor channel, then broke in two as her cargo of Leona crude oil poured from her. Her last morning was as fine as the *Torrey Canyon's,* although March 3, 1968, was a Sunday instead of a Saturday, and she met her death at eight instead of seven o'clock. Visibility was equally good and neither the northeasterly force four to five wind nor the 15-foot swells with a ship's length between crests presented problems for her. The *Ocean Eagle* was only a third the size of the *Torrey Canyon,* and carried a Greek crew of thirty-five instead of the latter's thirty-six Italians, but still she was a vessel of 18,254 tons deadweight and almost 600 feet long. That is a lot of ship, about the the size of big tankers before they grew so rapidly to become supers, mammoths and oilbergs.

The unlikely fate of these two fine vessels had more in common than weather, nationality of registration and their 16-knot speed. Their masters had made good their landfalls after uneventful voyages, bringing them that much nearer vacation and comfortable retirement, when their performance of duty began to suggest negligence. Why they were unable to respond in a moment of stress is probably as little known by them as it is by us. Basic precautions for sailing unfamiliar waters with heavy traffic were ignored, aids to navigation were not utilized, plain common sense was abandoned and confusion and its ally, fear, were permitted to join the watch. It was almost as if these masters were determined that their ships must not escape, and to those who witnessed the results of the oil pollution, their punishment—the beach—was not enough. There was no way to get them to provide compensation to those they had injured economically. And for the destroyed life of the sea, sky and the shore, no compensation was possible.

The proximity of Puerto Rico and its beaches to the United States made this disaster big and immediate news. The fact that the *Ocean Eagle* was smaller than the *Torrey Canyon* wasn't too reassuring—her cargo of 5,689,488 gallons of black death still endangered the island's ecology, economy and way of life, and to American readers and viewers it was a disaster happening not to foreign shores but to their sun-kissed and fun-blessed sea and beaches. Mass concern for the environment, which was born of the *Torrey Canyon*'s death, was about to grow. A sense of urgency was introduced into the deliberations of Congress, industry and government laboratories began working under pressure and Madison Avenue spiel tanks worked hard at rewrites. The message was that the U.S. consumer cared about his living space not merely as a political concept and repository for the possessions that made for the good way of life, but as a resource to hand on to the future reasonably intact. The environmentalist, who had been seen as an erratic vegetarian and dreamer in health shoes, had been joined by the consumer. Unlike the voter, who does not always vote, the consumer always buys. The environment was about to become a big issue, and the impact of the *Ocean Eagle* on this process was so effective that she didn't need company for emphasis. She had it, though, even if in smaller headlines, when the Greek tanker *General Colocotronis* stranded on a reef off Eleuthera, the Bahamas, on March 7, 1968. This was four days after the *Ocean Eagle* stranding and eight days before the *Torrey Canyon's* anniversary, and it was just as unlikely and unnecessary a disaster as theirs.

The Indians called Puerto Rico "Borinquen," but the Spaniards gave them better reason than a change of name to curse the island. Seafarers, old-timers at least, say a change of name can put a curse on a vessel, but for all her having been christened *Ocean Trader* on her Belgian launching in 1953, then later called *Maritime Trader*, the *Ocean Eagle* gave no evidence of a hex. When she neared the San Juan channel, however, she was about to join the buried timbers and rusting iron of many a ship which are the reminders of Puerto Rico's curse. The reputation of the channel as a maritime death trap is almost as bad as that of the Scilly Isles, where the *Torrey Canyon* stranded. Of the seven vessels stranded at San Juan channel in the previous five years, all were foreign flag, three were total losses, and while most did not have a local pilot aboard, one, the *Guadaloupe*, might have done better on her own. Her stranding was the result "of confusion on the part of the helmsman, due to both Pilot and Master alternately giving orders to the wheel." Another, the *Venus*, grounded during steering failure—the "Master rang up full astern, the engineer on watch answered with full ahead." The cause of the *Loch Garth* stranding was more colorful, being put down to "the Master's error in buoy identification because of bird droppings," and the loss of the *Catalina* is at least more understandable, her master having "failed to use his anchors" after she lost power. It is said in that port that while not all of these shipmasters may have been aware of the local curse, most either did some cursing of their own or heard some from the insurers.

The owners of the *Ocean Eagle* were Trans Ocean Tankers Corporation (60 percent) and Northern Transatlantic Carriers

Corporation (40 percent) of London, and the agents were Norland Shipping and Trading Corporation of New York. The charterer was Kupan Transport Company, a subsidiary of Gulf Oil Corporation, and the cargo consignee was Caribbean Gulf Refining Corporation of San Juan. Her navigational equipment was in good order and consisted of gyro and magnetic compasses, radar, Fathometer, radio direction finder, sextant and a chronometer. No structural damages were sustained or repairs made on her in the previous two years, she had been in severe weather in the North Atlantic without incident, and no structural defects or excessive deterioration in the hull were noted during her dry-docking at Liverpool in September, 1967. There were no known cracks in hull or piping prior to the casualty, there was no history of fractures or structural weaknesses, and the vessel had not undergone any structural alterations. She was, in fact, a fine ship and kept up to the standards of her American Bureau of Shipping classification.

The *Ocean Eagle* sailed from Puerto La Cruz on her voyage No. 168 at 14:50 hours on March 1, her mean draft of 31 feet 2 inches being 6¾ inches above the proper tropical loadline. Fresh water, used for boilers and galley, was discharged to lighten her, and although about 85 tons of bunkers (fuel) and water were consumed on the voyage, she was still 5½ inches over her loadline. This, together with the distribution of her cargo, was later to give rise to both criticism and hard questioning. There wasn't much else to find fault with concerning the voyage, except for the discovery that the course recorder tape was six hours ahead. It was an unimportant detail but one that admiralty law reputations can be made on, and it is the kind of thing that the *Torrey Canyon*'s master would have been displeased by—a late tape is not routine. It functioned properly in other respects, registering that on March 3 course was set at 274 degrees (all bearings true). Culebra Light was abeam to port at about 8 miles, and this course was designed to parallel Puerto Rico's north coast. As with everything else on the voyage, it did that as planned and the speed, as also planned, averaged 14.1 knots.

It was just another voyage for the *Ocean Eagle*'s master, Captain Stelios Galaris. A tall, thin and youthful looking Greek

Clemens Kalischer

Clemens Kalischer

for his thirty-six years, Captain Galaris held an unlimited Liberian master's license and a Greek first mate's license. He had served aboard the *Ocean Eagle* since 1964 as chief officer, except for a couple of months in 1966 when he acted as master, and had held command since December, 1967. Panagistis Michalopoulus, thirty-four, was chief officer. He had been sailing on the *Ocean Eagle* in that berth since December, 1967, with a Greek chief mate's license, having been on her in the same capacity from October, 1966, to May, 1967, with a temporary Liberian license.

Both officers were on the bridge as the vessel approached San Juan, as was a helmsman. Captain Galaris had been there since 21:00 on Saturday, and the first link in the chain that was to mean the end of the *Ocean Eagle* was forged at 04:00 Sunday in the form of his being unable to raise the San Juan pilot station. He became increasingly anxious at the prospect of entering a strange channel with a reputation for being tricky with his ship in an overloaded condition. Oddly, he seems not to have thought of standing by outside until such time as he was in contact, but this may have been due to his desire to be sure he was docked with the high tide. He shifted to radio telephone at 05:30, raising an unknown answerer, and was later assured by the Puerto Rico lighterage radio that a pilot boat would be standing by. He felt more confident until he discovered that it was a mere 30 feet and had neither radio nor loud hailer.

The wheel was manned by the helmsman, who had been standing lookout, when the chief officer secured the automatic pilot at 06:00 and then logged "End of Voyage." With the vessel a little more than 3 miles off the San Juan channel at 06:08, speed was reduced to half. The view from the ship was one that has excited many tourists—El Morro Castle, 400-year-old Spanish fort, was to the east off the port bow and palm-lined white sands glittered to starboard against the azure sea in the morning sun. The Bacardi plant was a little farther west and those famous greeters of San Juan, the brown (or West Indian) pelicans, escorted the ship as they did most arrivals. These great birds were seen as such a good welcome symbol by the Puerto Rican Commonwealth government that thought had been given to including them on the official seal, but not much was heard of the idea after the *Ocean Eagle's* cargo was spilled. The few still around were reminder enough of the disaster.

Four minutes after the first speed reduction, the master ordered slow ahead and from then on links were added rapidly to the *Ocean Eagle's* chain of death. The helmsman reported steering difficulty, probably due to the following sea together with reduced speed, and the course varied as much as 15 degrees between 06:06 and 06:13. The vessel still had considerable way on though, in effect coasting on the following sea, and she was to some degree out of control. Had he originally reduced his speed farther out, her master wouldn't have had to worry about overrunning the channel entrance, or about becoming increasingly misaligned with it.

Although Captain Galaris was to testify later that he approached slightly to the east, the evidence developed was that he was to the west and becoming more so, due to the wind and loss of steering control. At 06:13 the vessel was on a rather variable course of 195 degrees, while the bar channel range, marked by lighted buoys, calls for 180. A pilot cannot go wrong, theoretically, if he steers in accordance with the range marking the dredged channel, but this assumes that the vessel is in proper alignment, under suitable control and that enough power is applied to make an abrupt easterly turn to port soon after she has passed El Morro. The *Ocean Eagle* did not meet these conditions and worse, her master was both making some wrong decisions and avoiding some right ones. His earlier anxiety about not having been able to raise the pilot station had turned to anger at the failure of the pilot boat to come out far enough. And soon his vessel would be trapped in a channel narrower than she was long, for which she was improperly headed, and with no real possibility of backing out.

Speed was increased from slow to half at 06:28, presumably in an attempt to regain steering control, but only three minutes later stop was rung down. She was then drifting in that following sea with considerable headway on, and the control problem had become worse than ever. The last entry in the bridge bell log was at 06:33 when the engine was put at half-ahead again. It would be interesting to know if the engine room bell log agreed with the bridge log, but it was not recovered from the wreck. Nor was it alone in being reported missing—quite a few ship's papers, all of which would have been useful, failed to turn up. Among them were the bearing book, the captain's night order book, azimuth book, compass log, engine log, oil record book and two applicable charts. Had these documents been recovered, however, they would not have explained why Captain Galaris did not wait for the pilot to come out to him to board, instead of, as it appeared, deciding to go it alone and then changing his mind. Nor would they explain why he had waited so long to cut his speed initially, why neither his fathometer nor radar were in operation, why no one was standing lookout and why he remained alone on the bridge with only the helmsman for assistance once he had sent the chief officer forward to the fo'c'sle head to see to the anchor windlass.

When the *Ocean Eagle* was close enough in, the assigned harbor pilot, Captain David T. Gonzales, had the pilot boat maneuvered along the starboard side of the *Ocean Eagle* and made three attempts to board. He was unable to do so because of the ship's 4-knot headway and the 15-foot swells, his boat being a poor launching pad from which to grab a Jacob's ladder. He was also unable to communicate with the vessel's master, either to get him to stop or to warn of the reefs on the west side of the channel. Hand signals proved as useless as his voice without even a megaphone, and Pilot Gonzales ordered his boat to head in so that he could get a second pilot boat standing by up-channel to alert tugs. The master of the *Ocean Eagle* later testified that he took this, together with the hand signals which he had not understood, to mean that he should follow the pilot boat in, and thus another link was added to the chain. The second pilot, a Captain Rivera, lost no time in contacting tugs, which got under way as soon as their skippers secured their coffee mugs against the swells to come. Captain Galaris, seeing that his command was only about 700 yards north of the entrance buoys on a heading of 202 degrees, sent his chief officer to the fo'c'sle head to direct the bos'n in dropping the starboard anchor. There was considerable disagreement later on how much anchor chain was let out and whether or not the anchor did reach the bottom or was merely carried lowered to be ready, but it was established that the engine was put full astern and that by 06:51 the anchor had been dropped. By then, the buoys were 5 to 10 degrees off the port bow, and there was still headway on. The bow overran the anchor, causing the chain to tend aft with such strain that additional chain had to be eased out by careful braking of the anchor windlass. Four or five shackles were let out (a shackle, or shot being 15 fathoms, and a fathom being 6 feet). Soon the bow was swinging to starboard and the stern to port across the channel, so now not only was the ship in imminent danger, but she also stood a good chance of blocking the channel.

The deteriorating situation had one advantage: the *Ocean Eagle*'s port side now afforded a lee, and Pilot Gonzales took advantage of it to board. He hurried to the bridge where he found an "excited" master and the engine full astern but headway still on—she was a hard ship to stop, the *Eagle*, and she was going to be even harder to get rid of. Another hard task is to imagine the scene on that bridge when these two captains met—an angry master and an outraged pilot—whose careers and even lives were in peril. The U.S. Coast Guard Board of Inquiry brought out the dialogue, and with it at least some of the tension.

Q. What were your first words to the Pilot?
A. (Captain Galaris, after much thought): Good morning.
Q. He was excited?
A. Hadn't met him before, so I didn't know. I was nervous—excited, mad. Pilot said he was waiting since 05:45. I told him about trying to get hold of him and nobody answering.
Q. Did Pilot say, "You are standing into danger"?
A. Don't remember. Think so.

When Pilot Gonzales, a small, intense, middle-aged man, took the stand, several things became clear. He wasn't about to let Captain Galaris, whom he described as running around in excitement, put the blame for the casualty on him. Also, the Board of Inquiry found it was facing quite a communications problem—English, Spanish and Greek were used, in addition to an occasional bit of Portuguese and some Brooklynese. In spite of the efforts of two skilled interpreters, it took a lot of reinterpretation and defining of terms before the testimony became clear, or even made sense. It was also clear that Pilot Gonzales wasn't going to go in for any maritime courtesies, and that when he boarded the ship, Captain Galaris hadn't either. Instead of "Good morning," he testified, he was asked a surprising question.

He say, "Why did you board from the port side?"
I say, "Never mind that, Captain. Your ship is in danger."
He say, "My mistake—I am sorry. Engine is full astern."

In order to head her properly for the channel, the pilot ordered full left rudder and dead-slow ahead. Slow ahead was suggested by the master in order to regain maneuvering ability, and it was so executed (the working relationship between master and pilot is that while the pilot directs a vessel's movements, the master remains responsible). The ship responded in due time and by 06:57 the swing to starboard was checked and replaced by one to port until her heading reached 258 degrees. She rose and fell with the swells coming from three points abaft the starboard beam, and while she was not yet out of danger, she was under control at last and tugs were on their way.

The master and the pilot felt better about their predicament, but they didn't have much time to enjoy it. The *Ocean Eagle* struck bottom (or a reef or submerged object, according to some accounts), and this was repeated at least twice. After the third contact she sagged amidships, then oil gushed from near no. 6 cargo tank. Steam began escaping from ruptured lines on deck and the master and the pilot looked at each other.

"The ship struck like thunder," Pilot Gonzales testified, "then she shook."

Captain Galaris went back a bit to give his version of the grounding:

With slow ahead, I ordered the Mate to weigh anchor. Five to seven minutes pass, the ship not moving. Then I feel a slight shock —hit. I told Pilot to turn right and take me out to sea, but he said "reefs" and showed me old wreck there.
I asked Pilot where was soft bottom after two more hits, then

oil came from both sides of ship. I saw from beginning my vessel
was doomed!

The *Ocean Eagle* continued to float freely, if sagging, and
after the second engineer reported no damage to the machinery
spaces, the master ordered full ahead in an attempt to ground
her. He thought better of this shortly, however, as he feared
the rotating screw would endanger crew members on abandoning. He then ordered the chief engineer to secure for abandoning.
Next, he gave the order to abandon and blew the ship's whistle
(others were to deny this, and it does seem that the crew didn't
wait for orders, whistle or anything else to man the boats). There
is doubt as to when the anchor was dropped, or if already
dropped, raised and later dropped, just as there is as to who
raised the anchor ball (the maritime signal flown from the
foremast to indicate a vessel is at anchor) and when it was done.
There is no doubt that Captain Galaris failed to transmit or
display a distress signal, though, and there is none that the
Ocean Eagle's midsection was surging up and down about 10
feet. Her starboard anchor chain tended forward, as she settled
to a generally northerly heading and continued to spew oil. It
spread rapidly.

A Coast Guard helicopter arrived within a half-hour, by
which time two of the ship's lifeboats were standing by, together
with two tugs, the pilot boats and a Coast Guard utility boat.
The master, who remained aboard alone, dropped the port
anchor, then flew the international signal "Not under Control."
But by then, she was under control, even if done for. Asked by
the Board of Inquiry to tell in his own words of the grounding,
Pilot Gonzales shook his head in wonder, then held out his
hands to illustrate his helplessness.

A. Oil was coming out, was no one on bridge and I call on
   radio for help. Tell Old Man (the Master) to rig a line for
   the tugs.
Q. What did the Master say?
A. A mystery. Talking quick, that's sure!
Q. What happened next?
A. Old Man went to his room, then all leave ship—no words
   said.

Captain Gonzales left the ship in a lifeboat, and on reboarding later to "discuss things" found the master packing his suitcase. It took courage for the pilot to return and it took even more for the Master to have remained aboard—in every tanker casualty there is danger of explosion, and the heavy smell of crude oil vapor made the danger seem acute. Among the personal gear the master collected was a sharply cut bright blue suit; also, he needed to collect himself—there were a lot of questions coming up and they were big ones.

The bow and stern sections of the *Ocean Eagle* parted at 09:45, the break being at the point of sag aft of the midships deckhouse. The stern drifted southerly to ground on the west side of the channel between buoys no. 2 and 4, while the bow remained at anchor 450 yards north of no. 2 buoy and just west of the channel boundary. About an hour later the tug *Katanya* put a line aboard and pulled northwesterly without success. The stern wasn't tried, being hard on and in such shoal water that it was impractical for a tug to come in close. When the Coast Guard placed a lighted wreck buoy to warn off traffic, the *Ocean Eagle* became a wreck officially. In fact, she was a double wreck and a double threat. Crude oil, still flowing from both the bow and stern sections, was to present a major pollution problem, and either section could shift back into the channel to endanger other vessels. And before San Juan was to see the last of her, she would cause many a winged, swimming and crawling thing to die.

"If she flies again, that *Eagle*," a fisherman said, disgusted, "she'll do it submerged. And after the harbor pirates are through with her, there won't be much to sink."

There was almost as much confusion ashore that Sunday morning as there had been aboard the ship before she was abandoned. Among the rumors spreading throughout San Juan was the claim that "a tremendous noise like an explosion shook everything" at El Morro, and another said that the stranding was the result of the master's not realizing his command was longer than the channel was wide (500 feet), and thus he stuck her across it in trying to turn around. Among other untruths being circulated were that the master had panicked on being unable to raise the pilot station and had locked himself in his cabin, that the chief officer drunkenly dropped the anchor without orders, forcing the ship onto reefs and that the disaster had been caused by the pilot's fear of boarding in view of the high seas. In addition, San Juan was supposed to be facing imminent danger of fire from the spreading crude oil, the failure to ignite the *Torrey Canyon*'s oil on the sea having already been forgotten, or never appreciated.

It is true, however, that President Lyndon Johnson happened to be weekending at Puerto Rico's Ramsey Air Force Base, as attested to by a press photo of him driving a convertible with top down and his dog's ears up. It is not known whether he was sipping branch water when he is supposed to have used the hot line to the Pentagon to order the brass to "get off the pot and on the spill," but it is known that his visit prompted a critical editorial in the San Juan *Star* entitled "L.B.J.'s Goof." In it he was accused of "bad manners in not extending his greetings to the people of Puerto Rico and the government that represents them. He might have considered his visit in the same light as a visit to another base. However, the circumstances are different and the President should have realized it."

Disasters, whether natural or man-made, affect the poor most and the *Ocean Eagle* spill was no exception. By the time her bow and stern had separated, her cargo was working its way east along the coast to La Perla, a slum inhabited by squatters. La Perla, despite its fine view of the sea, is a grievous sight and the commonwealth government had been unable to decide whether to raze it and remove its denizens to the interior where they would be out of sight, or to clean it up and maintain it as a tourist attraction to illustrate the degree of poverty before Operation Bootstrap, a New Deal economic assistance program. Nature took care of the cleanup to some extent the previous December, when heavy seas swept in over the rocky shorefront and demolished over two hundred shacks called home by those who lived in them. One of these owners by seniority of possession, an old woman, sat on an oil-blackened rock a couple of days after the stranding, shaking her head at the lifeless Caribbean and rocking back and forth in grief.

"Ah, the poor sea," she moaned. "The poor, still sea!"

Word of the disaster spread quickly, and by the time the

church bells of San Juan had finished summoning worshippers to Sunday morning mass, the ramparts of El Morro were crowded with people using cameras and binoculars. It was a dramatic sight, for not only was the channel below stained by the still-flowing oil, but black spume from the seas smashing against the bow section had discolored the white deck house, turning the pilothouse ports opaque and making the slippery decks and rails glisten. Pilots of incoming planes had begun pointing out the wreck to their passengers, a practice later discouraged by tourist interests. The industry didn't need a massive spill added to its problems, which included a continuing water shortage, growing discourtesy by hotel employees toward guests and incendiary acts said to be the work of Puerto Rican nationalists, the Independentzias. Hotel managements got busy reassuring their guests that there was no real pollution threat to their beaches, and those who complained that the air was thick with the smell of oil were told it was caused by the agents used to control the menace.

The air became heavy with more than crude oil Sunday afternoon, and at night the vapor glazing auto windshields made driving hazardous. Old San Juan lay under a blanket of the stuff, and of reassuring words. The commonwealth government, through acting Governor Guillermo Irizarry, instructed Public Works Secretary Francisco Lizardi to inspect the area of contamination by helicopter, then announced that the commonwealth intended to avoid damage to the beaches and coastline. A spokesman for the Caribbean Gulf Refining Corporation, owners of the *Ocean Eagle*'s cargo, announced that Gulf was gathering detergents and would be flying in experts to combat the pollution. It was reported that 28,000 gallons were on order and would be sufficient to clean the seas. In addition, Gulf planned to fly in a plastic boom to control the oil, having ordered over a mile of it. The vanguard of what was to become an army of representatives from the manufacturers of detergents and dispersants arrived Sunday night, briefcase and sample-equipped.

The warning by the U.S. Agriculture Department's San Juan office of the threat to marine life and birds was seconded by a marine biologist of the commonwealth's Department of Agriculture, who speculated grimly about what could happen to coastal plant life. While the U.S. Coast Guard was primarily concerned with the hazard to navigation presented by the two hulks, it took pains to confirm that the channel buoys were in proper position and set up a patrol of the area. Captain Warner Thompson, U.S.C.G., wore two caps with scrambled eggs—as captain of the port and commander of the San Juan District with headquarters at the La Puntilla base. A large, jovial officer who had developed excellent relations with both the commonwealth government and the people of San Juan, he became a stabilizing figure during the crisis. Mrs. Thompson, aided by Coast Guard base volunteers, gave treatment and shelter to over 70 pelicans early in the crisis, making a major humane contribution.

The U.S. Navy also became active Sunday afternoon, both by word and deed. An emulsifier called Wyandot 20 was spread on the growing slick, and while it is normally used for naval bilge and machinery cleaning, it was said to be effective. Its degree of toxicity was not mentioned, nor was the fact that the resulting emulsion promised to be difficult to collect. The point was that action was being taken, if only of a preliminary nature, and that with an estimated 1,000,000 gallons of crude spilled by nightfall it was about time "a can-do outfit got busy." It was estimated by Navy sources that 1 gallon of emulsifier was required to dissolve 2 gallons of crude, meaning that 500,000 gallons would be needed to treat the present extent of spill. Per gallon cost of the agent was unavailable, as was an opinion of Gulf's estimate that 28,000 gallons of detergent would do the job. No one was burdening the acrid air that evening with mention of the 4,700,000 gallons of cargo still aboard the hulks.

The swells eased a bit on Monday, which would have permitted operations to begin on the hulks if there had been a plan and equipment to execute it with, and the White House announced that President Johnson had ordered that all possible assistance be rendered to the people of San Juan because of the menace threatening them. The Coast Guard was concerned over the possibility of the stern section sliding back into the channel and blocking the city's lifeline, and a meeting was attended by representatives of all interests involved—federal, commonwealth, tourist, shipping and those directly concerned with the vessel. Plans were developed to off-load the oil from the stern section into barges, then tow the hulk out to sea and scuttle it.

"Talking about off-loading a wreck," said a Navy tug skipper, "is sure easier than doing it."

Approximately 10 miles of the best Condado beaches were oil-soaked by Monday night (though public relations downplayed it) and most of the harbor lay heavy with oil. The commonwealth announced an all-out attack with chemicals on the "grave threat to our economy," and the Public Works Secretary predicted that the prevailing currents would help his crews leave clean beaches behind as they worked along the shore. It was not mentioned that eight hotel beaches were closed, that reservations were being canceled, that the crude continued to flow and that the spill was now put at 2,000,000 gallons.

Tugs had another unsuccessful try at moving the bow, according to the Coast Guard, and it was announced that a new attempt would be made on Tuesday with a pair of powerful Navy tugs from the Roosevelt Roads Base. An expert from the Murphy Pacific Marine Salvage Company of New York, who had studied the situation, wasn't encouraging. He described the bow as being held by rocks or ledge, and called it "a tough one." He wasn't happy about the stern either. Both sections presented problems because of the sea conditions frequently prevailing, and he said that if the top 4 feet of oil in the 15-foot-deep tanks could be removed, they would be doing well.

It wasn't a good Monday for San Juan, although some felt that at least it was a relief to have gotten beyond the bland reassurances that had come with each tide. A local shipping agent complained that maritime concerns were losing thousands of dollars a day because of safety restrictions put on channel traffc due to the danger posed by the hulks, and the press recorded the first attempt to use the crisis as a political weapon. A statement was issued by the chairman of the Commonwealth Committee on Beautification and Natural Resources in which it was suggested that the San Juan Port Authority might not be supervising navigation adequately.

Another controversy was generated by Kenneth Biglane, of the

Federal Water Pollution Control Administration, who had witnessed some of the *Torrey Canyon* cleanup efforts. He stated that widespread use of chemical agents was being made to save the beaches rather than the ecology, and he favored herding the oil to areas where it could be collected and pumped into receiving vessels or vehicles.

"Sinking it or breaking it up may help hide it for a while," a visiting ornithologist claimed, "but it's not that simple. Beaches will become quagmires, the sea floor a bed of asphalt and sensitive flora and fauna extinct."

The battle between detergent and emulsifier salesmen was intensified by a statement from Public Works Secretary Lizardi, who said that although booms and telephone poles would be used to collect the oil, he intended to continue with chemical agents as long as they did the job. He added that there was no use in treating the beaches until the water was cleaned up, and he thought it might be possible to try oil skimmers. More salesmen with antioil samples arrived on the scene, and the argument grew over whether it was more effective to form the oil into balls which sank, to disperse it by causing it to foam or to break it down into layers of its various components. The claims were loud and large, and a local detergent agent offered an unconditional guarantee that his product would not injure marine life. He was willing to treat San Juan harbor at a discount and would personally replace all injured organisms.

"Who is this guy?" a competitor asked.

"God," another answered.

The salesmen, who became known as de-oilers, spent a lot of time bombarding officials with the merits of their products and gave so many demonstrations of sinking oil, raising it, dispersing it and collecting it on one hotel beach that the sand became unstable. A guest, rashly ignoring warnings to neither swim nor use the beach, went down to his knees in the quicksandlike substance. He was pulled out, a layer of black gum covering his legs, and complained of a tingling of his skin similar to sunburn. The products employed at San Juan came in many forms, and among them were Ameroid, Penetone, Nabsoil, Mistron Vapor, Ekoperl and Sierra Talc. Special claims for nontoxicity were made for such agents as Polycomplex A and a Standard

Oil of New Jersey product called Corexit. It was to be energetically promoted and used on another big channel spill, that of Platform A at Santa Barbara, and although its efficiency is no longer questioned, its toxicity factor still is.

Many similar agents had been tried in the *Torrey Canyon* disaster with pretty much the same findings and results, but at San Juan the lessons had to be learned over again. In spite of claims to the contrary, no fully satisfactory agent turned up there, nor did a wholly effective technique. The best approach still appeared to be collection of the oil, then onshore disposal. The collection presented major problems, however, and the effects of wave and wind action were only one of them. Suitable equipment wasn't available, and the only skimmer at the scene, a 24-foot craft with a production of 50 gallons an hour in still waters, would have taken three years to clean up the oil spilled by then. It was believed that now that the experts had found out what was needed, they merely had to find it. However, it turned out that they would have to create it.

A marine biologist, Maximo Cerame Vives, of the University of Puerto Rico, said that not only were all detergents harmful, they could kill the coral off Candao. He reported that already sea urchins, spiny lobsters and some fish were dead, and that there would be worse to come. That long Monday, the first day after the *Ocean Eagle* stranding, ended on a cheerful note, even if there were those who knew why it was sounded and how inaccurate it was. Pan American, Trans Caribbean and Eastern Airlines, noncompetitive for once, announced that there had been no appreciable effect on travel to San Juan because of the spill, and there was no reason why there should be.

Navy tugs worked most of Tuesday night trying to move the bow section, having set up their towing gear during the day, and the operation was impressive. It failed, however, to do more than reassure the public that an effort was being made. In this it had something in common with the inspection visit of a V. I. P., Joseph Moore, commissioner of the Federal Water Pollution Control Administration. His presence proclaimed the concern of the federal government, but his statement on Wednesday was neither revealing nor reassuring—the two hulks contained a lot of oil that could escape into the sea. A Navy spokesman didn't have much comfort to offer either. He pointed out that the previous night's towing effort of four hours had moved the bow 150 feet, and that while this was progress, it was slow going. Observers on El Morro agreed with the "slow going," but to them the hulk's move looked like a very small 150 feet.

"Fifty is closer," said an off-duty chief petty officer, "and the way they wrestled, it maybe stretched that much!"

The Navy's big effort was scheduled for Friday at the 02:18 high water, when an armada of six vessels, led by the U.S.S. *Preserver*, a large rescue salvage vessel, went into operation. It was pointed out that a lot of horsepower would be represented and that with all the towing gear available there would be a lot of leverage too. It was decided that both the bow and stern sections would be towed 100 miles offshore to be sunk in the Puerto Rican Trench, a depression of 18,000 feet. The Coast Guard said that the oil would offer no pollution threat, without going into details, and the scuttling could be done by .50-calibre machine gun fire. In the meantime, use of detergents in deep water had been suspended, it was announced, because the major slicks had been eliminated and the balance was spread too thin for the chemicals to be effective. It was also reported that a plastic boom had been placed around the stern section Tuesday night to contain the leaking oil, but that it had carried away. The oil had resumed its former flow, and in order to save the Condado Lagoon, emulsifiers were being spread on slicks near the Dos Hermanos Bridge.

The Seventh Coast Guard District, Miami, announced that a Board of Inquiry was scheduled to investigate the stranding and would be headed up by the commander, Rear Admiral P. G. Prins, U.S.C.G. An officer explained that a definite reason for maritime accidents is sometimes difficult to establish, and that the board might be limited to determining what probably happened. Admiral Prins was asked by the acting governor if there was any way to prevent similar accidents. "The only sure way I can think of," the admiral was quoted as saying, "is not to allow any tankers in."

It was hoped that making the hearings public, unlike those in the *Torrey Canyon* disaster, would be helpful in securing a federal grant to help with financing the harbor channel improvements. They were needed, the channel not being known as one of the trickiest for nothing—a pilot must know what he's doing, do it, and have the guts to stay with it. Even before the *Ocean Eagle* disaster, the U.S. Army Corps of Engineers had scheduled public hearings to discuss a $15,000,000 improvement project. Governor Sanchez had sent a bill to the commonwealth legislature that would require a licensed harbor pilot aboard all larger vessels entering and leaving. A San Juan booster in the Port Authority, however, questioned the hazards the channel offered. He claimed that since 3,500 vessels had used the port in 1957, the danger couldn't be so great. He was not heard from again, but then not much has been heard of the improvement project either.

On Wednesday people began to feel that not much was being done to solve the crisis that each breath of oily air reminded them of, and an editorial in the San Juan *Star* entitled "Emergency" summed up the growing concern:

It is becoming painfully clear what an enormous task the Commonwealth Government and other concerned entities have on their hands in cleaning up the *Ocean Eagle* mess. Four days have passed since the tanker split in two sections and little of a remedial nature has been accomplished.

Lack of experience and equipment for dealing with such a situation is, of course, impeding progress. But this unfamiliarity and uncertainty also seems to be inhibiting some immediate measures that could be undertaken. Coordinating officials must realize that there has to be a mobilization of labor to clear the oil from the beaches; plain manual labor but in large quantities. Sand has to be shoveled, shoreline oil patches have to be scooped up and trucked away, equipment must be borrowed, leased and, in cases where absolutely necessary, purchased.

This is an emergency of the highest order.

Thursday did not mark much progress in solving the *Ocean Eagle* problem. Again, Kenneth Biglane of the F.W.P.C.A. warned that cleanup techniques could be as dangerous to marine life and beaches as the spill, and he cautioned against detergents, saying that they should not be used where wildlife is valued. As to the beaches, he explained that once oil reaches the substratum of sand, it performs as a corrosive, the biodegradable detergents being susceptible to bacterial decay in the water. He recommended the practice of skimming and rounding up the oil at points along the coast, where it could be sucked up by septic trucks. Such trucks, normally used for sewage collection, were in plentiful supply.

The effects of the oil on wildlife had become obvious by Thursday, as had the lack of planning and organization for its care. At La Perla a pelican completely covered with oil was picked up, its only movement an occasional blink of one eye. It was treated by a bath in gasoline to cut the oil, and after being rinsed in fresh water, was allowed to dry in the sun. A few hours later its rescuers were surprised to find it still groggy, and wondered if they should have used wine. While the lessons learned in bird treatment during the *Torrey Canyon* spill had had little circulation, at least the volunteers who set up an unofficial aid station for shore birds at Isle Verde knew enough to stay away from such agents as gasoline. Household cleaning and laundry aids, including one application of Brillo, were used at first, then Lestoil and Ivory soap. Eventually mineral oil was found to be harmless and fairly effective in cutting the crude.

An octopus, lobsters and sea urchins were washed up on the beaches that afternoon, and the Public Works Commissioner warned that expected heavy swells might be enough to slide the stern section into the channel, facing him with another 4,000,000 gallons of oil to combat. The Weather Bureau said that such seas were not expected and didn't know why officials were expressing concern. Another area of concern, less mysterious, was raised by the Popular Democratic party in a demand that the government protect the people from fish and pigs contaminated by the oil-polluted water. The government did not reply, perhaps because it was puzzled as to how pigs, which neithtr drink nor swim in sea water, could be contaminated.

Dissatisfaction with the control and cleanup efforts grew in San Juan, and the press pictures of salesmen with hand squirt guns and powder cans didn't help. The Coast Guard's defense was that it had neither sufficient manpower nor equipment to accomplish the job, but at least a statement by Captain Thompson cleared the air.

"It's an impossible job," he said. "Nobody knows a heck of a lot and we are just stumbling along."

As if to capitalize on the discomfiture of the Coast Guard, the Navy made an optimistic announcement—preparations for off-loading the oil in the bow section were under way. The Army had an offering too. The Murphy Pacific Salvage tug *Curb* was under contract to the Corps of Engineers, and on its arrival Friday, work would begin on off-loading the stern section. Much was made of this news, but it failed to impress hotel guests. Their mood was as acrid as the smell of oil, their expressions were as dark as the sands and their opinions as caustic as the agents in use. A few found diversion as sidewalk superintendents, watching laborers with shovels on the beaches and the antlike procession of wheelbarrows filled with soiled sand. The outboards and skiffs trying to maintain the light booms in generally futile attempts to keep new oil off beaches which had been cleaned for the third time offered some diversion, but it took the tourist industry thinkers to come up with what they called an oil-spill plus. The beauties of Puerto Rico's interior were extolled, and while some visitors did investigate the rest of the island out of frustration, it was the beaches that had brought them there and not the Rain Forest, scenic mountains or primitive villages. So many thousands gathered at El Morro for a view of the source of pollution that the Municipal Golf Course became a giant parking lot, and there was a welcome sales upturn on cameras and films. One dealer complained, "Developing they'll do at home. Here, all that develops is 'phew!' "

Caribbean Gulf, self-effacing owner of the *Ocean Eagle's* cargo, was loath to claim credit for picking up as much of the cleanup tab as they did. The less connected with the disaster they were, the better, they felt, and not even the rumor that oil collected from the beaches was being delivered to the plant free, was denied. "The commonwealth rakes up the oil," it went, "and Gulf rakes in the money."

Probably less oil was being hauled to the refinery than to the municipal dump, where it was discharged from cesspool trucks backed to the edge of a great mountain of garbage. It flowed down sinuously to a marsh below, then oozed its way to a fetid creek and, presumably, to the ground water. The harbor was a concern of the commonwealth Department of Health. Its secretary, Dr. Manuel Torres Aguiar, advised a ban on commercial fishing in San Juan Bay, and the director of the Environmental Health Program, Dr. Fernando Padro, stated that the water was badly polluted and went on to say that it hadn't taken the slick to make the fish inedible—they were that already, the bay being classified as an industrial area. It had been so ever since prosperity came to San Juan, he said. The federal government, not to be outdone, also warned of the effects suffered by fish through an advisory by the Interior Department.

The Navy had another unsuccessful try at moving the bow section, perhaps as a warmup for the big Friday pull, and a spokesman on the *Preserver* estimated that getting it off the ledge holding it could take anywhere from three days to several weeks, a pretty free estimate at best, but no one was making bets on the stern section. Because of breaking seas, riled by the shoal water, it went unvisited all day. Criticism of the continuing flow of oil from the bow was defended by the Navy as a necessary evil. Oil had to remain aboard to prevent the hulk from shifting, it was explained, and because of the hull's condition some loss was inevitable. Why the tanks were not flooded with water for ballast instead was not explained, but it was pointed out that Navy personnel were doing a conscientious job under difficult conditions and that a pulling force of more than 120,000 pounds of thrust was available to move the bow. Some experts objected, and with good reason, that the hulk represented not *pounds* caught by ledge but thousands of *tons*, and until the Navy either off-loaded the remaining oil of lifted the derelict with some giant helicopter, there wasn't much point in boasting about horsepower.

As with the *Torrey Canyon* disposition problem, fire and explosion was raised as a solution, but was rejected. The possibility presented a real threat for the stern section, and it was one that the Murphy Pacific Salvage people had every intention of avoiding. That section had ceased to ooze oil from its compartments, but a survey of the hulk suggested that there was still enough oil aboard to cause major pollution if more bulkheads gave way. The engine room was flooded, other compartments were heavy with oil vapor and the atmosphere was like that around a bomb that would be happy to go off. The salvage crew were going to keep their fingers crossed and, as one swore, toes too. The *Curb*, a former World War II Navy salvage vessel, was able enough, but along with her salvage gear had a look of time about her. Some of her pumps were originally designed for steam power, being later converted for compressed air, and diving helmets—large, brass teakettle affairs with many a dent—were in evidence. It was clear that more modern and lighter equipment would be required if time was to be made on removing the stern section. If Murphy Pacific didn't have it, the Corps of Engineers would know where and how to get it. They are great believers in equipment, the Engineers, and they believe in the best.

"They can afford to," says a civilian salvage master. "It's our money."

Questions were being asked about the plight of the pelicans by Friday, and other than that they were in a bad way, there were no answers. The brown pelican is a ponderous, aquatic bird weighing up to 50 pounds and has, as does the cormorant family, webbed toes. It has a wing spread of over 5 feet and flies with its long neck retracted, the broad bill resting on its breast. Its flight is a joy to watch, as lines of pelicans skim the water with occasional, powerful wing strokes, the bill ready to scoop fish. Attached to it is a sack for storing food, of which, due to the bird's size and efficient digestive system, it is a large consumer. They are less dramatic than eagles, perhaps, but far more touching, and on occasion, humorous. Their takeoffs, reminiscent of early amphibian planes, need room, and on land they get around with a fat man's waddle, sometimes using their wings to maintain balance. Their method of fishing is almost as efficient as their digestion, and it is done at some speed. Skimming the surface, they will plunge with open beak, sending up a shower of spray, and if the prize is not too big, will regain altitude without having to go through the laborious takeoff. Their immersion does wet them thoroughly, however, and after the spill this was with more than water, which meant loss of flight ability. Between ingesting crude oil from contaminated fish and frequent preening, they were done for, but it is a question whether toxicity or exhaustion and starvation caused greater suffering.

Their way of dying is eerily human. The birds often pair off in their distress, and as the dying victim eases down to the ground, wings limp, it gives an occasional shudder and gasp. Its mate will stand close, then extend a protecting wing over the victim until the death tremors have passed. Eventually, the wing is slowly lifted, and after a pause which has a look of mourning, the mate turns away and with a slow, lumbering stride goes off by itself to huddle with wings down and eyes closed. After a bit, it will stand determinedly, then with a shake and wing flap, goes about its business. It does not return to, or even seem aware of, the body.

The commonwealth Fish and Wildlife Division had planned to retrieve the sicker pelicans in the harbor area on Thursday, but on its postponement tourists and civilian volunteers assembled under the Constitution Bridge and went into operation. Oil-drenched pelicans were gathered from the marshes and sandbars north of the bridge by slum children, the volunteers being leery of quicksands and the black, odiferous mud. Payment was a dollar a bird and capturing them took some doing. Unable to fly, the birds had become afraid of the water and had to be pursued across the marshes in waist-deep ooze until they became exhausted and collapsed. They were then dragged to the bridge by their long necks or a wing, both birds and boys becoming thick with oil and mud. After securing the birds with clothesline, the volunteers clamped the powerful bills shut with rubber bands and set to work with cleansers and rags, which soon were in short supply. It was planned to put the sicker birds, whose condition was judged by the fight they put up, out of the way. That raised the question of how best to do it, and a vacationing college student tried neck wringing. To wring a neck as long and flexible as a pelican's takes some doing, certainly more than the student was capable of. Outraged protests by both bird and onlookers put a stop to it and a presumably more humane suggestion was offered. A baseball bat was borrowed from a small boy, who soon regretted his cooperation. Then a man stood on the neck and held the wings, while another swung at the head. The first blow missed, the next connected, but it took several to do the job. Oil and blood stained the ground, the boy ran off without his boat and a few of the volunteers followed. It was decided to let nature take its course, and the cleaning operation resumed in silence under the bridge.

The operation was conducted on more efficient lines Friday, the commonwealth having employed fishermen in skiffs to collect the birds from the water, or failing that, to herd them onto the marsh for capture. A Fish and Wildlife representative, Felix Inigo, pointed out that the fishermen knew the waters and the birds' habits—also, fishing having been suspended, the men were out of work—and added that the treatment the birds were given at the Agriculture Department's laboratories at Dorado was experimental because little was known about how to proceed. The same held for the techniques used by the Puerto Rico Humane Society, however great the concern on the part of personnel. By nightfall, there were still numerous pelicans on the marshes—oil-soaked, hungry, sick and unable to fly. They squatted in the mud as if brooding, occasionally shuddering and opening their sticky bills. Some roosted on old tires and timbers, and every now and then others would give the water a try. None could take off.

Something of a production line was in operation under the bridge Saturday. The frightened, helpless birds were sprayed with Lestoil after being secured, then bathed in fresh water. It was an arduous, dirty job taking about a half-hour for each bird, after which they were allowed to waddle about in the sun to dry off being being boxed for trucking to the Humane Society, where milder agents were used. The problem was the same as with the *Torrey Canyon*'s victims—how to remove the crude without cutting the natural oils vital for insulation, proper flotation and flight. Preening was encouraged—it was vital that the waxy substance excreted by a gland on the birds' backs be distributed through their feather covering. Since fish were in short supply and hand feeding was required at first, nutrition was a problem.

It was solved at the Coast Guard base where 100 pounds of whiting was presented by local supermarkets and an additional 400 was purchased by base personnel at a discount. In addition to Hexachloryphyl, Magnus Hand Cleaner was tried there and castor oil was used as an agent to clear the intestines of crude. The base reduced the intake of food gradually as the birds gained strength, and they were made to fly. The hope was that they would not end up as permanent residents, but some refused to stray far from their handlers. Of those who survived, a few became mascots and others would check in for a handout regularly.

Accurate figures of the growing toll in marine life were hard to come by, one bay man claiming that figures were meaningless.

"Like the pelicans," he said, "sea creatures come and they go, and they'll come again. So will oil."

The Catano fishermen were less sanguine, complaining that not only were people afraid to buy local fish, but even fish imported from the south was spoiling on their stands. The commonwealth was petitioned to provide financial support and compensation for damage to their nets, many of which had been ruined, and for their buoys and lines. Statements by experts that appeared in the press added to their problem—predictions were made that some species of fish might survive for as long as six months, during which time toxic residue could be passed to humans. The symptoms, new to neither residents nor tourists, took the form of indigestion and diarrhea. A press agent said that at last they had something which wasn't Puerto Rico's fault to blame the *turista* on.

The figures for economic losses were hard to come by too, but here it was simply a question of their not being released. Reservations were said to be off at least 10 percent, and as one hotel operator explained, in addition to the immediate loss there was the future to reckon with. He expected that it would be months before the oil was completely removed and that during this time the island would acquire a bad name. He wondered if the beaches would ever be as good after the exposure to crude and chemicals, even though thousands of cubic yards of sand would be replaced. Nature, he said, still makes better beaches than man. And as for the oil that was being sunk, who knew when it would reappear? Standing on an oil-polluted beach watching the rollers coming in to break not as surf but as ledges of crude, it was hard to be optimistic. They fall with a plop as if they were solid, and black sea spray rising from the reefs takes some getting used to.

In the Navy's heralded Friday towing operation on the bow section, the powerful *Preserver* was equipped with a massive chain instead of 2-inch steel cables, which had parted in an earlier effort. It was hoped that the lack of stretch in the forged links might help to shake the hulk loose, but not apart, as some feared. She and five other vessels gave it all they dared, ending up with worse than failure—new oil poured forth, and a lot of it. The swells which had been looked to as an ally, together with the high tide, now turned out to be a hindrance. Work had to be suspended on the stern section, and the twenty-four-hour patrol by Coast Guard picket boat to check on the hulk's position and harbor pirates was called off. It was getting late in the day to worry about souvenirs, according to a collector who was said to have gotten off with the captain's navigating chair. The ship's clock, bell and binnacle, he reported, were already safe ashore.

The heavy weather continued through Saturday, straining bulkheads and plating, and oily seas stained the bow section deckhouse as black as its sides. The hulk shifted position that night, a parted cable dangling from her fo'c'sle head on one side and a length of anchor chain on the other. The *Ocean Eagle,* her two halves adding up to more than a whole, was a derelict, a danger, a polluter and an embarrassment to the commonwealth and, thanks to the Navy failure, the federal government. The channel was closed by the Coast Guard because of the hulk's shift in position, and shipping interests lost no time in complaining about their losses. Defensive statements that the closing was only temporary and that the off-loading and removal preparations would resume as soon as the weather moderated didn't reassure anyone, nor did the suspension of cleanup efforts. As soon as they were resumed, the Public Works director said, Ekoperl would be used on a larger scale. He praised the ability of this treated rock compound to absorb oil but not water, and there weren't many competing salesmen to object—most had gone home with fairly full sample cases and very empty order books.

With Monday's moderating weather came a sunny announcement from Governor Sanchez describing the new, improved plans for the bow section. He admitted that it was still spilling oil and was hard aground about 200 yards from its former position, for which he blamed the weather. He praised "valiant" Navy efforts, saying that it had been decided that empty tanks would be flooded with seawater to act as ballast to keep the hulk in position, and so would the other tanks as they were emptied of oil. The bow operation was to be the responsibility of the Navy, while the Army Corps of Engineers would be responsible for the stern, employing the Murphy Pacific Salvage Company.

Captain Bernard Peters, U.S.N., chief staff officer of Service Squadron 8, commanded the bow operation, assisted by Commander J. H. Boyd, U.S.N., as salvage master. Captain Peters, a trim officer of slight build and rather Royal Navy manner, took obvious pride in his unit. Its members did the Navy credit, even if they went about things with a more dashing air than their unglamorous support service called for. The stern section operation was headed up by Lieutenant Colonel John F. McElhenny, U.S.A., who was deputy district engineer at Jacksonville and assigned to interoceanic canal studies. At one point in his career he had attended the Navy War College at Newport; by the time his *Ocean Eagle* assignment was finished, he was promoted to district engineer as a full colonel. At San Juan he was assisted by a small but efficient civilian staff transferred from other Engineer Corps assignments and they managed to ride herd on the Murphy Pacific operation without getting anybody's back up. This was an accomplishment of some size, for the salvage problems rose, so did the pressure, to say nothing of the Corps' desire to finish work on the stern section as quickly as the Navy's work on the bow. For all that the latter faced tougher sea conditions, the stern was a larger undertaking. It contained the propulsion and pumping machinery with innumerable vapor-filled compartments which required first venting, then sealing. There was a multitude of hull openings to close and there were some problems of stress also, both because of the way the hulk lay and the unequal weight distribution. A tanker's stern is meant to be a part of a whole, not an entity unto itself—things had gone so hard with this one, it was as if the stern were saying so.

The first order of business for the salvors was to put aboard the tools and equipment needed. There was a lot of this, and because of the weight, a handling problem arose. It wasn't practical for the *Curb* to come alongside to place it with her cargo booms due to her draught, and there would have been some reluctance to do so even if there had been enough water—if the hulk blew, there would be a good chance the *Curb* would go with her. A stiff-leg crane on a barge was engaged to handle the bigger units, such as diesel generators and air compressors, but to get a sea condition quiet enough to avoid stoving them in took some patience. Smaller items, such as pumps, suction and discharge hoses, patching material and other salvage gear, were raised by block and tackle from the M boat, a borrowed Navy landing bessel. She took many a knock against the hulk's plates, thanks to the seas encountered, and so did the *Curb*'s two motor lifeboats doubling as tenders. It was a hazardous, ungainly way to supply the operation, and having to manhandle the gear on oily decks wasn't any better. Even getting the salvage crew aboard wasn't always easy—mastering a swinging Jacob's ladder from a small boat in 10-foot seas needs timing, agility and courage, as well as expert boat handling. Portable items had to be hoisted, and if the hitch slipped or the hoist failed, it was a long way down to the bottom, which is where the tools liked to go. If one fell while getting on the ladder from the fantail's rail, it was a good 30 feet to the combing seas, which were still preferable to landing in the boat or between it and the ship's side.

Once aboard, there was the feeling of dread common to wrecked vessels. It comes from a stillness not found on a ship afloat and from the feel of power not yet dead—a destructive force that can be released at the wreck's will. It is as if one's destiny has been turned over to a thing with a mindless logic expressed in the coldness of sweating steel bulkheads. There are memories crying out not to be forgotten, and an assortment of odors fighting for recognition. On the *Ocean Eagle* there was the smell of crude, the engine room supplied a mix of lubricating oil, brass polish and pipe insulation, and the alleyways that of moldy bedding and soiled work clothes. The after end of the deckhouse was strong with the odor of rotting food in the walk-in freezers and the product of backed-up sanitary lines. The noises aboard were not reassuring either—water dripped, leaking oil plopped from strained bulkheads and deck plates creaked as the hull shifted slightly on the bottom. These noises spoke of those who had sailed her and the pride some took in her.

Evidence of the rush to the boats was on the mess room tables—food-caked plates, congealed coffee mugs and soured wine there wasn't time to toss off—and on the galley range were huge pots already growing a variety of multicolored moulds. Personal articles littered the decks of cabins, chest drawers hung out, lockers gaped open and half-packed valises and sea bags lay about in both the crew's and officers' quarters. The luggage in the latter was of better quality, just as the officers' staterooms were decorated with glossy pinups, while the crew's quarters displayed pictures of loved ones. It has been suggested that the officers, being more sophisticated due to their better education and longer sea serpice, were less dependent on reminders of home. Certainly their accommodations were sophisticated enough, providing a luxury neither group enjoy in Greece—those of the master, chief officer and chief engineer rivaled the best hotel suites. Reading tastes paralleled the difference in decor, unlicensed personnel going in more for educational works, while the officers preferred comic books and pornography.

As was the *Torrey Canyon,* the *Ocean Eagle* was a happy ship and the presence of wine and spirits helped to compensate for the difference between hers and U.S. pay scales. There must have been a good supply aboard, but pirates, in spite of the seas and Coast Guard patrols, had done well for themselves. Only empty wine flagons were left and it must have pained them to have passed up dry stores, ship's linens and gear. Their small boats were up to sick bay items though, and syringes, surgical instruments and drugs had disappeared. As the days passed, the salvors stripped the wreck of souvenirs, considered traditional, if illegitimate, booty. Eventually even the brass porthole fixtures began to disappear (they can be made into fine end tables) and the engine room wasn't spared either. That vast cavern, once glossy white and glittering with polished brass, was an awesome sight from the fidley (funnel) grating. At least 15 feet of oil and water had flooded it and this dark lake stirred occasionally, releasing gaseous bubbles with a digestive lethargy. It was possible to make out the submerged turbines, pumps and generators, and the waste of so much good design, workmanship and power was as depressing as the lifelessness. In spite of the hazards of slippery steel ladders and gratings topside, the roll in dictator and various gauges had been removed and tools secured to the bulkheads soon disappeared too. There was an indecency about this stripping before burial, but as one souvenir collector said, studying his wrecking bar, "Maybe we call a ship she, but it's still only a thing."

The stern section represented more than the scrap value of its hull, but at $18 per ton there was a lot of that too—perhaps $75,000. Much of her machinery could have been overhauled and then have brought another $50,000, and there was even interest in trying to save the entire unit for jumboizing with another forebody. It would have had to have been removed from Puerto Rican waters, however, but towing to Miami could have been done for $5,000. To have made the hulk seaworthy would probably have run not more than $50,000, so there was a chance for a good profit. Liability coverage would have been extremely high, though—a lot could go wrong on such a tow and no underwriter is eager to be associated with a name as black as the *Ocean Eagle*'s had become. The possibility of salvage was settled by the authorities, commonwealth, and federal, who wanted to see the end of the *Ocean Eagle*. The bottom of the sea was the place for her, the quicker the better, and no one was going to stand in the way.

Murphy Pacific, under pressure to expedite the off-loading and eventual scuttling was reinforced by the arrival of the salvage tug *Cable*, a sister ship of the *Curb*, fresh from her work on the S.S. *General Colocotronis* at Eleuthera. It was not so much that she and her equipment were needed, but her salvage crew was, and with them work proceeded faster on the stern section. A different kind of reinforcement appeared in the person of the operations manager of the Merritt division of

Murphy Pacific, Captain Robert K. Thurman. Merritt had been part of the venerable Merritt, Chapman and Scott firm before it became a stock manipulation. Captain Thurman had been a Navy salvager and served in the Arctic. His mission was to head up the operation in consultation with the salvage master, Captain Henry C. Halboth, and as a man who liked to work, he liked to see others work. The pleasure he took in this was not shared by all—salvors don't go for drivers.

"Bosses got to live too," said a welder, putting his can of beer down, "only they don't live so long. We work, they worry."

The presence of Captain Thurman, together with longer work hours and the receipt of modern salvage gear, made progress on the hulk more evident. This was in spite of, as a salvor put it, reflecting the traditional view of the presence of brass, the daily visits of Colonel McElhenny. Salvors have an air of independence which says time is their servant, and Colonel McElhenny was wise enough to overlook their manner. He concentrated on the progress being made, but for an Army regular it can't have been easy. The level of oil and sea in the engine room dropped steadily, thanks to submersible pumps, and cargo was off-loaded by the ship's own pumps into lighters alongside, power being provided not by her boilers but by air compressors. It took a lot of air, just as the submersible pumps took a lot of electricity, but by this time the compressors and generators brought aboard had the capacity to handle the job. Work was speeded up throughout the hulk, almost as if the crew had caught the tempo of the equipment.

As San Juan underwent its second week of suffering from oil pollution, heavy rains helped flush some areas of the bay and the combination of bacteria and evaporation began to break up the slicks. By midweek, divers had located a long indentation in the bottom plates of the stern and were taking underwater measurement of plate thickness by micrometer, in addition to other tests of metal strength and erosion effect. It was ascertained that both plating and rivets were under considerable stress, resulting in a decision to handle the hulks more gently for fear of their breaking up and spilling more oil. Spill containment was still being tried and high hopes were held out for a giant boom Murphy Pacific was building at the Coast Guard base.

Later known as the Merritt Navy boom, its construction was headed up by an elderly salvage master, who had recently discarded a trunkful of logs and photos of his World War I salvage operations, among them the scuttled Imperial German fleet. His disregard of their historical interest was indicative of his view of the interest the press took in oil pollution.

"We've always had spills and we always will," he grumbled. "If only you pencil pushers would lay off, shore folks would relax. It isn't the oil that messes things up, it's the talk!"

The boom used 55-gallon drums as floats, tied together by steel cables to support plywood panels with an apron of weighted plasticized canvas. Although portable, it was a massive rig and handling had to be done by crane. It represented both good design and workmanship, but was never tried—the oil was off-loaded from the hulks before its completion and no one had either the time or the patience to undertake experiments. "We know it will work," Captain Thurman said. "All we need is another good spill to show what it can do."

The Navy continued with the off-loading of the bow section often working well into the night, and by the end of the month it was estimated that a "mere" 350,000 gallons of oil remained in the stern section. The cost of work on that section was put at roughly $1,125,000, which was offset to some extent by the oil recovered and delivered to the Gulf refinery. The total cost of cargo removal from both sections and their scuttling is a figure hard to come by, but the best guess puts it at close to $2,500,000. The loss by then to the commonwealth economy was both large and uncalculated. It was not a figure responsible sources wanted to publicize.

"All that would do," said one, "is scare away tourists. They're leery enough now."

"Call it many millions," said another, "but not hundreds of them."

One loss the work on bow and stern did not lead to, surprisingly enough, was that of life. The nearest approach to it occurred during scuba-diving operations on the bow section. It was storming with force four winds, seas close to what they were when the *Ocean Eagle* stranded, and there was a strong current. Hard-hat divers would not have gone down under such conditions, but the pair of scuba divers who had been sent by a New York marine surveyor weren't to be put off by sea conditions, a roiled bottom or an inappropriate platform to work from. This had to be a tug because of the seas, but it had too much freeboard and was too unmaneuverable to be either convenient or safe.

"You have to really be a diver to go down when it's like this," one said.

"Or nuts," added his mate, helping him with his air tanks.

They became separated below and the first diver, a lean, intense man no longer young, surfaced unexpectedly some distance upchannel from the tug. Maneuvering to bring him aboard was a tricky business, the location of the second diver being unknown, and when he was finally pulled over the side he was tired, cold and pale. The failure of his mate to appear only added to his disgust—it had been dark below, the current was strong and it was all work. The tug headed back to the hulk slowly, pitching steeply in the seas, and those aboard hoped that the second diver would surface soon, but not too close to the plunging bows or churning screw. Turning, the tug came in closer to the hulk than intended, and it was then that the overdue diver, younger than the first and a lot heavier, came up between the hulls and ripped off his mask. Fast throttle work by the tug skipper saved him from being crushed, together with instant response by the Caterpillar diesels. When he was at last hauled aboard, being freed of his tanks, he took a long breather and shook his head.

"It might just be," he said, "I'll learn enough to be scared some day."

The crowds on El Morro continued to watch the operations on the hulks and the Coast Guard Board of Inquiry had almost as good a view from the lawn of the La Puntilla base. The board was convened March 10 in a screened porch of the reserve officers' recreational building, a flag-decorated space about 75 feet by 30 with a tile floor. A large goma tree and hibiscus hedge graced the front lawn and beyond the bulkhead was the busy channel with the menacing sections of the *Ocean Eagle*. The board was chaired by Rear Admiral P. G. Prins, U.S.C.G., a genial, substantial man whose shiny bald head suggested a country banker. He was flanked at a long table by the members of the board, Captain E. H. Daniels, U.S.C.G., who acted as recorder, and Commander J. S. Lipuseck, U.S.C.G. All wore dress whites with ribbon bars, as did their host, Captain Thompson. Two other Coast Guard officers were present in civilian clothes, Rear Admiral Louis M. Thayer, U.S.C.G., (Ret.), a member of and observer for the National Transportation Safety Board, and Commander M. E. Welch, Jr., U.S.C.G., technical adviser. Also part of the proceedings were a court stenographer, interpreters, counsels for the ship owners and cargo owner, and underwriters for the hull and liability coverages. Representatives of interested parties were also present, such as federal, commonwealth and Liberian authorities, maritime unions, port interests and the Pilots Association.

Communications were a problem in spite of able interpretation. The *Ocean Eagle*'s officers spoke through interpreters, as did the pilot in some of his testimony, and the frequent periods required for translation and retranslation, defining of nautical terms and clarifying of legal points provided opportunities for witnesses to bend testimony to their needs and for counsel to obscure, evade or confirm matters according to their objectives. The chairman and members were at something of a disadvantage in having to deal with admiralty lawyers of considerable standing over finer points of the law—they had neither the background for such a specialty nor the virtue of experienced counselors. The atmosphere in the hearing room was on the tense side, for many causes were being pushed. The master and chief officer were anxious to avoid blame, as were the owners and hull underwriters. The liability people would have been happy if evidence showed the buoys were out of position, cargo owners would have welcomed evidence of hull failure, commonwealth interests were ready to shift responsibility to their federal opposite numbers and the pilots hoped to lay the blame where they insisted it belonged—on the master—and he was to work hard to return the compliment.

For those who tired of the drama in the hearing room, there was the channel with its traffic for a distraction. Much of it was commercial, ranging from cruise liners to trawlers spreading antipollution agents, but there was considerable salvage, Navy and Coast Guard activity too. The noise from the frequent coming and going of low-flying jets, amphibians and helicopters was as disagreeable to members of the board as were the blinding rays of the setting sun, which they faced daily.

"Real judges would move," a wire service reporter guessed. "But flag rank ones don't dare—they're afraid it might seem a concession."

An early witness was the *Ocean Eagle's* chief officer, Panagistis Michalopoulus. He was a heavyset man who showed considerable anxiety, only part of which could have come from the fact that when sitting in the witness chair his legs were too short to reach the floor. His pauses before answering questions seemed endless, his speech was deliberate and he was a stickler for exactness in translation. He lost no time in trying to make clear that neither he nor the master was to blame for the disaster, and in obscuring both the positions of the vessel and anchor use. The anchor subterfuge was probed by hard questioning—was it lowered only one shot to be carried ready for lowering, or was more let out and did it catch? It was an important matter, bearing on seamanship, vessel control and position. Yes and no answers wouldn't serve; it's hard to cover yourself that way, whereas language difficulties and technical definitions help. An example of how the finer points were disputed among the board, counsel and the witness was the agreement, reached after long discussion, that the record should speak of the anchor's position in terms not of how far from the bottom it was but how much below the surface.

The chief officer had been ordered to the fo'c'sle head, and however open to the weather, it was a refuge from discovery of the truth. His station at the time of the disaster allowed him to appear to know little of what had gone on, even including the ship's position and time of day. But, strangely, he was able to back up later testimony where needed. He established that all tanks, except for the wings, had been filled to within 5 feet of their tops and that the overloading was the fault of the shore—in spite of being warned to reduce the rate of flow, they had pumped too much and too long.

Wisely, perhaps, the board decided to follow more relaxed rules of evidence in order to get at the facts more readily, but further exploratory discussion couldn't be avoided—how long it takes a windlass to winch in 70 feet of anchor chain, whether 90 feet of chain in 50 feet of water is enough to swing the bow 45 degrees, and if so, how long it takes. It was less that the board was running out of patience than that it was running out of time—it had been a long first day, too long for the facts ascertained. It looked as if it might be a long voyage to the truth about the *Ocean Eagle*, as one counsel observed.

"Even all the way to Monrovia," agreed another, referring to news of a Liberian inquiry.

Loyal to the master, Chief Officer Michalopoulus was adamant that the order to abandon ship was properly given and that the latter did not shout to the men running for the boats, "Stop! Stop!" He wasn't too clear about what he was doing on the fo'c'sle head during the fifteen minutes that passed after the order was given and before he abandoned ship, and he wasn't much help in regard to the bos'n either. The bos'n wasn't sure of anything, except that since he didn't wear a watch he couldn't help with the timing of events. He was as respectful a witness as one could ask for, even if he wasn't helpful and the first session ended with the board squinting into the sun. They rose in evident relief, as an aide frowned at a heavily loaded tourist boat coming downchannel for a look at the hulks. Called the *Pirate Ship*, its list was reminiscent of that of New York's Statue of Liberty sightseeing boats when tourists crowd one rail. Here there was an additional hazard— the *Pirate Ship* rolled heavily as she turned broadside to the swells by the bow section. It was clear from the officer's look that on future trips fewer passengers would be carried and concentration would be on the less exposed stern section.

The helmsman began the second day of hearings. This nervous, middle-aged Greek, however respectful, didn't speak English or wear a watch either. He had no recollection of engine orders and the telegraph wasn't visible from the helm. His recall of the stranding and abandoment was clear though. The ship struck three times.

Then, whole place shook. Captain, he say, "Ship broke—abandon." I go starboard boat, port boat already down, radio man and Bos'n in. Steam lines rupture, I go, too—not losing for time, either.

He described the master as exicted, saying that he sent the chief officer to the "foxhole," by which it was developed he meant the fo'c'sle. At this point in the testimony, a Coast Guard outboard attempted to corral a pair of swimming pelicans, directed by officers in a picket boat. The birds made such desperate attempts to take off that the hunt was called off for fear they would harm themselves, just as the helmsman was explaining that he knew nothing about the *Ocean Eagle's* courses. It was easier to steer for a shore point than use the compass.

"When you're young, that is," chuckled Admiral Prins, off the record.

The testimony of the chief engineer, an engaging man proud of his engines, was concerned with bunkers (fuel), which he put at 3,000 tons with consumption of 82½ tons per day, and water carried—75 tons, of which the boilers used 25 and the domestic system 8. After the master phoned that the ship was "cut," he said, an order was rung down for full ahead. Soon after came a stop order. The reason he didn't remove the engine logs was simple enough—he "didn't think"—and the suggestion of a possibility that the ship might have leaked made him raise his arms in surprise and say loudly, "No!" The translation of his answer to the question regarding his opinion of the master brought more than one smile to the hearing: "The Captain loves his engineer."

Captain Galaris, for all his eleven years at sea, had more the look of a press agent or promoter than shipmaster. His prized blue suit didn't go with his earnest manner, but that discrepancy pleased members of the Pilots Association—for them, the worse the impression he made, the better. The voyage, it developed, was a first for him in two ways—he had never entered San Juan harbor before and he had never sailed in an overloaded condition. The latter he put down to the shore "giving too much too quick," but he wasn't let off so easily.

Q. Why was it not pumped back?
A. No.
Q. Why wasn't it done?
A. This is not done.
Q. Are you aware it *is* done?
A. I haven't heard of such things.
Q. Did you ask permission?
A. I ask for regulation. Book didn't say so.
Q. Did you ask formally?
A. No one can give information.
Q. Because of a language problem?
A. Nobody to ask.
Q. The port captain?
A. Spoke to man who came for orders—don't know who.

The problem of pumping the cargo back, apparently, lay in the fact that the supplying tanks fed through gravity from a hillside, the result being that the ship's pumps had insufficient power to overcome the head. The master was quick to deny improper loading, pointing out that he had approved the chief officer's loading plan. He listed the cargoes the ship had carried in addition to crude, known rightly as "dirty" cargo—bunker fuel, vegetable oil and molasses, but no naptha or gasoline.

"If her cargo had been either this voyage," one of the admiralty lawyers said during a break, "we'd be even harder up for answers. It would just be a case of X marks the spot."

Questioning soon led to the anchor controversy and whether the ship had been properly aligned for the channel. It was clear that neither the board nor counsel were satisfied with the answers, and during an off-record discussion of how best to get at the facts, the master looked at the stern section of his former command, his hands tightly clenched. He had worked hard to conceal his anxiety and anger, but in this unguarded moment both showed—his face was haggard, he wet his lips and his forehead glistened with sweat. He watched a trawler pass, spreading an absorbent called Ekoperl. Forming a cakelike substance, it absorbs oil and little water, is relatively easy to collect and is said to be nontoxic. It was not as effective as hoped, however, partly because instead of being spread, whole bags were dumped intact. As to toxicity, it was impossible to ascertain the effects on seabirds, which hurried to sample it, among them several swimming pelicans.

Under cross-examination regarding anchor use, Captain Galaris said that he had ordered it lowered by one shot.

Q. How would one shot of anchor chain help the ship?
A. To have it ready.
Q. Do you usually drop anchor when approaching?
A. No.
Q. Why here?
A. Bad weather.
Q. Were you in doubt about port?
A. Sure.

Testifying about the events immediately after the grounding, he seemed more relaxed. His manner said here was a master in control of a crisis situation, doing his best to save his crew from danger and his ship from becoming a hazard to navigation.

A. Pilot he left bridge. I call engine for all speed to get ship out of channel and aground. I gave alarm, told Chief Mate to drop starboard anchor and let out much chain. There was no way on ship and when aft port life boat being lowered, I saw propeller turning. I stopped engine, told Chief Engineer to stand by and crew to abandon ship. The mid-ship lifeboat was checked to be sure it lowered, then all hands ordered to abandon ship, except Chief Officer. Chief Engineer to abandon when all secure.

Before the examination returned to the boarding by the pilot, an item of interpretation was cleared up—the phrase at issue was "one long ton" not "one good ton." As the sequence of events was gone over again, Captain Galaris began to lose his composure and he froze for some time on one question. It had been asked in a deceptively casual way by counsel.

Q. The channel depth is 38 feet and the vessel's draft was only 31—why did she strike if she was in the channel?
A. I cannot explain.

Q. Until the first hit, did you believe you were standing into danger?

A. I asked Pilot to turn starboard to take me back to sea.

There was a pause after this, and during it the only sound in the room was the occasional turning of a page of notes by board members or by counsel. The hearing was recessed, the master rose with a slight bow to the board, then went out to the bulkhead. He seemed a tall, very solitary figure in bright blue with heavily padded shoulders. He looked down at the oily water, and after a bit, a pelican flew past. Captain Galaris looked up, shielding his eyes to follow it out of sight. It was the first seen on the wing since the inquiry had begun.

Counsel questioned Captain Galaris sharply the next day and it wasn't long before he was wiping his brow with a handkerchief as blue as his suit. A number of technical matters relating to the ship and its operation were examined—draft, freeboard and the amount of sea room required for a 90-degree turn at various speeds. The mathematics entailed had even the board looking anxious, and there was a sense of relief when the questioning turned to the pilot's attempts to board. It didn't last long, though—the master soon found himself on the defensive.

Q. Why didn't you wait there for the pilot?

A. I did.

Q. Why could you not insist that he come to you and board?

A. How can I insist?

Q. Why couldn't you stay there?

A. (After pause) I can't say.

Members of the Pilots Association listened with interest as the master's responses became angrier, and they began whispering among themselves when he accused the pilot of not coming out far enough, of not maneuvering the *Ocean Eagle* with more speed and of having failed to answer his radio calls. After a pause for control, he finished the attack.

"Pilot knows water best," he said, rather too loudly. "Master knows his ship best."

Pilot Gonzales, who held an unlimited master's license and

had been a pilot in San Juan since 1966, had been going to sea for thirty-three years. He recited how he attempted to board, in English with a Spanish accent, not failing to refer to the vessel's 4-knot speed, his attempts to warn her off and his decision to alert tugs. He made a good witness, and his sense of outrage was as effective an ally as Captain Galaris's anger had been an enemy. An item of importance for the record, and one of some embarrassment to the federal government's Coast and Geodetic Survey, came up in the form of sailing directions contained in the *U.S. Coast Pilot*. It is stated there that vessels are boarded by a pilot at the entrance buoys.

A. According to the sailing directions, you go to the entrance buoy according to it, but we never had that practice. We go outside two miles and get it inside.

Q. But you say it was your practice to go out a certain distance to meet vessels?

A. Yes.

Q. And what was your practice?

A. My practice?

Q. Yes.

A. You see, if a foreign ship is coming here for the first time, we always meet him outside. The pilots go outside and meet him two miles out. An inbound ship coming in always, always, stop the the vessel and making leeway. But they stop to pick up the pilot. They stop.

Under cross-examination, Pilot Gonzales requested use of an interpreter and proceeded to speak in Spanish. He held his ground in maintaining that the ship was in danger before he boarded, adding that he had done all in a pilot's power to save her, and this in spite of the excitement of her master (an allusion which is a reminder of the *Torrey Canyon's* officers running back and forth when she grounded). Pilot Gonzales's testimony revealed that the Pilots Association was a private body without official status, but operated under the Port Authority. The pilot he had dispatched to signal tugs, Captain Rivera, made an equally earnest impression, though he showed less outrage in describing his efforts to get the attention of the

Ocean Eagle's master. These included blowing his police whistle and waving his jacket (here again, one recalls the lobstermen's attempts to warn off the *Torrey Canyon*). There was a touch of wonder in his voice as he described the chief officer coming aboard the pilot boat.

He say Old Man want no tug or lines aboard. And he made me stand by so long, instead take him ashore. And the Captain, later he ask for chart of San Juan harbor!

Presumably, the master was afraid that if a tug got a line aboard there might be a salvage claim against the owners, but the Coast Guard decided that problem for him, as Captain Tyler Daniels, skipper of the tug *Catano*, testified. He gave a concise personal history—fifty-nine years old, master's license limited to 150 tons, an eighth-grade education with eight years in the Navy and forty-five years at sea. The description of his command was equally terse—160 tons (although this was more than his license authorized, no one would question *this* skipper about the violation), 95 feet long, 1,500 brake horsepower and diesel-powered. His answers were to the point and businesslike, if Brooklyn-accented, yet his listeners were able to discern under his words an unspoken opinion of the *Ocean Eagle*'s master and, perhaps, a few members of the admiralty bar present. After the Coast Guard took off the master, he testified, he was ordered to take her in tow. This he attempted with 1,500 feet of 8-inch hawser, pulling for two hours with the result that the vessel moved just enough west to clear the channel. He docked at 13:40.

"And that was the end of that," he said.

Subsequent witnesses consisted of Coast Guard officers for the most part, all of whom made a good impression with their dress whites, ribbon bars and well-organized testimony. A helicopter pilot described the slick as moderate to heavy for 16 miles, and another officer spoke of the ship's end—broken, streaming oil, held together only by her cables and piping, and working badly in a seaway. The chief officer was recalled for further questioning, and another party at interest would have been also, had he been available. This was Captain Galaris who, having been excused by the board, had left for Greece. His wife was expecting a baby momentarily, and he had departed with some good wishes, but not from the pilots.

"Let's hope he does better by his berth as a father than he did by that of a master," said a maritime union representative.

At 3:30 that afternoon, Admiral Prins looked at his watch, wrapped on the table and announced loud and clear, "The board is closed." Several of those in the room strolled toward the bulkhead for a last look at the hulks, as a pair of pelicans made repeated attempts to take off from the channel. The men turned away, then watched in silence as another, oil-soaked, waddled across the lawn with dragging wing in the direction of the commandant's house.

"Anybody got any answers?" someone asked.

The conclusions of the board, when finally released, were that the casualty was caused by "faulty navigation," that the breaking in two was caused by "(1) overloading (2) improper loading, (3) grounding," and that "the casualty could have been averted by prudent seamanship on the part of the Master by remaining a safe distance at sea until his vessel was lined up with the channel for a proper approach."

There are those who felt that in a case where a master lost a tanker worth at least $2,500,000, spilling her cargo to cause damage by pollution of unknown millions of dollars, together with unknown losses and suffering, that the board's conclusions were simply not enough. Its findings offended no one, save those who cared for the environment, the traditions of the sea and, in view of patently false testimony, truth itself. The recommendations by the board made them no happier: (1) vessels should be boarded at least 2 milts from the entrance buoys; (2) pilot boats and the pilot station should be adequately equipped with radio telephone; (3) pilot boats should be of adequate size and speed to enable pilots to board incoming vessels under adverse weather conditions; (4) and "that a copy of this report be forwarded to the Government of Liberia for information and consideration of appropriate action concerning the license of the Master of the SS *Ocean Eagle* for his part in the casualty."

"Of course, it isn't enough, and of course, it isn't right," says a maritime underwriter. "But how do you penalize a master and chief officer who do not sail under your licenses, or owners of a vessel not under your flag?"

"After all, the board does give Liberia a pretty broad hint as to what to do," agrees an admiralty lawyer. "Any broader, and we'd be accused of trespass upon her sovereignty."

The Republic of Liberia didn't need any hints, not after public reaction to its inquiry into the *Torrey Canyon* casualty. She was not about to be accused again of a "casual look at a casualty." The Liberian Deputy Commissioner of Maritime Affairs convened a Board of Investigation on March 14, 1968, in New York. The chairman was James V. C. Malcolmson, a marine architect and former Texaco vice president in charge of marine operations. He and a board member, Roy I. Melita, staff member of the Maritime Affairs office and former merchant marine officer, had served on the *Torrey Canyon* board. They were joined by two other members, George E. Henries and H. Barton Williams.

The board interrogated the master, chief officer, chief engineer and helmsman, but not Pilot Gonzales. That angry man, who actually had not been piloting under the authority of his U.S. unlimited master's license—a fine point but one relieving the Coast Guard of action against him had they felt obliged to take it—declined the invitation to appear. He is reported to have felt that he could not trust himself to be in the same room again with Captain Galaris, however bigger, younger and stronger the captain was. The board adjourned March 20, then reconvened on May 20 to consider the report of Raymond A. Yagle, professor of naval architecture and marine engineering at the University of Michigan, relative to the course recorder readings and the divers' examination of the *Ocean Eagle*'s bottom. On July 16 the board reconvened in London to hear additional testimony from the master, by then so thoroughly examined that presumably he could have no further "incorrect testimony" to admit to, a condition in which he was joined by his conspiring chief officer. Between them they gave birth to a triple-screw maritime crack: "Beware of Greek officers bearing Liberian licenses in U.S. waters!"

This time testimony was both more accurate and more colorfult—he first because even for a shipmaster the truth will out, and the second because of literal interpretation and attempts at English by witnesses.

A. The last I check of the distance at 6:40 about was, if I remember well, about half a mile. I little before I had seen a small boat in the middle of the channel. I continued to approach inside and I saw the little boat come close to me. That boat was the pilot boat. The Pilot tried to come to the starboard side, alongside of the ship, and he tried two times—but he couldn't. The weather conditions was heavy swell, and at the same time I sent the officer to the bow to be ready with the anchor. I don't remember how many times it was, but just one minutes, or minute, just one, and because I was close to the buoys, and the ship is pitching, I ordered the chief officer to drop the starboard anchor, just one side of the water.

He did that. Really, I don't know how time passes, but, again, minutes, but the pilot came up on the bridge and—
Q. Excuse me, Captain. He came around the other side, I presume?
A. I don't remember, because I didn't see him.
Q. All right.
A. And at the same time I gave order to the Chief Officer to heave away the anchor. The ship was then—how do you say that? A little to the right of the channel.

If I remember well passes the time about between five to ten minutes more or less. The ship has not a very well controlled, and the last check was about—I check the—the bow was in line with the No. 4—I think—yes, the second one red buoy, I think it is No. 4. In the same about time I hear a noise but it was touching—the ship touching the bottom.

After that, and in the time less of a minute I heard the second one stronger one, and then the third, another one, stronger than the first and the second.

When I feel the first one touching I told to the pilot, the ship touching the bottom. So you do the best you can. If you want make around the starboard, or to the port, if you want, and go out, and we have to try again to come in, because really the ship was to the starboard side in the channel.

He told me we cannot to make to the round starboard because, look, another ship has aground on there, and all the places is a wreck.

But, as I said before, the hitting of the bottom—

Q. Pounded?

A. Yes. Were coming and I go out to the starboard, or to the port side of the ship and just to see what happen, to see the water, or something like that, and I saw oil came out of the deck, between No. 6 and No. 7 tanks. At the same time I ask the pilot again, the ship is cutted, and if you know, or, if we can, to tell me some soft bottom to go to around to aground the ship.

I don't remember if he gave me any answer, and also I told him, because not so far away were the tugs, all the tugs were coming for assistance.

Also, I don't remember if he gave me any answer, but I lost him. I don't know where he been. He came down, out, another side of the bridge, I don't know.

Then the rest of the happening happened very, very fast, so I don't remember what is exactly the line.

I gave order to the engine room and I talk to the chief engineer, "The ship has broken and give me all the speed I had to ground the ship and to go far away of the channel."

Also I said to the Chief Mate, because still was in the bow to put the starboard anchor. Also I give signal with an alarm and then—How do you say it?

(The interpreter translates to the witness)

A. (Continuing) Distress, distress also with the whistle of the ship I gave the signal, seven short ones, long, and already the lifeboats were going down the water.

I saw if the ship was moving but I can't see any—I mean, any real movement of the ship, and because the aft port lifeboat was close to the water I said to the Chief Engineer by telephone, "Stop the engine completely." And I say to all the crew to go out, just aboard the ship. I must stay down and await my order.

Again I saw the condition of the ship. The oil was out and

before the ship start something like that, it was like this (indicating). And then I saw it very fast going down (indicating).

I make another phone to the Chief Engineer to cut off—to isolate down to the engine—

THE INTERPRETER: To isolate and stop the central electrical handle.

Q. Motors?

A. I mean the generator and the boilers to—

Q. Cut them out?

A. Yes, that is the correct estimation, yes. And to leave the ship. This is all the story. Let me know if I can to say anything else, or if you want anything else.

The hours of probing at the Coast Guard Board of Inquiry had failed to produce such simple testimony, but then, for the truth to out, someone must say it. Thus, the *Ocean Eagle's* anchor was dropped before the pilot boarded—not lowered one shot and then raised to be ready for dropping—and the ship was not in the channel when she grounded, but outside it and to the west of it. Had Pilot Gonzales been present, and had he been able to control his assaultive drives, would Captain Galaris have referred to his disappearance—"I lost him"—and would he have insisted that he gave the distress signal? No one seems to have heard those seven short blasts and one long, indicating that either the whistle malfunctioned or that the master was still clutching a falsehood. The chief officer, obedient to the end, followed in the footsteps of the captain's testimony, and once he had testified to dropping the starboard anchor a second time, questioning turned to the abandonment. After receiving the order, he said, he told the bos'n to prepare the lifeboats (a little late, it would seem, others having testified that they were already in the water).

Q. And then what happened?

A. I stayed on the bow. According to the order of the Captain to stay on the bow.

Q. Then what did you do?

A. I stayed there about fifteen minutes, approximately.

Q. Then what did you do?

A. Then I went to the bridge. I met—No, correction—I went to the room of the Captain, where the Captain was trying to collect the different things of the ship. And we were giving these things down to the lifeboat.

Q. To whom did the Captain deliver these things down to the lifeboat?

A. He was giving these things to me, and I was delivering these things to—and I was throwing these things toward the lifeboat. But I cannot say that, if all of them were going to the hands of the people or were going on the sea.

Q. To whom did you throw these things in the lifeboat?

A. There were in the lifeboat two second mates, the boatswain, this gentleman Kavadas. I don't remember which, whom else was there, but was one—I don't remember, one or two more people were there, persons were there.

Q. What did these things you threw into the lifeboat, what did they include?

A. I cannot determine. Whatever he was giving to me, the Captain was giving to me, I was throwing. But I cannot determine what was—all "higgle de piggeldy," all mixed up.

Q. Then what was the next thing that happened?

A. What I have last in my hands was the seamen's books.

The lifeboat was already gone. Because it was a swell, it was swelling and the sea was coming on the deck because the ship was already split and the lifeboat was going away.

I took the seamen's books and stayed on the bow for a few minutes. And then came the boat, the pilots boat, and took me. Then I disembarked and the only person who stayed on the ship was the Captain.

The Liberian board was quite concerned that the Chief Officer did not have a license in that grade, but only in the grade of second officer. The first the Maritime Authorities of Liberia knew of this fact was the evidence brought out in this investigation. The Deputy Commissioner of Maritime Affairs subsequently received his application for a Liberian license as chief officer. However, the fact is that at the time of sailing he was in a capacity for which he was not licensed and for which no waiver had been granted.

, The Board considers that the Chief Officer conspired with the Master to misinform the Board concerning the cause of the grounding and the casualty under investigation. In light of the foregoing, we recommend that his license be revoked.

The recommendation was carried out, the chief officer lost his second officer's license and one supposed he would be on the beach. However, he also held a chief officer's license issued by the Kingdom of Greece, and the board made no recommendation that Greece consider "appropriate action concerning the license," as did the U.S. Coast Guard to Liberia. Ship's officers' berths are short of occupants, ships must sail . . .

"After all," asks an industry apologist, referring to the false testimony, "shouldn't a chief officer back his captain?"

"But not full astern," answers a critic.

The helmsman, in spite of language problems, gave a dramatic account of the moment of grounding and one suspects that he was grateful his responsibility extended merely to the execution of orders.

A. After the lapse of some minutes I felt that the ship has hit something.

Q. And what did it feel like?

A. A trembling, not too strong.

Q. Did the Captain or Pilot say anything when you felt this trembling?

A. I didn't receive any orders from neither one. But they are going back and forth and shouting, both of them.

Q. Do you remember what they were shouting?

A. I don't speak English and I couldn't understand what they were saying.

Q. Then what was the next thing that happened?

A. After the lapse of some minutes, there was a second impact, and then a third impact. And then at the third everything was—it was—it went to hell, something like this.

Q. Much confused?

A. Much confused, yes.

Q. Did the captain say anything?

A. Neither one said anything, but both of them was going back and forth and they were in an excitement.

Q. After you felt the third trembling, what did you do?
A. In a few minutes the Captain says we were split and throw the lifeboats in the sea and abandon the ship.
Q. And what did you do?
A. I went to the right lifeboat and uncovered it.

There is a sense of loneliness in the master's testimony at the point wherein he describes his actions after his command was abandoned by all but him.

A. When all the people left out of the ship, also the Chief Officer, I have to go in the bow and I put it another one anchor, the port anchor, and I slack. I don't remember how many shackles. I put up there the black ball. And then I put some ropes both of the sides just in case for myself. Then I been up to the bridge, but I can't walk in the gangway, to go from the steps because one pipe, steam pipe has broken and the steam was out, and it was dangerous for me. I went up to the sun deck, and the rudder mast, I put up the two black ball. And just I am looking at the ship . . .
Q. After the two sections parted, you then left the ship yourself?
A. Yes.
Q. Where did you go?
A. To Coast Guard.
     Just a minute. I don't remember in the line, because the Coast Guard boat has to pick me up from the ship. And then I been to the tugboat. And then again to Coast Guard boat. And then to Coast Guard office. And then to our agent. So I don't remember when I be first. But I been to all these places.
Q. Yes, I understand.

The master didn't have any more use for wreck pirates than other mariners, but he may have experienced a sense of relief that any of the ship's papers left aboard were probably de-

Q. Captain, do you know, did anyone go back to the ship after it had parted and tried to get on board to salvage any of these records that were not available?
     (The interpreter speaks to the witness)

A. Yes. I did at the same time in the afternoon.

Q. And what success had you?

(The interpreter speaks to the witness)

A. Nothing. Because the Chief Engineer was with me, the Chief Officer was with me, also the wheelsman was with me and they—

(The interpreter speaks to the witness)

THE INTERPRETER: They stopped me.

A. They stopped me because it was dangerous to the bow section.

Q. So that as far as you know, Captain, no one has been back on board or has been able to get back on board to retrieve or to get the books?

A. For us?

Q. For anyone.

(The interpreter speaks to the witness)

A. I don't know.

Q. You don't know?

A. I know another one thing, the second or third day we tried the same exactly four Greek persons, me, Chief Officer, Chief Engineer and the wheelsman to be, to go up to the after section to take some things, new things from the crew. And from another people has been out, up to the ship, and they have take many, many things. They tried to cut the doors, and they have all over radios, open the— how do you say ship—

THE INTERPRETER: Drawers.

A. And many, many things was out of the ship.

Q. But you had no success in getting any of these books or records from the ship?

(The interpreter speaks to the witness)

A. No. Because all these things, my things was up to the bridge or to my office.

One of the first "Findings of Fact" that the Liberian Board of Investigation came up with was that although the *Ocean Eagle* had sailed in an overloaded condition that put her tropical loadline 7 inches below water, a new loadline convention was to go into force on July 21. It would have added 12¼ inches to her loadline:

Had this loadline been in effect on her sailing, her loadline would have been 5¼ inches above water and she would not have been technically overloaded. She would have been enabled to load a further 420 tons wih her designed 80 tons per inch immersion.

The board drew the conclusion "that on this evidence alone sailing in an overloaded condition, while a technical violation of the Loadline Certificate, did not in fact contribute to the casualty." In order to nail the lid shut on any further possibility that the "technical" overloading had contributed to the casualty, the opinion of Professor Yagle was quoted:

I am now absolutely convinced that the *Ocean Eagle* did run aground. The longitudinal gash in the bottom could only have been made by a ship moving over a sharp pinnacle of rock (or coral) and is not the sort of damage which could have been caused by a structural failure due to overloading.

The board wanted to bury speculation that the casualty was caused not solely by grounding as deeply as her bow and stern sections lie under the sea, and to this end came up with another "Finding of Fact":

The evidence before the Board now makes clear that the *Ocean Eagle* broke up as a result of grounding. This evidence includes the analysis and interpretation of the course recorder tape by Dr. Suarez, an expert in such matters retained by the *Ocean Eagle* interests, the London testimony of the Master and the statement of the Pilot as to events subsequent to 06:30. This finding is buttressed by the evidence of the diver who found physical markings on the *Ocean Eagle*'s bottom which clearly showed that she grounded and pierced the cargo tanks.

Even a quibbler would agree with the board's decision here, but he might be curious about some of the phrasing—a ship is either overloaded or it is not, and regardless of the future changes in loadline certificate, at the time of stranding she was overloaded and not merely "technically." Also, it is nowhere established that the overloading could not have contributed to the grounding—we are not told that without this additional weight she would still have touched bottom. Such a quibbler might also wish to know more about the expert Dr. Suarez, including his first name, the influence his retention by *Ocean Eagle* "interests" might have had on his findings, and how his study of the course recorder tape makes clear that the ship "broke up as a result of grounding." The quibbler wouldn't be happy about the validity of the master's present testimony in view of his earlier statements, described by the board as "perjurious," and even the diver's finding of "physical markings" wouldn't please him. The quibbler would also be worried by Professor Yagle's conclusion that "the longitudinal gash in the bottom could only have been made by a ship moving over a sharp pinnacle of rock (or coral)." Professor Yagle fails to mention that such a gash could also be caused by a *section* of a vessel moving over a sharp pinnacle, such as the stern section (there being no evidence that a matching gash was present on the bottom of the bow section). The record mentions several times that both sections moved independently at least once, that of the stern as far as a couple of hundred yards.

On a tonnage basis one out of every four ships using the English Channel is of Liberian registry, so it is important in view of the frequency of Liberian disasters that her vessels appear as seaworthy and well maintained as possible. Both Liberia and the *Ocean Eagle* "interests" would naturally prefer that the cause of the disaster be determined as human error— we all make mistakes, and besides, this one was made by a Greek.

The board also found that "there was no failure or defect in the equipment aboard the *Ocean Eagle* which could in any way have contributed to this casualty. The vessel and her equipment were at all times in sound condition and functioned properly. The *Ocean Eagle* had on board all necessary equipment, charts and publications." And so she did, says the quibbler, even if her master didn't use the depth recorder, radar, leadline, crew member as lookout, or the engine room telegraph to reduce speed well before he did—even a ship's length from the entrance buoy she was still under way at 4 knots. He didn't use the *Coastal Pilot* either (which is just as well, since it calls for the pilot to board at the buoy). The item of equipment he did make use of—the ship's megaphone—was done under a misapprehension and was useless. He had called to the pilot to go in, saying that he would follow.

The board also found that "the sole cause of the grounding was the error of the Master in allowing the *Ocean Eagle* to get out of control when he could have circled out to sea again if his chief concern was to obtain a pilot for entering San Juan Harbor." The quibbler would have liked an examination of why the master allowed his command to "get out of control"— was it inexperience (having been a master only eight months), panic at being unable to utilize the services of a pilot on his first visit to the port with a ship in an overloaded condition, negligence or aberration?

After saying that it "would have sympathetically received the true facts and taken into account various mitigating circumstances, the perjurious acts of the Master and Chief Officer effectively removes them from any sympathetic consideration of their problems," the board states in its recommendations that "the Master is also at fault for causing it to expend substantial additional time to determine the true facts and cause of the casualty which, in the last analysis, was rather simple. Therefore, for his errors in navigation and his contempt for the dignity of the board, we recommend that his license be revoked."

The quibbler would conclude here, and in so doing would restate in summary form his understanding of the Liberian findings: the *Ocean Eagle* disaster was caused by grounding due to the master's errors in navigation, for which defect, together with his contempt for the dignity of the Board of Investigation, his license was revoked.

"Call it a mild penalty of unknown duration," an industry critic has said, "an incomplete investigation, and an easy way out for all, except the victims."

Human victims, at least, did have recourse to compensation and it took the form of an action based on gross negligence, unseaworthiness (in that the crew was incompetent) and improper loading. It was brought by the federal and commonwealth governments against both the owners of the *Ocean Eagle* and her cargo. Total claims amount to as much as $10,000,000. The vessel's owners are represented by two firms, one of them a San Juan firm called Bird and Bird (surely an apt masthead under which to defend interests in a vessel referred to throughout the action as "the *Eagle*"). The other is the prestigious New York admiralty firm of Burlingham, Underwood, Wright, White and Lord. Together they filed a brief for plaintiffs (the owners) in the U.S. District Court of Puerto Rico, pleading for "Exoneration from or Limitation of Liability." The brief lists six attorneys headed by Eugene Underwood.

Mr. Underwood, a senior partner, is currently in his fiftieth year of admiralty practice and his oldster's geniality serves as an effective cover for a quick and subtle mind. An attorney, who has had his measure taken more than once in an action in which he opposed Mr. Underwood, was asked if this veteran with the grandfatherly manner might not be called the dean of admiralty lawyers.

"Dean?" he replied. "I'd call him our first fox."

The brief, running almost 200 pages, is as impressive a document as was Mr. Underwood's examination of witnesses at the Coast Guard Board of Inquiry. The first issue dealt with is the question of loading records, the complainants hoping to establish a history of overloading, but these were not available. In the words of the brief:

Nobody kept old papers. They were no longer useful and were too bulky to keep. No one had any reasonable basis to believe that anyone, including the claimants in this case, would have any interest in them. From the outset claimants have sought to cast plaintiff in the part of foreign villains who smeared their beaches with oil, walked away and then destroyed the evidence of prior misconduct. Moreover, plaintiffs too are victims—they lost a fine ship worth $1,500,000 to $2,000,000 and possibly twice that in today's market, due in part to the fault of the USA and the Commonwealth.

The tenets of admiralty practice are rather unexpected, such as that under U.S. law owner of a vessel can limit his liability to the value of the vessel at the time of the casualty, in this case the value being nil (discounting that of souvenirs, which the owners never had a crack at). If the owner can be shown to have been negligent, the picture changes, but if a vessel is on the bottom and is a shipper's sole asset, damages are not recoverable. It is odd, too, that in admiralty practice one can demonstrate how seaworthy a vessel is by citing her mishaps—the *Eagle* brief details four groundings, one bump, three occasions of damage by heavy weather and an encounter with a submerged object. Even the ownership of the cargo comes into question, the brief pointing out that the ship received the cargo "for the account of Gulf Oil Corporation to be delivered unto Caribbean Gulf Refining Corporation on payment of freight as agreed. There is no evidence that the freight was ever paid, or that the cargo was ever sold to Caribbean Gulf Refining Corporation. Gulf Oil Corporation was the owner of the cargo at the time of its loss." It would be interesting to know which, if either, of these corporations (hardly strangers to each other) claimed a tax loss on the cargo.

For the lay reader, at least, the brief confirms that the *Ocean Eagle* did not break up due to structural weakness or overloading, but because of grounding. In refuting the overloading, an apt simile is employed—"A shot glass is not overloaded just because the level of the contents rises above the 1¾ oz. mark—nor until the whiskey at least touches the rim." The charge of improper loading is dismissed on the basis of expert opinion in which it is mentioned that a sag in the hull of a loaded tanker of 6 inches is not unusual. While this speaks well for the flexibility of a hull, it also raises the question of metal fatigue—at what point does a hull tire of sagging and just give up? Cracks in tanker hulls came up for discussion too, one expert testifying that all an owner can do to avoid hull failure is to install crack arresters.

"There is no tanker built yet that is free from these nuisance cracks," he said.

The Navy is taken to task in the brief for having attempted to wrench the bow section off the bottom holding it without first off-loading the cargo, thus laying at least part of the spill and its effects at the door of the federal government: "It is apparent that the Navy's wrenching and hauling efforts resulted in the rupture or holing of various tanks, or collapse of their internal bulkheads, permitting 1,064,000 gallons of oil to escape to the sea." Both the federal ond commonwealth governments, together with Caribbean Gulf, are attacked for their use of detergents, the claim being that these entities knew beforehand of the adverse effects and hazards, including toxicity which can be harmful to marine ecology. The brief ends:

It is clear that the pollution east and west of the San Juan harbor entrance was in large measure due to the use of these detergents and chemical agents, creating an enlarged mass of contaminated material that was more easily and rapidly moved by the wind than would have been the crude oil alone.

The pilot boats come in for criticism too:

The Commonwealth went so far as to require that its pilot boats be painted black and display a white P on their bows, but there is nothing—not even one word—to establish the barest minimum standard for construction and equipment. Gonzales pointed out that his pilot boat was an ex-Navy picket boat used to take people ashore. That is quite different from bringing and holding a pilot alongside a vessel in 15 foot seas so that he may board safely. A square and surplus peg was provided for a round hole.

The causes of the casualty, claims the brief, were that the *Coastal Pilot* incorrectly advised that vessels are boarded at the entrance buoys, the lack of radio communication with the pilot which resulted in his hand signals being misunderstood, and the pilot's inability to board, so that the ship approached the buoys until with her reduced speed "she lost steerageway and strayed outside of the channel into shallow water and struck bottom causing her to break up."

Under the Limitation of Liability Act, liability of the owner of a vessel for any loss or damage incurred without the "privity or knowledge" of the owner shall not exceed the interest of the owner in his vessel. Plaintiffs need only prove that they were not privy to the fault for which they are held liable, in this case negligent navigation. "It has been universally recognized," claims the brief, "that the conduct or knowledge of the master is without the privity or knowledge of the shipowner, and will not defeat the shipowner's right to limitation of liability." It then proceeds to claim that the federal government was negligent in publishing misleading information (the *Coastal Pilot*) and in the manner in which it attempted to salvage the bow section and in using and directing others in the use of chemicals in cleaning up the spill.

A decision is not apt to be handed down in a hurry, for this could be a case in which important precedents are set. In the meantime, Mr. Underwood has a Cheshire cat expression when he considers the brief, and a few small claims have been settled, among them one for oil stains on a hotel carpet. Apparently, it was as impossible to save as wildlife, and the owner received $7,000 for a new one.

"Be nice if the pelicans could have bought new lives for themselves, wouldn't it?" asks an ornithologist.

Since nothing about the *Ocean Eagle* came easy, Mr. Underwood's "Brief for Plaintiffs" may not achieve the ends its language and quaintness merit. One does not envy the jurist who will hand down the decision, Federal Judge Sylvester Ryan, and on Wednesday night, April 3, 1968, Captain Peters wasn't to be envied either. His Navy salvage crew had lightened the bow sufficiently to turn it almost 100 degrees due north. It had taken a month to free the bow section from the ledge holding her, about 1,000,000 gallons of oil had been off-loaded, tanks had had to be charged with air and numerous risks had been taken. At 09:15 Friday morning the channel was closed to traffic and towing preparations were complete. The U.S.S. *Preserver*, determined not to undergo another fiasco such as had happened on March 9, when the bow section slipped away from her, grounded off Isla de Cabras and spilled hundreds of thousands of gallons of crude into the channel, fouled her towing cable. It was sometime before it could be freed, and the next event was to forecast a future one—a Navy tug collided with another salvage vessel, though without great damage. It was caused by an engine-starting failure, the Fairbanks-Morse engines on that class of tug being direct-reversible. (To reverse you have to stop a running engine, shift cams and restart it.) Next, it developed that the bow section was still caught, and the Navy, being a believer in horsepower, hoped that one big pull would free it. This time horsepower did the trick.

At 12:45 the *Ocean Eagle*'s bow was officially afloat and under tow to the nearest disposal area, accompanied by a cortege—the

Preserver towing a second salvage vessel and two Navy tugs sailing as escort. A barge was secured to the bow section's side loaded with gear and three air compressors to keep the tanks under pressure, a helicopter was overhead and two Murphy salvage vessels, the *Curb* and the *Cable*, took up the rear. The hulk appeared battered, her once white bridge structure blackened by crude from the oily seas breaking over it, and she looked as if she did not have long to live. Aboard was a Navy salvage crew of twenty-five men under Captain Peters, all wearing red life jackets and all glad the end was near. There was good visibility, a light ground swell and no apparent wind, the sea being still enough for a trail of oil to show up for miles behind. The Navy treated it with detergents.

"She's dirty to the end, isn't she?" observed an onlooker.

The plan had been to sink the bow 12 miles out at sea in a deep depression, but as the convoy was making only about 2 knots, at 16:00 hours it was clear that it would be dark before the spot was reached. Therefore, at 17:00 hours when the hulk was about 8.3 miles off San Juan with 4,200 feet of water under it, the *Preserver* slowed and took up the slack in the towing lines. The compressors were shut down and the salvage gear was transferred from the fo'c'sle head to the barge, which the Navy tug *Hackensack* took in tow at 17:25. A few minutes later another Navy tug took off some of the crew, leaving Captain Peters and seven others aboard. The towing line was winched in by the *Preserver,* and soon the hulk began to settle at its after end where the break had occurred. The cargo tanks were flooding, now that compressed air no longer kept out the sea, and valves installed for the purpose were opened to hasten the end. A problem in scuttling vessels is the tendency for compartments to hold air, which can prevent a sinking indefinitely. The Navy had taken no chances on being embarrassed by this, but as it turned out there was another embarrassment. Things went much faster than planned.

Those aboard had gathered on the fo'c'sle head as the angle of immersion increased, and soon the seas reached the after end of the deckhouse. As water began pouring from open port holes, strangely gorelike, the fo'c'sle head reared up so far that the hulk was almost vertical, literally standing on the sea. The men were out of sight, having climbed to the far side, and it was assumed that they were there being picked up.

"About time, too," someone on the *Cable* said.

The line was almost lost in a roar of steel against steel. The chain lockers had let loose and anchor links slid down the decks, raising a great cloud of rust scale. Then the hulk stood even straighter, as if reaching for the sky to save it from the sea, and gave an agonized twist to port. Suddenly, one after another, eight life-jacketed forms appeared and jumped a good 30 feet from the port rail into the sea. They landed safely and at once were swimming hard to clear the huge form hanging over them.

"That lousy Navy is disgusting!" the *Curb*'s skipper said.

The mate nodded. "They can sink ships in wartime, but they sure don't know how to do it peaceful."

When he added that it took a civilian salvor to really sink a ship right, it was pointed out to him that slavage duties normally call for raising ships, not sinking them. There was, though, a unanimous feeling aboard the *Curb* that the Navy was negligent in not protecting its men by having a rescue vessel standing by, and it later developed that such had been the plan, but the Navy tug assigned to the duty had suffered a starting failure —she lay a half-mile off, rolling helplessly in the swell. Other vessels headed for the scene at full throttle, reaching the men soon after Captain Peters was retrieved by the helicopter. All were wet, awed and in one piece.

"One thing you got to remember about these old diesels that use compressed air for starting," a first assistant engineer said, "you don't want to run out of it."

The bow section remained nearly upright for several minutes, murky water boiling around it, then began its slide down. It didn't take long, and all that was left was a hill of foaming water, broken up by rust-colored jets. Then even that was gone and the sea was still. The Navy signaled its certificate of delivery:

At sea 4 April 1968. This is to certify that the Liberian steam tanker *Ocean Eagle* (bow section) has been refloated from her stranded position near the bar channel entrance, San Juan Harbor, Puerto Rico and delivered to her new master, Neptunus Rex at latitude 18-36.3 north longitude 66-08.7 at 0418010 by the USS *Preserver*. Receipt of said vessel and her remaining cargo was not tendered.

B. Peters, Capt, USN

Witness: J. H. Boyd, Jr., Cdr., USN, Salvage Master.

The allusion to remaining cargo of this supposedly empty hulk was to cause the Navy its final embarrassment. For months to come oil kept appearing both at sea and on Puerto Rico's beaches, and there were those who were certain that the wreck was still up to her dirty work. A Navy car at the base didn't help the island to forget the disaster—its license plate bore a metal reproduction of the wreck going down and it carried the letters OCEAN EAGLE. The tourist industry wasn't any happier about this reminder than were the civilian salvagers, which didn't need to be told that the Navy had usurped what they saw as their role.

At last half the *Ocean Eagle* was out of harm's way. The final resting place for her bow section was in 660 fathoms of water (almost 4,000 feet) and, as a polluter, it must have felt at home. It lies a mere 9 miles from the U.S. Army explosives dumping area. Half the menace to navigation presented by the *Ocean Eagle* had been eliminated too. The Coast Guard issued a notice to mariners saying, "San Juan Harbor is open to entering and departing shipping. Bow section of tanker *Ocean Eagle* has been removed."

Rear Admiral Alfred Matter, U.S.N., commander of the *Caribbean Sea Frontier*, and Captain Peters presented to Governor Sanchez a souvenir of the *Ocean Eagle* disaster to mark their successful completion of the operation. It was a fused metal engraving of the bow section on a well-varnished wooden shield. The captain pointed out that it was "amazing" that there were no accidents during the month-long salvage work, and in view of what had nearly happened with the scuttling, nobody disputed him. The admiral added that nowhere in the world could salvage vessels with so much power and equipment be found, and a civilian reading the news story chuckled. "And nowhere in the world could so much money be spent on a scuttling," he said.

Both the Corps of Engineers and the Murphy Pacific salvagers were determined there would be no foulups with the stern section. As one official said, "It's not a question of trying to show the Navy up, it's just that we want to show them how it's done."

A first step in this direction was to assuage the ruffled feelings of the press, who had found information from the Navy hard to come by and interviews with responsible officials scarce. The salvage vessel *Cable* was assigned to carry reporters, still photographers and a film unit of the commonwealth Education Department. Aboard the *Curb* were to be Colonel McElhenny and staff, in addition to official observers. Murphy's completion of the off-loading of oil and preparation for towing the stern section to sea was reported in an announcement given by the company to *The New York Times*, in which it mentioned that both the salvage vessels *Curb* and *Cable* were involved in the operation and that a third sister ship, the *Rescue*, was off-loading oil from the Greek tanker *General Colocotronis* at Eleuthera. It was a busy month for Murphy Pacific and a tough one for the Caribbean environment.

Monday, April 15, was the day appointed for towing of the stern section, and dawn looked propitious—the sea was moderate, the tide near high, wind slight and visibility good. The Coast Guard closed the channel, in spite of objections by shipping interests, and the hulk had been moved the previous day just enough to be ready. It had come to life during the final off-loading and charging of the tanks with compressed air—first it trembled, then shifted and from a fixed point on the fan tail rail the shore appeared to move. All aboard knew that while it was not a ship again and never would be, it was afloat and towable. A ragged cheer rang out, a beer can went over the side and Colonel McElhenny gave a relieved smile.

"Operation scuttle, commence!" someone said.

As the *Curb* began to raise her anchor in preparation for getting into towing position, it fouled something on the bottom. Eventually, she freed her hook, and speculation was that the *Ocean Eagle* still hadn't given up her tricks—what had probably fouled the *Curb*'s anchor was her own, missing since the bow section had first shifted. By 09:50 the tow was under way at a speed of one-third ahead, later increased to two-thirds. It was a good clip for such an ungainly tow and one with a will of its own, as demonstrated by the tendency to yaw, but those in the escort were glad such good time was being made—he photographers wanted to be sure there was light for the scuttling shots. The vessels in the escort were the *Preserver*, (maybe the Navy didn't want to miss any Army foulups), the *Cable*, civilian tugs *Borinquen* and *Catano*, Coast Guard buoy tender *Sagebrush*, and close astern of the hulk and pumping air into her, the Navy M boat. Aboard this small craft in lifejackets were Captain Thurman, his assistant Ray Calhoun, a Navy demolition crew with their gear and a compressor with hoses.

At 10:30 the towing line was lengthened to 1,200 feet and a quarter of an hour later the tugs were dismissed. Things went so well that the scuttling hour of 16:00 was advanced to 13:50, by which time Colonel McElhenny felt she was in suitable position—8 miles out with a depth of 625 fathoms. On orders to sink being given, the compressor was shut down, hoses retrieved and the demolition party boarded the hulk with the satchel charges. They weighed better than 50 pounds each with their cords—thirty-two were to be placed in the engine room, two in the fire room and sixteen in the pump room. The detonator box remained in the M boat, to which the crew returned after the charges were set and cords connected. It was then that it was noticed on the *Curb* that the party numbered thirteen, a matter of interest to superstitious mariners.

The M boat backed off, trailing the cord, the order was given to set off the charges and the detonator responded promptly. The resulting explosion was a lot bigger than expected, perhaps due to the accumulation of vapors, and the concussion effect was noticeable on even the vessels farthest away. Pieces of the swimming pool and engine room ventilators dropped around the M boat, the occupants of which ducked and covered their heads. A member of the demolition party was to explain the size of the blast later by saying that the Navy wanted the Army to get a bang out of the way they did things.

"Funny," said a member of the colonel's staff. "There are still thirteen in the boat."

The hulk took her time in spite of the force of the explosion, and in truth, she was too handsome to have to be scuttled.

Her deckhouse looked well painted, her rails seemed trim and the davits were swung out as if ready to retrieve her boats after a drill. It did seem wrong that so much ship and machinery had to be destroyed.

"Sure," agreed Colonel McElhenny. "Just so it goes to the bottom. There's been enough harm done."

By 15:20 the funnel was awash and the fantail settled deeper until the break in the hull was raised high out of the water. It resembled a cross section of some great beast dissected by a giant saw, and the innards were cavernous. Soon the fantail settled still deeper, then the hulk slipped below the surface without a struggle.

"She's gone," someone shouted, calling it a she again at the moment of death.

The time was 15:28, making the end thirty-two minutes ahead of schedule. The fleet of vessels headed for shore, led at first by the M boat, but she was soon overtaken by the *Curb* and *Cable*. It was almost as if they couldn't wait to get away from the place, and eventually the silence in the *Curb's* wheelhouse was broken by the question of how one signals in Morse that a vessel has been scuttled. The closest anyone could come to it were the letters N N X. Looked up in the code book, it turned out they meant "I have sunk a vessel."

"The line belongs to the *Ocean Eagle's* master," a voice said.

A year later it was clear that no one knew what the *Ocean Eagle* disaster had cost—in dollars, wildlife or petrochemical public relations. Many didn't care, some were anxious not to know and others wanted no one to know. There were sources in the various categories from which estimates, at least, were available and to an informed judgment they seem not too far off. However, a lot depends on the bookkeeping. For instance, were the Navy's efforts handled as an overhead item, only direct purchases being charged against the operation? And what would be the civilian rates for the fleet of vessels employed?

The loss in commonwealth revenue has been put at $2,000,000; spill control, cleanup efforts and sand replacement, including offshore applications, $750,000 damage to boats and gear for fishing and pleasure, $60,000; lost man-hours and value of volunteers, $40,000; off-loading cargo and scuttling, $2,500,000; vessel loss, $3,000,000; cargo loss (allowing for oil reclaimed), $125,000; loss to San Juan shipping due to channel restrictions, $75,000, and to air and cruise lines, $90,000. The total dollar cost by estimate amounts to $8,640,000, remarkably close to the aggregate claims brought against *Ocean Eagle* interests.

Wildlife loss is even more difficult to determine, but there are two estimates regarding the effect on the pelican population which are accurate, being based on definite counts. At least 300 birds were killed out of a population averaging 1,000 (where the 700 others went during the time of major pollution is anybody's guess), and the recovery rate of treated birds did not exceed 2 percent (authorities agree that a 4 percent recovery for oiled seabirds is optimum). And yet, the *Orange Disc*, a Gulf Oil Corporation house organ, quotes the commonwealth Bureau of Sport Fisheries as saying that there is "no basis to assume that any of the species of birds in the bay were affected by the oil spillage of the *Ocean Eagle*." It is a curious claim, however understandable its circulation by Gulf, and particularly since the commonwealth Department of Agriculture had estimated a month after the disaster that "several hundred birds succumbed."

The cost to marine life is both more obscure and more controversial. The only definite finding is that all concerned with fish—catching, processing or devouring—are against pollution. Surprisingly, a Federal Fish and Wildlife Service biologist, Dr. John Pearce, found asphaltic-encrusted barnacles on the Catano beaches still alive. This was an area of heavy pollution, and it is theorized that the more volatile elements of the crude were oxidized and devouerd by bacteria at an accelerated rate due to the warm climate, and that the asphalt by itself does not have a toxic effect on barnacles. When a marine biologist, Dr. Maximo G. Vives, testified before a special commission of the Federal Water Pollution Control Administration, he recommended that studies be made on the effect of the pollution on wildlife. It seemed a reasonable suggestion, but it was in opposition to a view of another biologist, R. Keith Stewart, who four months after the event did a survey of the Caribbean beaches at Puerto Rico. He found the recovery of aquatic life encouraging, saying that "it would not appear necessary at this time to make additional studies in San Juan Harbor." The few studies that were made are both superficial and incomplete, and information available about the aquatic population before the spill is scanty.

"Counts in pollution effect depend on what you are looking for," Dr. Ray Johnson, of the Federal Fish and Wildlife Service, said.

"And on who is looking, and why," adds a spill commentator.

Much of San Juan's rocky shoreline was still black on the disaster's anniversary, although efforts to remove the stains from the more popular tourist areas, such as El Morro's shore, had been effective. Evidence of oil, including asphalt, kept turning up on beaches and waterways, and there was a running debate as to whether it originated with the spill or was a product of routine tanker operations. Agreement was general that it had to be coming from somewhere, that it would probably keep on appearing and that even the layer of chemically treated crude that lies 6 inches under some beaches is going to be around for a long time. Not all U.S. visitors who fly home well oiled owe it to San Juan bars, observed a local newspaperman, who happened to be standing near a 55-gallon oil drum on a Catano beach. This black, battered relic was one of many that had been part of the large boom built by Murphy Pacific and never used. They, together with their cables and fittings, had become just more debris littering the shore.

Elements of the *Ocean Eagle,* some of which disappeared through the work of wreck pirates, were now in greater evidence. One of her lifeboats, still black with crude, lay on its side in a shipyard, and the ship's handsome binnacle graces a local seafarer's house, Casa Mar. Occasionally, a brass porthole fixture is sold for a price said to be nearer that of gold, and at least one bar flaunts a life ring so black the name *Ocean Eagle* can just be made out. The tattered remnants of her supposed pennant hang in another bar, the owner claiming that if the colors are wrong it is due to the oil stains.

The pilots have been instructed by the Port Authority to wait 2 miles outside the channel for arriving vessels, and orders for a pair of new pilot boats have been placed. They are to be radio-equipped, and although they would be larger and more powerful, pilots are quick to point out that boarding 2 miles out in heavy weather would still be a problem. As to channel improvements, such as widening, easing the first turn and considerable deepening, the only progress visible was in the cost estimates—they went up. And so entrance to the port is still tricky, and while maintenance dredging in a sweeping operation did level off the bottom to some extent, not all the underwater obstacles were removed or identified. One near buoy No. 2 is thought to be the missing *Ocean Eagle* anchor.

"One thing we know it can't be," says a tug skipper, "is the captain's blue suit. He left his reputation here, but not that."

The petrochemical industry continued to come under attack for water pollution, and it was heavy enough for a time at Guernica for it to be rumored that a proposed marine biology laboratory to be established there under federal funding would be canceled. Defenders of the industry point out, as is customary, that its economic contribution to the island is large and that the demand is growing. The manager of Caribbean Gulf, George W. Blanchard, Jr., was not happy at being reminded of the *Ocean Eagle*, or at the prospect of his company getting further press exposure. He felt that for Gulf to have had 1,400 deliveries of oil by sea with only one spill is not a bad record, and he is right. He is also right in believing that it is impossible to guarantee that it will be the last, but he is probably wrong in thinking that next time, thanks to the experience gained, the effects will be less disastrous. He may also be wrong in his refusal to recognize the public relations value of these 1,400 deliveries —in pollution practice, it is not true that the less said, the better. The facts won't make the oil go away, but they do help those who try to.

Two years after the disaster, the name *Ocean Eagle* began to elicit only vague memories, and it has ever been claimed that the *General Colocotronis* spill at Eleuthera was worse, but that because of lack of news coverage no one heard about it. San Juan was more concerned with the deteriorating tourist business, the freshwater shortage and firebombings by the Independentes. It was an event people wished to forget, less because they had happier things to think about than because the *Ocean Eagle* had made their lives harder. And for most Puerto Ricans that was no change.

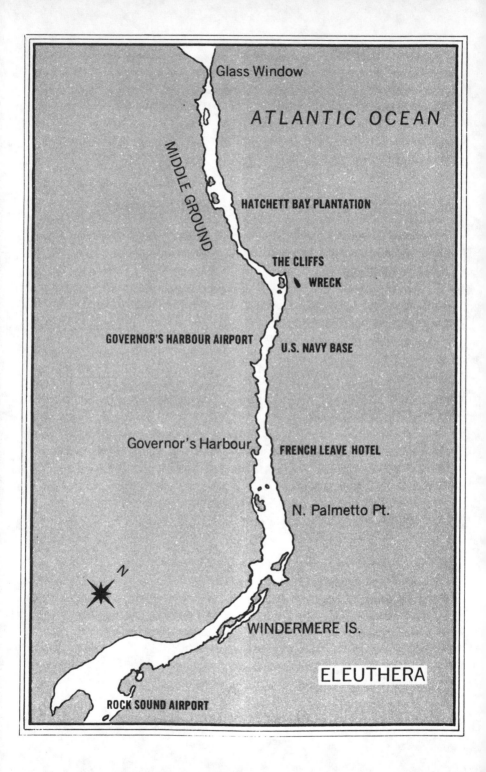

CHAPTER 3

"NOT A GREAT DAY"

The M.S. General Colocotronis
Stranding

THE BAHAMAS ARE said to average an island a mile, there are so many and they stretch so far. Those called out islands can still seem just that when visited by boat in heavy weather, even far out. One of them, Eleuthera, became a place of detention for recalcitrant slaves from the Carolinas in the seventeenth century (its name means "freedom"!), but today's detainees are voluntary. They exchanged what they saw as bondage to the U.S. Internal Revenue Service for what can sound like expensive exile.

"Instead of working for Uncle Sam," says a former New Yorker, who has developed an intolerance for the sun, "I spend my hours looking for shade and the rate comes high."

Another distinction for the Bahamas was the early reputation of a wreck per island, a total helped by shipwrecking. Spanish

Wells was as noted for this grim practice as it was until recently for its insistence that all blacks be off the island by sundown. A disapproving member of an old family notes that the regulation made the nights no less dark.

"The days, though," he said, "seem brighter now."

Early navigators were as leery of the islands as are contemporary yachtsmen, who do well to heed this seventeenth-century warning: "The coasts of them are dangerous, and bad to make, and ships that shall be neer (sic), or amongst them, must keep the lead always giing and a wary pilot." Masters of today's giants, navigating more by electronics than dead reckoning, consider themselves as far above such precautions as their towering bridges are higher than old-time poops. Wary pilotage is still required, though, and so are competent masters, as the late Thorkild Reiber, chairman of Barber Oil Company, made plain in a 1969 interview. Then eighty-six, this aggressive, stocky titan who helped build the Texas Company into Texaco, Inc. (a name he despised as being meaningless), was proud of having held not only a master's license sixty years earlier, but a pilot's for each port of regular call.

"I tell you there can be only one captain on a ship," he said, sounding like one. "And he has to be all captain, from sailing until docking. Take the *Andrea Doria*—her officers were running and yelling all over the bridge, and the *Torrey Canyon* wasn't any better. When her captain took that short cut, he let chance command his ship. He should have known better—did know better—and look where it got him!"

There are times when no one is on the bridge of some vessels on long hauls, particularly at night. This is denied by the industry, but the fact remains that the watch officer may fetl the need of visiting the head or catching forty winks on the chart room settee at the very moment that the helmsman, who doubles as lookout, housekeeper and runner of errands, is in the pantry assembling the night lunch (no less substantial for being gratuitous). A vessel steaming under automatic control can't get into much trouble, the claim goes, except when making her landfall or in crowded sea-lanes. Small craft on a converging course either give way or they're in for it, taking with them some rust, and how many of these have been buried under mountainous bows in fog or at night only the sea floor knows. The unwritten rule of the road now says that evasive action is the duty of small craft, since they can handle it, just as maintaining schedule is the tanker's—and to do this, her master steers a straight course at constant speed come weather, yacht, dragger, or sometimes, and perhaps realized too late, another tanker. He will respond to an S.O.S., though—it is a tradition of the sea, and besides, his ship could be in the same boat. The latter line was spoken by a master who, feeling that puns made the Persian Gulf run bearable, added that a sharp lookout is the other fellow's lookout.

"A lookout ashore can't do any more about comets running into us than one at sea can do about small craft," points out a marine superintendent. "Tankers just aren't equipped to play hide and seek."

Those who would apply U.S. Coast Guard licensing requirements to personnel on all vessels in American waters insist that ships registered under flags of necessity, as they are known to shipowners, but as of convenience to labor, sign on crews of such humble background that they see size and power as making them invulnerable. The result, goes the claim, is sloppy watchkeeping. The reverse, however, is claimed for the engine department—black gang members are said to be so mistrustful of machinery that they practice constant throttle fiddling and excessive burner adjustment under way. Foreign flag casualties please those who would have the U.S. merchant marine be number one—you don't see U.S. flagships breaking up all over the world, right? Actually, these casualties are in proportion to their numbers, and the more ships a nation has, the more that can get in trouble. Even with that wary pilot.

A foreign flag tanker that did not enjoy such services, alas, found herself doomed only four days after the *Ocean Eagle* stranding. This was a Greek, the M.S. *General Colocotronis*, which ran herself on a reef 1,000 yards off the east shore of Eleuthera the night of March 7, 1968. This she did in spite of shore lights blazing a mere mile and a half to port with dead ahead those of a U.S. tracking station at James Point, and had anyone been on the fo'c'sle head, the sound of heavy surf on the reef would almost have to have been heard over the noise of the bow wave. Nevertheless, she steamed ahead at full service speed as if she had all the ocean in the world, bringing to mind the *Torrey Canyon*, until she, too, came to a shattering stop.

"There's something about today's tankers," says an expert in marine casualties, "that makes each stranding more unbelievable than the last."

Almost as soon as news of this latest casualty appeared in the press, she became known as the *General C.*, and it was said by those who came down to the beach the next morning for a look at her that her full name would have sunk her if the reef hadn't. Its origin was cleared up by a marine underwriter in New York, who could afford to talk lightly about it since his firm did not hold a binder on her.

"It seems that General Colocotronis was a hero in the Greek War of Independence," he explained, "and it turns out that Eleuthera means freedom, so the *General* ought to feel right at home there. Trouble is that being held by a coral reef, the only thing about to be free is her cargo."

Except for being diesel-powered (the M.S. meaning "motor ship"), she and the *Ocean Eagle* could have been sisters. The *General C.* was 18,718 deadweight tons to the *Eagle*'s 18,254, her 255 feet of length made her only a little shorter, her crew consisted of thirty-one Greeks instead of the *Eagle*'s thirty-five, both carried a little over 18,000 tons of Venezuelan crude and they operated under charter, the *General C.*'s being held by Humble Oil Company, a subsidiary of Standard Oil Company of New Jersey. The *General C.*'s voyage, too, had been routine —she was out of Amway Bay, Venezuela, and bound for West Palm Beach—and rumors about her stranding reached shore with the first of her cargo. One, disproved by the court of enquiry, was that all aboard had turned in, including watch standers, and another claimed that her course had been improperly plotted from sailing, but that her master couldn't be wrong, in spite of being almost able to touch the shore. An excuse said to have been offered by him that his ship had grounded due to engine failure is in its casual disregard for truth a reminder of a couple of other tanker masters, and as with them, investigation brought out the absurdity of the claim —the number of bottom plates rolled back and the nature of propellor damage established that she must have stranded while under way. His failure to send out an immediate distress call is a mystery still unsolved, and the guesses range from the master's inability to appreciate the situation to his wild hope that he could get her off unaided with no one ashore the wiser.

The call was picked up by the Miami Coast Guard. It asked for immediate assistance with position given as Eleuthera's east coast, later pinpointed by the Bahamas Air Sea Rescue Association as off James Cistern. The association, known as BASRA, is a voluntary service operated from Nassau, and one of its most active members is Captain Harold Albury, the Hatchet Bay Dockmaster. A local boatman summarizes the esteem in which he is held on Eleuthera: "Trouble doesn't come in these waters Sarge can't handle."

The nickname was earned by Captain Albury's drillmaster's way of going about things when he first moved to Eleuthera from Abaco, but his manner has eased enough so that the skippers of most visiting yachts call him Harold, a holdout being the master of a 175-footer with scrambled eggs on his cap brim. Captain Albury's middle height, weight and age almost make his blue eyes and deep chest unnoticeable, and even the casually spoken claim of being able to swim farther than he can walk is apt to go unremarked. In spite of having left school as a sixth-grader, he was in command of a commercial schooner with a crew of ten by the time he was twenty, which is consistent with a heritage of seafaring, even if those of his forebears who were wreckers spent more time watching the sea than following it. He may not be thought of as the wit of Hatchet Bay, but he loses no time in answering when asked what kind of man can he be to have swum fourteen miles in search of a drowning victim. "The kind with flippers," he says.

The first Captain Albury heard of the *General C.* was at six o'clock the next morning after the stranding when BASRA raised him by radio telephone, and he wonders if he will ever hear the last of her.

"It was not a great day either," he recalls. "Winds were 18 to 25 knots out of the northeast with an overcast, seas were running a good 4 feet inside the reefs, tide was about high and they were to kick up more with the ebb. It was a day for working on gear, but a rescue setup was wanted, so it was go down and do it."

James Point reef was about right for a careless navigator to fetch up on, he figured, and he lost no time loading a Boston whaler into his Volkswagon pickup—when there may be survivors on a wreck, you move fast. Then he drove to the Governor's Harbour police station for help from the "Red Stripes." The whaler was put on a trailer and an inspector and three constables followed with it attached to a Land Rover. On the way to the beach he picked up a friend, George Bicknell, who had shared other missions.

"Better men don't come," Captain Albury says, "but before we finished that day's work, I was wishing George didn't have a wife and children."

They were sons, he said, with the casual air of a man who has only daughters, all five of them. He and George Bicknell had their first view of the *General C.* from the cliffs above the beach and they didn't like the look of her. She was big, Captain Albury says, and clearly a hard case. She lay obliquely in a northerly direction to shore, with a 10-degree port list, seas were breaking clear up to her wheelhouse, and a crowd of crew members in oilskins, heavy clothing and life jackets were huddled on the beach. They were wet, cold and afraid, and a pair of lifeboats were being knocked about in the surf.

"They jabbered away, seeming just about lost," he added, "and there wasn't a word of English among them."

Captain Harold counted twenty-three, and just as he was thinking that wasn't enough for so big a tanker, one of them grabbed his arm and pointed at the ship, saying, "Buddy . . . buddy . . ." A U.S. Navy four-wheel drive truck appeared with a second Boston whaler, followed by officers and men from the nearby Navy tracking station. It offers a hospitable sign at the sentry box on the road leading to it: "Welcome—although small, this is one of the most attractive, friendly and efficient stations in the world."

One of the Navy men had just enough language facility to decide that the language spoken by the men on the beach was Greek, that the man concerned for his buddy was the second mate and that on the ship were still the master and radio operator. The chief officer then joined in what was becoming a chorus of "Buddy . . . buddy . . ."

"Think we'll make it?" George Bicknell asked Captain Harold, as they considered the surf booming on the reef.

"Haven't been bested yet," the latter answered, turning to the trailer with the whaler.

She was only a 13-footer, though powered by a 20-hp. Johnson, and the decision to launch her was one that Captain Albury felt he had to make. There were quite a few people on the beach by then and they seemed to agree with the senior naval officer's refusal to let his men launch their whaler.

"For George and me, it was our job," Captain Albury says. "For the others, it would just have been heroics."

The two ship's officers insisted on going with them, and to Captain Albury that had a certain virtue—one of them could help hold the boat off if they boarded, while the other could act as guide aboard. Neither he nor Bicknell knew what they might find, or indeed even how to find it. They didn't take time to worry about equipment, which was meagre enough—a couple of gas tanks, 15 feet of bowline and a pair of paddles. They didn't lack for hands to help with the launching, the boat with equipment not grossing more than 500 pounds, and it seemed that a lot of people wanted to be part of the rescue mission to a point, which was the surf line.

"That tanker looked even bigger from the whaler," Captain Harold says. "We steered for the reef at half-throttle, watching the seas and how they worked on it, to see the best way through. They were big—12 to 15 foot—and while I hadn't taken on bigger ones with a whaler, I had handled others as big, so why not these? All it took was doing, and between us, George and I weren't short on that."

The wreck was a good 1,000 yards beyond the reef, itself a mile out, and the way seas were breaking right up to the pilothouse, he didn't think it would take long for her to start breaking up.

"If that happened, those aboard were for it," he said.

When they reached the reef, he saw a break in the cresting seas and with some fast tiller work he had a try at getting through. He was about to shout a word of encouragement to the others through the spray when a heavy sea caught them abeam, then broke. The boat shipped enough water to kill the motor, then they were flooded by a second crest. Captain Albury broke the motor loose and dumped it overboard in the hope of remaining afloat.

"I needn't have bothered," he says. "A third wave, a monster, threw us out of the boat and flipped it end over end."

They swam for the boat, and as they reached it, Captain Albury looked over his shoulder. "A sea was working toward us like a mountain building, and we had to get clear of the boat."

He pulled one of the Greeks from the gunwale just as the comber broke on the boat. They didn't see her again for a minute or more, and when they did, she was upside down and, due to the ebbing tide, quite a way out. The chief officer was even farther out, but there was no sign of the second officer. Wearing a heavy overcoat, he had failed to surface after the comber caught him.

"In that sea, you were lucky to be able to breathe," Captain Albury explains, "but George and I did all the looking we could."

Presently, a Coast Guard amphibian circled as low as 50 feet above the waves, and dropped life rafts near the chief officer. He swam to one and climbed in, but by the time Captain Albury and Bicknell gave up their search, the rafts were too far out. The tide and surf made it impossible for them to swim over the reef to quieter water inside, so there was nothing to do but try to survive with the help of the whaler. They developed a technique of holding on until a sea was about to crest, then getting clear of the boat. They would swim up the mountain hanging over them, and when the boat reappeared, sometimes 400 feet away, they would swim to it and wait for the next onslaught.

"Timing was all," captain Albury says. "That and not too much thinking."

After a couple of hours, Bicknell called that he was getting cold. The sea temperature was almost 70 degrees, even if it didn't feel it, but with fatigue comes cold. Captain Albury reassured him, saying that he was just shook up a bit.

"A time like that," he says, "it's no fear, or you're done. Panic is the killer, not the sea."

As the tide turned, the seas drove them over the reef, and in the quieter water they righted the whaler and crawled in. They headed for shore, using the seat slats for paddles, as the Navy whaler came out to take them in tow, its crew well life-jacketed. There was enough of a sea running even there for Captain Albury to injure his leg in fending the other craft off, and as he observes, had he been hurt earlier they would never have made it. A jeep took him from the beach to the tracking station where he was treated, hot-showered, coffeed and blanketed. There he was joined by Bicknell and the chief officer, whose life raft was also brought in by the Navy whaler. One who saw him on the beach said that he had the look of a man who wasn't sure he was alive, and breaking his hold on the raft had taken some doing.

"You couldn't come any closer to drowning than we did that day," Captain Albury says. "We were at the door and the door was open."

The nor'easter continued for several days, making it impossible to search for the second mate's body. It was never recovered, nor was one of the rafts which also disappeared under one of those mountainous seas. In due course, Captain Albury received an official commendation for his heroic attempt, the letter closing in the hope that next time he would be equipped with life jackets, and a U.S. Navy officer received a decoration for that whaler's work.

"It must be a special medal for Yank heroism inside reefs," observed a local boatman.

Among those on the beach that morning was David Mitchell, a member of BASRA and proprietor of Eleuthera Water Sports, Inc. A small man who shows the effects of polio suffered as a child, Mr. Mitchell watched the rescue attempt from the dunes in the company of Captain Albury's wife.

"I don't know to this day why she didn't ask for a look through my field glasses," he says, with his marked British accent, "but I know that I am happy I was rude enough not to offer them. I mean to say, no wife should see her husband battling seas like those, to say nothing of the absence of life jackets. You know, of course, that Bahamians are notorious for their casual attitude toward the things—they bloody well have to be forced to stow them aboard!"

Mr. Mitchell feels that Captain Albury undertook the attempt against his better judgment, but he admits that it would have taken a hard man to turn down the pleas of those on the beach. Had there not been such a language barrier, it would have been understood that the master had chosen to stay aboard, as had the radio operator.

"No matter," Mr. Mitchell continues, "the thing is he decided to make the attempt, and I give him full marks. You know, after that monstrous comber struck the whaler, the poor blighters were fighting the sea for two hours!"

While no one ashore knew it, or rather none was able to make it clear, had Captain Albury made it out to the wreck, Mr. Mitchell feels, it is unlikely the master would have come ashore, or permitted the radio operator to. The latter was taken off by one of Mr. Mitchell's boats four days later when the seas moderated enough to make it possible.

"He kept saying 'clean water—clean water' in his broken English," Mr. Mitchell says, shaking his head at the recollection, "and I didn't catch on at first that he meant fresh water for drinking. I mean to say, his wild appearance and gesture, not to mention his almost hysterical attempts to talk, were quite a contrast to the chief officer when he was taken out of the life raft. The radio operator was on the edge, you might say, while the chief officer was in shock—deep shock."

The radio operator was given water at Mr. Mitchell's house, in addition to other potables which, together with a full dinner, calmed him down even if they didn't improve his English. He was clear enough about the master's reason for remaining aboard. The master had insisted on remaining to prevent his command from being seized for salvage, and by the time he was willing to abandon her, it was too late—the sea had taken over. He himself seems to have remained because he feared the master.

128 *Disaster By Oil*

"His English was so broken and his fright so great," Mr. Mitchell continues, "for a bit there was neither stopping him nor understanding him. 'I nearly go crazy,' he said, and 'afraid captain will cut my throat. And no food, bad water—only waves to kill ship.'"

According to the radio operator, the middle-aged master had received a letter at Aruba, the effect of which was that the crew did their best to stay out of his way, and while several objected to his bullying them, no one dared protest. Guests at Governor's Harbour, who were having predinner cocktails at French Leave (a well-known beach resort), were startled by hearing the ship's engines. While numerous conjectures were made on her standing in so close, they didn't realize that they were seeing a fine vessel being driven to her death.

"Obviously, conditions aboard were unhappy," Mr. Mitchell says. "My guess is that the course was improperly plotted long before the southern end of Eleuthera was sighted. Not only that, but the crew members who knew it were too frightened to do anything about it. They just rode with it, as it were, and when she struck, pandemonium erupted. I mean to say, even though the fathometer was out of order, they couldn't have helped seeing the tracking station lights ablaze, in addition to those of the airfield beacons.

"As near as I could make out from the ravings of my no longer so thirsty dinner guest, the burners for the cargo heating coils had been started earlier in preparation for unloading at Florida. Right off, the crew panicked at the thought of an explosion and took to the boats. Mind you, the blighter's English was such that I am a little uncertain that I have him right on all points, but I did gather that the crew rowed about in that dreadful sea until they'd had enough, then reboarded again. One party of them were wrecked coming ashore over the reef, and this group I picked up on the beach track. A sorry looking lot they were, too."

Mr. Mitchell shook his head in admiration of Albury's courage and boatmanship, and said that he must know James Point reef pretty well by now, having performed another rescue there. A tug called the *Delaware*, which had been converted to a yacht, had grounded there on a September night in 1966 following a birthday party aboard in honor of the owner. A teen-ger was at the wheel, according to Captain Albury, who adds that as many a lost vessel has demonstrated, experience is not always the determining factor in marine disasters.

"This rescue turned out to be more of an undertaking than it should have," Captain Albury explains. "I lost a good two hours trying to locate the *Delaware* due to an improper posi-tion having been given, and when I did find her she was al-ready breaking up—awash and six survivors the worse for wear and tear. I got them off with my whaler, but it was slow work going through the reef—the night was black, there was no communication with the wreck, and I had to depend on the Coast Guard's dropping of flares both for picking my way through the surf on the reef and for returning to the wreck.

"I do know that reef well now, but it doesn't make me like it any better. It's a bad one and I've had enough of it. Not that that means I'll not be fighting it again before I'm done."

Captain Albury projects a feeling of satisfaction at a job well done as he talks about the *Delaware*, for all the difficulties en-countered, but his expression is sombre when he considers the case of the *General C*.

"I can see my mistakes," he says with firmness, "but I'm glad I did what I did that day."

Although in the salvage world a stranded vessel is called "the wreck," she isn't officially one until proclaimed a C.T.L. (con-sidered total loss). This implies abandonment by the owners and is done only with permission of the underwriters. It lets both parties off the hook (a maritime term for anchor) of liability for what damage she and/or her cargo have caused, or may. In this period of enormous claims for damages caused by maritime pollution, freedom from liability is harder to gain and, indeed, ship owners and underwriters may not be free of their wreck until she is either up or on the bottom. In the latter case, as the dark suspicions regarding the source of the continuing presence of oil on Puerto Rico's beaches suggest, she had better be clean.

"Oil is harder to hide than find," tankermen say.

Unless a salvager can claim the wreck after abondonment, giving him a chance to come out of the operation with a profit, he works on a per diem basis or for a flat fee. These rates, substantial and confidential, vary according to how busy he is, his salvage ability and the hazards involved, but if it is a bargain for the owner, the salvager has a poor head for estimating. He works against high risks, both in financial terms and physical safety, and good salvage awards are rare. It is also a competitive business and an example of how competitive is the fact that the *General C.* had not only Murphy Pacific's salvage vessels *Cable* and *Rescue* standing by for a few days after the stranding, but also a Moran tug out of Miami, the *Alice Moran.* Moran Towing is not primarily a salvage concern, but a tug skipper is always happy to get a line aboard a wreck— if he can't work a salvage contract, he still may have a claim which will have to be paid off. For its part, Murphy Pacific is not above accepting an occasional long-haul towing job for her salvage trips. These former Navy ARS vessels are powerful oceangoing vessels and have to earn their keep, even if it doesn't keep the salvage crews busy.

In marine casualties it is the underwriters, guided by their counsel, who call the shots and the successful ones lose no time in doing just that. The *General C.*'s owners, Astro Constante Cia, Nav. S.A., of London, were insured by the West of England Steamship Owners Mutual P. & I. Association (a protection and indemnity club). Such a club, seen by some shipmasters as a weapon held over their heads by underwriters, is a group effort in which ship owners share the risk, for marine loss experience can be disastrous in a bad year. Aside from spreading the risk, it comforts the underwriter with the feeling of company in the lonesome moments that come with news of a disaster.

"We can still be sunk," observes one, "but it's nice to know that the bubbles going up are not yours alone."

West of England's New York manager, George Freehill, youngish and personable, has a commitment to his work that seems pretty total, and this condition appears to stem less from ambition and conscientiousness than from real interest. It was he who, after consulation with the *General C.*'s owners and charterer, contacted Murphy Pacific for discussion of a salvage contract. Peter S. Barracca, now Murphy's president, came up with a plan for off-loading the cargo preparatory to scuttling after consultation with Murphy's Captain Thurman, who headed the *Ocean Eagle* operation.

Neither Mr. Barracca nor Captain Thurman was about to offer any guarantees of success in view of the wreck's exposed position and the weather expectations for the time of year. Among the other problems were whether barges or another tanker would make the most practical receiver reservoir, how to secure them and how to heat the cargo so that it could be pumped easily (crude is gummy and flow-resistant until it reaches about 100 degrees F.). It was impossible for the salvors to give a firm estimate of time for the work, which on a per diem basis is always a matter of concern, and it soon became apparent that they were not to be given their heads—Captain Sven Madsen, of Esso's marine operations department, was assigned to oversee the operations.

Captain Madsen is a small man and he occupies a small post, relatively, in a large company (Esso being merely one of Standard Oil of New Jersey's operations), yet in experience, expertise and imagination he may be one of the monolith's largest personnel assets. He is much freer in his thinking than most who follow the sea, willing to innovate and yet confident that what he wants can be tried with minimal risk. A thorough professional, independent and of great integrity, he raises a double question—how do giants of the petrochemical industry manage to hold such men without affording them greater recognition, and why do these men stay there? In Captain Madsen's case, the second question is answered by his hope that through thinking such as his, shipping techniques can be improved and sea pollution reduced. The first question is harder to answer, but the industry tends to promote financial men with public relations awareness. An example of the industry's esteem for this quality is the current plan to change Jersey Standard's name. After much research, a computer gave birth to a name— Exxon, one which could offend no one (an earlier computer choice turned out to mean "stalled car" in Japanese)—and the cost of promoting it, changing bill heads, gas station and facility signs, etc., has been estimated at from $60,000,000 to $100,000,000. The figures are large enough to make the consumer wonder if an equivalent investment in pollution control research wouldn't do more for the giant's image than a new name.

Murphy Pacific insisted on a hold-harmless agreement to protect them against oil pollution claims resulting from the salvage operations, which was granted, and the hull underwriters were worried about this too. As it was, they were stuck with well over a half a million dollar loss for the hull, and they wanted no part in pollution liability, or for that matter, salvage expenses. Murphy also was able to get agreement for reimbursement for tools lost and equipment damaged in the operation at cost plus a percentage, in addition to any additional expenses they might incur. It was an agreement, everything considered, that satisfied the parties concerned, the owners, the P. & I. Club and Esso. The operation promised to be one of significance in the shipping world—a successful off-loading of a tanker in an exposed position with accompanying pollution prevention could do much for the industry generally, and it could also change the world's way of looking at pollution risks. It could be demonstrated that spill controls are within the art and purse of those who cause them, and that, in his quiet way, was just what Captain Madsen intended to achieve.

Even before the March 9 arrival of the salvage tug Cable for standby duty, it was clear the General C. was doomed. A night of grinding on the reef had opened most of the tanks which hadn't had their double bottoms ripped out by the grounding, leaving only three intact. The engine room was flooded,both propeller and skeg (rudder support) had been carried away, and even if she could have been torn loose from the reef, there would be major pollution and probable sinking. Aside from this, the heavy seas had caused hull cracks and would complicate salvage efforts. Those of the Cable's crew who hadn't experienced the roll of an ARS in a seaway were learning something new about discomfort, but they were as little able to prevent it as they were to halt the growing pollution problem. Crude from the General C. poured from her as she continued to open up, and her bunkers—in this case not Bunker C, used for oil fires under steam boilers, but the more volatile diesel fuel—were leaking too. A 5-mile-long slick was off the outer reefs and some had worked its way onto Eleuthera's famous sands, colored pink from rose coral dust. Detergents were being flown in from Miami and New York, but fortunately self-appointed experts and chemical salesmen were in short supply due to their preoccupation with the *Ocean Eagle*. There would be less misapplied knowledge and disregarded common sense at Eleuthera, but the familiar black carpet was growing on the beaches and gave every sign of having moved in to stay.

"It was smelly stuff," recalls a beachfront owner, "and gluey too—like putting your feet in tar."

Other witnesses were fascinated by the numbers of shoes and boots abandoned to the oil's grasp by the curious, it being simpler to walk out of footwear than to attempt to retrieve it. The caustics tried in removing the oil gave rise to some new forms of the old hootfoot, but did lead to the discovery of the effectiveness of baby oil.

"It does as good a job removing crude from feet as it does with diaper rash," says an innkeeper. "We call it sole food."

Murphy's New York office, which has a fine view of the harbor and an even finer collection of salvage tug models, ordered the *Rescue* to the wreck scene—atitude 25°20'3"N and longitude 76°20'.5W—on March 12, after receiving the go-ahead from George Freehill. The *Rescue*, which is stationed at eye West, was commanded by one of the firm's ablest salvage masetrs, Captain A. Kirchoff. His log for March 4 opens the salvage report: "Arrived 07:30 at wreck, rough seas and swells, wind NW force 4. Anchored in 9 1-2 fathoms with 3 shots of port anchor chain, unable to lower launch due to weather. Salvage crew turned to, making up saddles for buoys and beach gear."

By evening, the heavy weather had increased to such an extent that the starboard anchor was let out with four more shots of chain and two of the four engines were running slow to ease the strain on the chains. The *Rescue* spent the night being worked over by the seas, pitching and rolling heavily, as did the *Cable*. The latter was ordered to the *Ocean Eagle*, and the next morning, faced with force seven winds out of the northeast, the *Rescue* proceeded at reduced speed on a southerly course to seek shelter in the lee of Wemyss Bight, a little south of Davis

Harbour, which is on the west side of Eleuthera. She lay there out of the weather for a couple of days, returning to the wreck on the 17th. It was still too rough to board, however, but that didn't prevent Madsen from turning up on a landing craft at noon. He conferred with Captain Kirchoff aboard the *Rescue* and that afternoon a working party finally went on the wreck. The balance of the salvage crew took soundings and rigged tackle for a stern-to-stern unloading operation, it having been decided to use a tanker for off-loading rather than barges, so the wreck's heating coils could be activated by the tanker's boilers to facilitate pumping. One unpleasant chore aboard the wreck was the disposal of a large quantity of meat spoiling in the freezers, the odor of which was strong enough to overcome even that of the crude. "And that," as a diver said, "takes some doing."

The next three days were occupied in transferring salvage equipment to the wreck, all hoisting aboard having to be done by hand since she was without power, and in setting out anchors, tackle and buoys for securing the reservoir tanker in 7 fathoms. The tackle employed was of the heaviest, but by the end of the 23rd the sea had so "made up" that operations were suspended and the *Rescue* had to again relieve the strain on her anchor chains by using her engines. She headed back for the shelter of Wemyss Bight at first light, where she was joined by a supply vessel, the *Magar Arrow*. On the 24th the launch *Delphine* put aboard George Freehill, a couple of Esso officials and the fire superintendent of the Bahamas for a conference on procedure and pollution control.

The weather didn't moderate enough to return to the wreck until the 26th, when more gear was put aboard under difficult working conditions—big seas were still running, the decks were slippery with oil and spray, and gear being hoisted had a way of swinging about as if determined to connect with a head. Again the sea made up on the 27th, with winds of 35 knots and heavy swells breaking over the wreck, and so it was off for the shelter of Wemyss Bight. There work was done on flotation gear for the discharge hose and steam-heating lines, and by 07:30 on the 30th the *Rescue* was maneuvering alongside the wreck once more to put aboard pumps and air compressors. All hands agreed that the real fun would start with the securing of the reservoir tanker, the *Esso Margarita*, which arrived on the 31st. Using the moorings ready for her, she was carefully winched into position under the direction of the salvage master in one of the *Rescue's* launches. It was tricky work with far more of a sea than was welcome, but by 10:30 that night the *Margarita* was in position, secured by her bow anchors, four moorings and with four nylon lines to the wreck's stern. She lay about 70 feet from it, and as an observer said, "sweet as you could ask and in spite of it being April Fool's Day."

Steam lines for heating the cargo and discharge hoses were hooked up, and by the next day, when the forward tanks had been warmed to 90 degrees, pumping was begun. Before noon, however, a 6-inch discharge hose parted and some fast work was done on closing scupper drains to prevent polluting the sea further. Sawdust was spread on the decks and by dark almost 3,000 barrels had been discharged. After a pump failure, the hands turned to for loading aboard the wreck thirty barrels of detergent from the *Margaret of Exuma*, a barge, and with pumping resumed, the *Esso Margarita* had nearly 10,000 barrels aboard by the next morning. The weather then took a hand and she was hove up on her anchors to keep clear of the wreck. The seas worked her over properly and the nylon lines had to be replaced, but in spite of her touchy position, pumping continued through the night.

The decks became increasingly hazardous for the salvage crew, in spite of liberal treatment with a compound called Slix ("Couldn't they think of a less slippery name?" asked a pumpman), and by April 4 a new problem arose—fresh water was in short supply. This, of course, was necessary for the *Margarita's* boilers and such had been the consumption to make steam for the heating coils and pumps that she was down to a supply of 400 tons with a consumption rate of 88 tons per day. One steam line was shut down, reducing the discharge rate to 230 barrels per hour, and on the following day steam was used only for heating, the pumps being run on compressed air. By noon, the *Margarita* had 27,000 barrels aboard, and after stripping pumps were employed to get the residue from discharged tanks, the pump lines were blown out with air to prevent spillage on being disconnected.

On April 9 the *Margarita* let go her lines and hove her anchors to join the *Esso Peru* offshore for transfer of cargo and the taking on of fresh water and bunkers. Detergents were applied at the wreck site and aboard the other vessels, and at first light on the 10th the *Margarita* returned to maneuver into position for more off-loading. By the end of the next day, the wreck's fore-tanks had been emptied and crewmen worked hard with detergents to clean up its foredeck in the face of rising seas. By that night the decks were awash once more, complicating the work of the salvors, and more lines had to be put out to hold the *Margarita* against heavy seas abeam. At 22:50 she requested suspension of pumping to allow for adjustment of her position, which was becoming increasingly difficult to maintain, but an hour later she was back in business and cargo was again being pumped. The next couple of days are ones the salvors are content to forget, for they not only had to work under dangerous conditions and in heavy weather, but they also had no relief—it was too rough to rotate watches from the *Rescue,* and meals of cold food, soggy with salt spray, became hard to swallow, almost as hard as the odor of crude was to breathe.

At last, on April 12, it became apparent that the *Margarita* had taken aboard just about all the cargo she was going to get, and in spite of decks being awash, hoses were blown and disconnected and at 09:00 mooring lines were let go and the salvage crew returned by launch to the *Rescue.* Off-loading was ended, theoretically, but a hitch, and a literal one, developed—the *Margarita* couldn't free herself of a forward mooring. It had to be cut away by torch, an unwelcome operation aboard tankers, and during it her port anchor chain broke. It was a near thing for a bit, but she "came out of it clean." More important, the off-loading operation had been a success—82,300 barrels had been taken on without serious injury, major pollution or, in spite of the uncooperative seas, too many gray hairs. After fresh water was transferred to the *Rescue,* she sailed for Aruba, West Indies, looking as fit a ship as her crew was efficient.

"That Esso fellow," a salvor said, referring to Captain Madsen, "knows how to do things and he isn't afraid to do them."

The *Rescue* sought shelter again at Wemyss Bight, returning to the wreck on April 15. She encountered long, heavy swells, which caused severe rolling and made coming alongside the wreck to take off salvage gear impossible. An inspection on the latter found pumps and hoses torn loose from their lashings, the midships shelter deck flooded, and several tanktop covers, their lugs broken off, had been torn loose. Oil was leaking from No. 7 port tank and No. 3 starboard, in addition to the engine room, and detergents were applied. Deterging continued the next day, another forty drums being deliverd, and work was begun on making all tanks airtight preparatory to their being charged to lift the wreck off the reef. Tank vents were plugged with wooden stoppers, the pump room was sealed off after having been deterged, and so were several tanks. The *Bahama Developer*, a supply vessel, arrived on the 17th with more detergents, and sixteen barrels were applied to the engine room and four to the fireroom, after which the contents were mixed by the stream from a 3-inch-high pressure pump. The next day the seas were easier and the *Rescue* was able to come alongside to take off gear and to apply more detergents. Work continued on making the hull airtight as manifolds (piping distributors) were assembled for installation on tank tops preparatory to compressed air charging.

On the 19th the *Margaret* was moved alongside to provide a diving platform for the wreck's bottom inspection and the *Rescue* sailed for Nassau, being out of fresh water. The diver, Arthur Steber, found numerous cracks below the waterline, bottom plates rolled back and the rudder lying 75 feet away. The wreck was caught by the reef for most of its length. His report says it well: "Keel crushed and buckled, numerous holes, rips and tears, plates missing and rolled up, skeg and rudder missing, only one good blade of propeller. What a mess!" It was clear there was nothing for it but sink the wreck.

On the 20th, after a morning of working on the air hookups, the salvage log notes that the crew "knocked off for home cooking at noon." Tanks were charged in the afternoon and found to hold air at 4 pounds pressure. The *Rescue* returned the next morning, but on the day following the weather made up once more. Work on the air charging proceeded nevertheless, compressors being refueled in preparation for towing to the grave site, loose deck plates were welded, if a little tentatively because of the presence of vapors, and numerous gaskets were replaced. This work continued for the next three days and on the 25th, with the tank tops secure, part of the salvage crew returned to the *Rescue* for rest. The diver found loose rivets below the waterline leaking, which had to be sealed, and there was oil seepage from the after tanks. The wreck was allowed to settle once more, as a safety measure in view of the heavy seas, and detergents were applied to the tanks. As much as 10 pounds of air was put on the tanks during the next couple of days, and so busy was the salvage crew plugging air leaks that meals were eaten aboard the wreck in shifts. It was not a happy time, but the wreck was almost ready for her last voyage and all involved were looking forward to it.

Before first light the morning of April 28 the wreck became lively, the tanks being charged, and the *Rescue* took up the slack in the towline attached to its stern. At 05:20 it began to swing slowly to starboard, and an hour and a half later, the *Rescue* had a line on the starboard bow and had swung it off-shore. Mooring lines were still holding, the intent being to take no chances on the wreck's getting out of control. One of the lines parted shortly, and then things happened fast. The bow swung in an arc of 200 degrees, but the *Rescue* stayed with it and was able to free the hulk from the reef at 09:00. She towed it clear of the moorings to an anchoring position, and there was general relief, both afloat and on the beach and cliffs, which were crowded with onlookers.

The rest of the day was spent in removing salvage gear from the wreck and the *Margaret* continued to spray the area with detergents. Although crude was still present, it was under control. As for the wreck, she rode easily at anchor, rising to the swells and occasionally taking a bit of a roll. Being light and with little ballast, she had so much freeboard she seemed a very giant of a ship. To shore watchers, she had the look of a ship reaching upward to sail the sea of the sky, and it was hard to realize that such an able-appearing vessel was doomed.

To seafarers, she looked a ship ready for a repair dock, a world with its own language and customs.

When a vessel is berthed in a dry dock and the water is discharged, she is known as on dock and dry. Today's tankers are so large that drydocking can be a problem, and in some cases as much as 200 feet of a ship will project beyond a floating dock, seeming to teeter on air. Once braces and keel blocks are driven in place, the shave and haircut begin (sandblasting, then antifouling and anticorrosive applications). The work is said to be in hand, the office begins keeping track of the charges (drydocking is figured on a basis of about $.40 a ton) and marine surveyors in boiler suits go over her so that she can be certified seaworthy. Surveyors are serious, conscientious types and operate with a "show me" style but they are more relaxed than Coast Guard inspectors. These go by the book and are apt to be inflexible, but it can be said of both that a payoff is almost unheard of—the calling has its own pride, which keeps those who look for faults in a vessel, and those who would conceal them, straight. Even in dry dock a ship has the feel of life about her—she gives an impression of restlessness, as if she resented being invaded by strangers who explore her secrets and bar her from the freedom of the sea. An oceangoing vessel in dry dock is an awesome sight—you are looking at steel plating 10 stories high with a propeller perhaps 40 feet in diameter and a rudder 30 feet high. The sheer bulk of the hull makes it understandable that it can take 6 miles to stop when under way at full speed.

"With some of them," says a port engineer, "even if the watch is ready to jump for the throttle—and except for sea trials they aren't—you have to allow as much as twenty minutes."

In U.S. southern yards blacks do the work below the waterline for the most part. It has been said that it is not work for whites, and that blacks feel at home in the dark and heat under a ship's belly. They don't mind being covered in grease to protect their skin on a paint crew, it is added, or being swathed in coverings to protect them from the dust of sandblasting. There's a lot of sledgehammer work below the waterline, which is also done by blacks—they seem rather above what they are doing, as if they survive through overlooking it.

"Someone has to do the heavy work," says an assistant dock superintendent. "Blacks are good at it, I'll give them that."

Big ships are made of small places, it has been said, and no one who has crawled in and out of double bottoms, fore and after peaks, or in chain lockers will dispute it. These are solitary, claustrophobic places in which one wonders if life still exists outside the steel closing one in. Crawling under 1,000 feet of bottom can also be unnerving, and awareness of the 50,000 tons of steel above, which seem to teeter on keel blocks for all its vast width, doesn't help. Blacks in oilskins seal the overboard discharge lines dripping in the darkness by hammering home wooden plugs, somehow adding to the menace in this awesome, dank world which exists 40 feet below the waves at sea and which most seafarers prefer not to dwell on.

"A tanker's life is a battle against corrosion," say dry-dock men. "If the sulphur in crude doesn't eat her guts out, sea salts will eat their way in.'"

The average tanker loses 2 percent of her steel each year, and although new anticorrosive and antifouling treatments help, power plants still tend to outlast hulls when properly operated. The latter can be salvaged for use in new forebodies, but when the hull goes to the shipbreaker, that is the vessel's end, and for him the less woodwork the better. Getting rid of wood costs money, but cutting up steel *is* money. He looks forward to the day when ships are made so they can be cut entirely by torch with no ripping out by wrecking bar.

"Antiquers go for mahogany rails and oak decking, but we haven't time to bother with them," explains one of the bigger shipbreakers.

Although the *General C.*'s scrap value wasn't going to benefit anyone, at least her wood and steel didn't have to be separated —they were for the deep along with her cargo residue, and they were to stay there. As salvage master, Captain Kirchoff was taking no chances on the weather's making up once more to thwart this end and he made the *General C.*'s last day a long one, both for her and his salvage crew. By the first hour of April 30, her tanks were under air pressure and a nylon towing line was in place. Just before two that morning of moderate swells and wind, the order was given to slacken her anchor chain, but it fouled in the hawse pipe with 5 shots out. It could neither be let out nor heaved back aboard, an inauspicious beginning for the *General C.*'s final trip, and there was nothing to do but sever it. It was burned through with a cutting torch (which with links as heavy as a man can lift takes time), then was let go with a buoy secured. The buoy line parted, however, and the anchor is on the bottom yet.

The crew was taken off, it being estimated that the air charge in the tanks would hold for about eight hours, and the tow got under way. Good time was made, the wreck behaving in spite of having no rudder. A little after nine speed was reduced because the wreck had developed a pronounced list to starboard, and a scuttling party was put aboard. There was danger of the wreck capsizing, which would mean the possibility of·her floating upside down indefinitely as a hazard to navigation. The scuttling party went about their mission of opening tank vents and sea valves with a will—they wanted to see the last of her, but they didn't want to go with her. They were back aboard the *Rescue* within half an hour, and "not sorry, either," as one observed.

The towline was heaved in, having been cut at the eye aboard the wreck, the launch was hoisted and secured, and then it was just a matter of waiting. There wasn't much of that to do, as it turned out, for the *General C.* went down stern first at 10:35 at latitude 25°50'N, 75°46'W and in about 300 fathoms of water. Her epitaph consisted of some oil mixed with detergent, spreading a slick of perhaps 300 feet in diameter, a life raft which bobbed up to the surface and eight empty detergent barrels. The *Rescue* stood by for a respectful period.

On the way back to the wreck site she assisted a disabled tug drifting off San Salvador Island with two barges, then spent a day at James Point hawking (submerged looking) for the *General C.*'s anchor. The ship's carpenter used a water glass on the launch and he didn't give up happily (an anchor of that size is worth money), but finally the *Rescue* was ordered to proceed to station. She arrived at Kingston, Jamaica, at 14:14, May 5. To use Captain Kirchoff's log entry, "All engines off line

—*Rescue* secured to Station Pier. This closes case of *General Colocotronis*. Alfred Kirchoff, Salvage Master."

As usual with strandings, particularly when there has been enough oil pollution to attract public interest, cost figures are hard to come by. A reasonable estimate of the cost of off-loading the *General C.*'s cargo, use of detergents, equipment hire and an overhead allowance for the *Esso Margarita*, less value of salvage cargo, is estimated at $400,000.

"If the *General* didn't cost them more than a half-million aside from hull value," guesses an underwriter, "they got off cheap."

Captain Kirchoff was careful to submit an inventory of "Expended, lost and damaged items," in which he listed work gloves, flashlight batteries and hacksaw blades. In a separate inventory he listed items salvaged from the *General C.*, and in this he did not neglect to mention that they were "used, broken, soiled or in bad or poor condition." Included are a bed, sofas, chest, ship's stores and canned goods, fans, small refrigerator, and various items of radio receiving and transmitting equipment "damaged in handling." The conscientiousness of such a listing is unusual in the salvage trade, given as it is to unspoken recognition of the rights to booty, and a couple of items mentioned at the bottom of the list give, perhaps, a clue.

Taken by Capt. Madsen: 1 motor lifeboat given to *Esso Margarita* —1 steering wheel given to *Esso Margarita*.

Doubtless, the motor lifeboat was sold to benefit the *Margarita*'s slop chest fund and it would be nice to think that the wheel graces Captain Madsen's den. Surely, both he and Captain Kirchoff earned at least one souvenir by their expert planning, able operation and courage. It was as fine a piece of salvage work under adverse conditions as the tanker industry has seen, and one hopes the lessons learned will be utilized in the next tanker disaster. For it's coming up, and may the salvors be as able.

The *General C.* stranding was notable for more than oil spill control—for the first time in a warm climate a spill came under scientific examination. Such a study was provided not by public authorities but by underwriters, a group that has been more interested in keeping pollution disasters quiet. The general manager of the West of England P. & I. Association, R. S. Fort, M.C., commissioned two marine biologists to go to Eleuthera during the off-loading. The decision must have taken almost as much courage as Mr. Fort's winning of his Military Cross—not only was it in effect an industry admission that spills were here to stay, but also his choice of scientists presented a problem. Molly F. Spooner, M.A., Ph.D., and her husband, G. Malcolm Spooner, M.A., M.B.E., of Britain's Plymouth Laboratory, had done a study on the *Torrey Canyon* spill which was not entirely complimentary to either industry or government. The Spooners point out that oil on the sea exposed to the sun's rays undergoes evaporation of its lighter elements, particularly in warm climates, and there are times when this natural remedy is preferable to chemical applications. At Eleuthera there aren't many seabirds, the shallows being too prevalent to permit diving by pelicans, and sea gulls are present inly in summer when they nest on uninhabited islands. Commercial fisheries didn't have to be considered either, but the effect on tourism caused much concern. Attempts were made to minimize the effects of the stranding, and actually the pollution was limited to a few miles of undeveloped and inaccessible beach due to the prevailing winds, current and profile of the shore line. The Spooners estimate that only one seventh of the 18,000-ton-plus cargo escaped into the sea, although other sources put it at at least one-fifth. There was always a chance of an offshore wind blowing the slick seaward to threaten beaches in greater use, and it was for this reason that it was decided to attack the spill at the wreck site and in the shallows inshore.

Oil is not destroyed by dispersive efforts, but undergoes structural change. Its disappearance is the result partly of evaporation, partly of oxidation through ultraviolet ray catalysis, and by bacterial action, although this is inhibited by chemical agents. The slicks were fairly thin in comparison to the *Torrey Canyon*'s, because of the smaller amount of spill and the warm air and water temperature. The Spooners confirmed some of the *Torrey Canyon* findings in regard to the use of oil-spill dispersants, solubilizers and detergents. Adequate mixing, also important, was accomplished by propeller action, turbulent wave condition and high-pressure jets. Detergents and dispersants tested are of three types—kerosene-based, water-based and chalk- or silica-based. Among those in use at Eleuthera were Enjay 7664, the low toxicity of which the Spooners confirmed, Polycomplex A, which is water-based, Magnus, an oil-based agent in use for some years, and a compound made by Drew chemical found to be a skin irritant. Kerosene-based agents are the cheapest in first cost, but their irritant and toxic effects require masks and protective covering, which in warm climates is a problem.

The Spooners make some recommendations for spill cleanups utilizing natural and local substances which, while they haven't been tried to any extent, seem practical for warm areas. They point out that a spill of thick oil may be attacked with coral sand, which acts as a blotter and produces readily collectible residue. The James Point beach, for instance, acted as a sponge, and when oil appeared on the French Leave beach, it could have been treated with sargassum weed to bind the particles together for collection. This weed, which is in plentiful supply, could be used on the sea as a collecting agent, and sea grass, washed up on the beach in big clumps, proved a fine oil collector also. Burning of oil-soaked weeds and grasses was tried but with only fair success. The fires couldn't make much headway against sand and wet growths, and the result was considerable air pollution. Coral sand is mobile enough to be able to cover oiled beaches on its own if one can be patient, and this natural process, the Spooners feel, is far preferable to the use of chemical agents. The latter, in combination with oil, can form a slurry which is removed by sea action, leaving the coral base of the beach exposed.

"Bare beach bases we can do without," a government official said. "We have enough of a problem with bare bottoms on them!"

At James Point, the oil leaking from the *General C.* was blown toward the reef, where it was churned by breakers before being carried onto the beach, permitting both structural breakdown and oxidation. The beach absorbed the mix in layers as the result of tidal action, then was covered by blowing sand to await formation of the next layer. Such layers, mixed with oiled sea growths, built to a thickness of about 2 inches, and in the shallows other layers of oiled weeds formed to a depth of a couple of feet. In time the lighter elements washed onto the beach for natural covering and erosion by bacteria. Applications of detergent were employed after the off-loading was completed by spraying from a small boat inshore, and by a pump on the beach to treat the breakers.

Reefs which had been blackened by oil began to appear lighter in color within a couple of weeks, partly as a result of chitons feeding on the oiled coral with their magnetite-capped teeth. This produced gray feces instead of the usual white found when their diet is algal cells. Had the reefs been treated with detergents, the oil would have sunk into the porous rock instead of remaining on the surface, and would have killed off the browsing fauna, as happened in Cornwall during the *Torrey Canyon* spill. There it was established that if left alone, limpets would browse on oil without apparent harm. They can pass oil well enough, even if it does not have food value, but their rate of absorption is slower than that of chitons. A suggestion has been made to raise chitons commercially as an aid in spill cleanups, but there are unknowns.

"Let's first find out what else chitons do beside wear away coral," a marine biologist suggests.

Toxicity test experiments were carried out by the Spooners in their makeshift French Leave Laboratory on small fishes from reef pools, gastropods, spider crabs, bivalves, sea urchins and chitons. Indications were that Enjay at 100 parts per million is not toxic even if it did suggest an irritant effect, Magnus showed toxicity at 10 parts per million for pinfish, while the Drew compound was found to be rather more and Polycomplex A somewhat less toxic. In earlier tests, Magnus was found to be nine times less toxic than an agent in much use at the *Torrey Canyon* disaster, British Petroleum's 1002. In general, the Spooners found that toxicity levels of agents used at Eluthera were low enough to suggest that with the careful applications employed, no toxic effects of consequence are to be expected. One spill-control device experienced the same failure at Eleuthera as elsewhere—the oil boom. The jagged coral had its way with it so that it required much maintenance, and it was viewed as "chiefly of psychological value."

One recommendation resulting from the Spooner study is the warning to "allay public fears and explain courses of action, especially if it is considered best to do nothing." For officialdom, there is only one thing harder than to explain doing nothing and that is to admit that there is nothing to be done. Among other recommendations are assessment of chemicals used in cleanups as to their biodegradibility (ability to be decomposed by bacteria) and investigation of natural causes of oil-spill degradation. Perhaps most important of all is an investigation of oil-sludge bacteria.

Research into the basic chemical process by which microorganisms eat petroleum hydrocarbons is being conducted by Esso Research and Engineering Company, a Humble Oil affiliate. Microorganisms do the dirty work at a Humble refinery in New Jersey, where a biotreatment plant takes process water contaminated by organic compounds and, after skimming off residue oils, transfers the water to lagoons in which live microorganisms in the form of a brown bacterial sludge. After the water is well mixed into the lagoon, the microorganisms convert the organic chemicals into carbon dioxide and water, and the effluent is drained into a settling tank. Eventually, the organisms sink to the bottom and are returned to their lagoon, with the water left clear and clean.

The devouring of hydrocarbons is done by enzymes, biocatalysts capable of changing one compound into another without being changed themselves. Those that favor crude oil have been identified, and breeding attemtps to produce stronger strains that can attack other kinds of oil are under way. Particular emphasis is being placed on a strain for use on oil spills and in line with this is an investigation of the fate of oil slicks at sea which are not treated. Today's guess says that the microorganisms that digest oil, converting it into water and carbon dioxide, become food for larger organisms, which in turn are eaten by fish. One technique developed to use microorganisms in controlling oil spills employs cultures frozen into a powder so concentrated that one billion cells can be placed on a pinhead.

In laboratory tests they can disperse an oil spill into droplets while reproducing simultaneously.

"We're learning to cooperate with nature," an Esso spokesman explains.

An environmentalist chuckles at the line. "By which he means that if they don't, there won't be any nature left."

The importance of keeping the public informed during an oil spill has also been urged by a Florida lawyer, Dewey R. Villarel, in a paper delivered at a seminar on recent developments in admiralty law. He urges that the attorney representing the ship owner acquire a professional public relations team, in addition to organizing a news conference with the master so that he can be interviewed within controllable limits. While such a suggestion, of course, is more concerned with managed information than full disclosure, it is a step forward. Other hints for the attorney include being sure the spill is from the ship he represents, and informing the Coast Guard that while the client may clean up the spill, the attorney does not consider it his duty and that the owner may seek idemnification for the expense incurred. It is also urged that the attorney order the master to forbit law enforcement officers boarding his vessel to collect samples of the oil, for there is always the possibility of suppressing evidence obtained by unlawful search and seizure. The attorney is also advised to have ready marine biologists and zoologists who can rebut claims of extensive damage to wildlife, for without these experts he may have difficulty refuting such claims. And in case the attorney may think cleanup costs are a minor part of a spill's damage, he is told that oil cleanups average $3 per gallon.

"We don't cry over spilled oil, we bleed," says a spokesman for the American Petroleum Institute, an industry lobbying and public relations group.

The findings of the Bahamas government inquiry into the stranding of the *General C.* were released on April 19, 1968, and they were not unexpected. The cause was found to be "faulty, inefficient and inaccurate navigation" and the Court of Inquiry, consisting of the chief magistrate of the Bahamas and the inspector of lighthouses, declared that "the Master and Chief Officer were mainly concerned in varying degree with the stranding." The terse announcement is consistent with the government's desire to have as little publicity as possible, even to the extent of ignoring the victory achieved in the off-loading and the spill control. "Oil" is such a bad word that often it is called "tar," and the source of its disrepute was once said to be the U.S. tankers sunk in World War II. Diving teams, however, found the hulks of those tankers that they dove on free of oil, and it is now generally admitted that a more likely source is the shipping of oil in the amount of 10,000,000 tons annually. Between bilge pumping, tank washing, ballasting, and loading and discharging, some is bound to end up in the sea even without a casualty. And it does, daily.

A year after the stranding of the *General C.*, James Point beach still had a slight smell of crude, long rollers easing in from the reef had a brownish color, and a swimmer came out with a bronzed tint never achieved my mere sunbathing. There was enough light oil in the surf to produce a rainbow coloring, and to make the breakers fall with a "ka-plink" instead of "a-harsh" sound—for an active sea it was too still. On the beach were a few reminders of the stranding—a post dug in as a deadman mooring with rusty cable attached, a couple of lifeboat flotation tanks, numerous Drew chemical drums, an oil-blackened Jacob's ladder and one broken oar. Under the beach, about a foot down, was a black, asphaltic substance similar to crude after its lighter elements have been dissipated.

Two years later, weather conditions approximated those Captain Albury had to contend with in his rescue attempt. A nor'easter blew for several days, tides were abnormally high, the sea bottom was roiled and innkeepers worked hard to free their beaches of debris. Included in this was driftwood, sea grasses and numerous plastic containers and bottles. While the dumping of garbage at sea may not be a serious pollution threat in the ocean itself, it is becoming one on the beaches. A container or bottle will usually sink before reaching shore unless it is sealed, but if it is, as were those on Eleuthera's beaches, it is almost bound to end up ashore. It has been suggested that the reason people seal a container before throwing it overboard is an unconscious desire to see it float rather than sink. Whatever the cause, said a laborer on one beach, all bottles at sea should be stamped with this tiny piece of advice, "Drink it, then sink it."

Another problem faced by beach owners three years after the *General C.*'s end was a serious infestation of blackheads, small pieces of asphaltic substance not unlike those kicked up by tires from the potholes of New York streets. There is a difference though, and it is appreciated as soon as one of these lumps is stepped on or squeezed—the outer layer of blackened sand acts as a container for a gooey mass which has all the look and smell of congealed crude. It has the same staining effect too, and responds to baby oil as does the real thing. Few of these lumps exceed an inch in thickness, usually they are spherical with a width of not more than 2 inches, and on some beaches they were so thick it was impossible not to step on them. The source of this nuisance, which riles visitors much as the sea is roiled, is unknown. The two main theories ascribe it either to passing tankers washing their tanks and discharging the dirty water, which is prohibited but still practiced, or to a source even the mention of which causes an ominous silence. This is the possibility that the blackheads are formed either by sea action on that portion of the *General C.*'s cargo sunk by chemical agents, or from what remains within the hull. It is known that no matter how deep oil may lie in the sea, it can still rise and undoubtedly will if it can find a way to do it. It is also known that such infestation of blackheads occurs only after a good blow.

"It's not going to give up blowing," says a property owner in boots, raking his littered beach, "and my guess is that bloody tanker is going to dribble out her poison on us for years to come."

At least, there was no trace of the golden glow of lighter oils on this second inspection, nor was there any sign of oil a foot below the sands if it was still there, it would have been buried far deeper by then. The coral reefs in some locations showed oil stains, however, and at least a few people maintained that they go back to the stranding, neither time nor tide having been able to remove it.

"And there's been enough of both, too," says one of them. Most of Eleuthera's residents look back on the event as one that did them credit—many helped in any way they could to make the pollution control effort easier, supplying equipment to aid the off-loading operation and offering hospitality. There is relief that the world press was too busy with the *Ocean Eagle* to give the story much space, for an oil spill, no matter how well handled, scares off tourists. Today, Eleutherans are less interested in discussing the *General C.* stranding than their economic plight—1971 was not a good year, visitors not only being fewer but more careful in how they spent their vacation money, and no improvement is seen in 1972. An influx of long-haired surfers doesn't do much to take up the slack, and even if it did, they wouldn't be very welcome.

"It isn't that they sleep on the beaches, or spend no money," a black constable, immaculate in white jacket and helmet, explains. "They have a way of looking at things we don't. This makes them a bit of a luxury, do you see?"

His black superior with a neatly trimmed moustache, recently returned from a police course in England, had a ready answer to the source of the beach blackheads. He insisted that they couldn't be solely from the *General C.*, for islands all through the Caribbean faced the same problem and had been unable to solve it.

"You may be sure," he said, gesturing with his swagger stick, "if that tanker were the cause, our government would have eliminated the condition long since."

He didn't go on to say how this would be done, but if the continuing and costly problem of oil on the beaches could be solved at Eleuthera, that fair island wouldn't need tourists—it would have converted oil into gold. But even those who have made walking on the moon possible have yet to come up with the magic to make the seas clean.

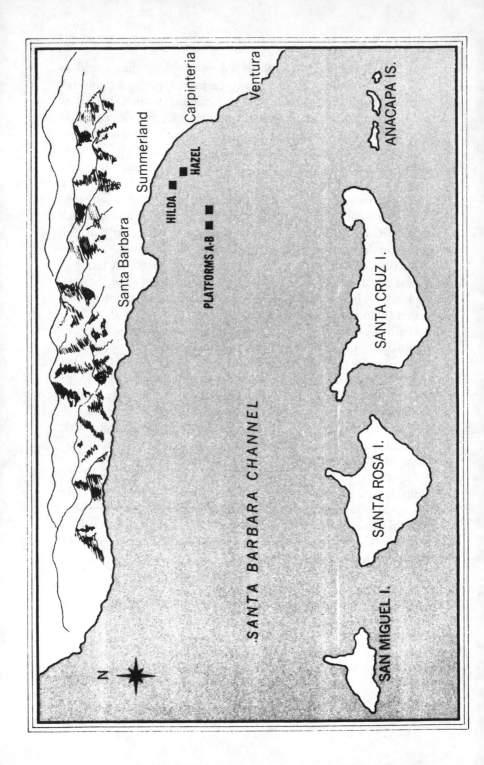

CHAPTER 4

"PROBLEM PLATFORM"

The Santa Barbara Channel Disaster

THE DAY BEFORE the anniversary of the *General C.*'s stranding, the United States government opened bids for oil-drilling leases in the Santa Barbara Channel. Involved were seventy-one tracts of 9 square miles each, twenty-six oil companies and a total price of $603,000,000. Except for those bidders who hadn't been able to top the record prices, all participants came away happy—the federal government was in pocket for over a half-billion dollars at a tight-money moment, and the oil industry not only had won the right to tap a major reserve of oil, but they had also defeated the people of Santa Barbara County and City. These citizens had hoped to prevent further channel drilling in order to avoid diminishing its scenic value and what they were certain was a threat to the environment. They protested that the channel bottom was unstable and earthquake-prone, and that it had seeped oil naturally for so long that early mariners used the slicks as an aid to navigation. They tried to convince the federal government and the oil industry that it was not a safe area in which to put up drilling platforms, let alone put down wells. They pointed out that the state was so concerned about its waters inside the 3-mile limit that their drill regulations were more severe than those of the Department of Interior. The experts scoffed at such fears, seeing the Santa Barbarans as privileged reactionaries who would hold back progress and deny both the community and the government added revenue. Even worse, they would deny the nation a desperately needed defense material—the one and a half billion gallons of crude oil under the channel.

The people's defeat was softened somewhat by a sop—a 2-mile zone in which there would be no drilling for the present and which adjoined a state sanctuary along 16 miles of coast. But the vanquished saw only a victory for greed over responsibility, and they weren't reassured by the fact that the lease winners were so anxious to get going that men and equipment were on the move the very afternoon of the bidding—with offshore oil, time is even bigger money than with onshore operations, and neither high water nor citizens brought low can be permitted to stand in the way. The federal government as managing agent for the landlord (the people), through the Department of Interior's United States Geological Survey (U.S.G.S.) acting as building superintendent, was empowered to see that the tenants (the oil companies) fulfilled the obligations of the leases they held. And the public relations staffs for those tenants promised the landlord that he would see what such substantial and imposing tenants could do with his property—within no more than a year, one P.R. man predicted. And he was right, dead right.

Just about a week short of the lease anniversary, the landlord found out what at least one tenant could do. On Tuesday, January 28, 1969, Well No. 21 under the Union Oil Company's drilling Platform A blew out and a massive mixture of crude oil and gas came roaring up the drill casing out of control. Word of this accident so dreaded by drillers didn't get out until the next morning, when the Santa Barbara *News-Press* was called. The caller remained anonymous, either because he didn't relish being known as an informer or because he knew the fate of those ancients who were the bearers of ill tidings, but his information was complete enough. A new well was nearing completion, being the fifth drilled from the platform capable of putting down more than twenty, when it blew without warning as a drill bit was being extracted. The sea around the platform, he said, was boiling with gas-charged oil. By the time the *News-Press* reached appropriate city and county officials, who thus heard of the menace for the first time, the well had been out of control for almost twenty-four hours. This time span had been chosen by a Union vice president, John Fraser, as all that would be needed to bring the spill under control, or even stopped altogether. That was a Wednesday, and those who read it in their evening papers knew by the end of the week that the prediction was as far off as successive Union reassurances, and as understated as the admission by Union's president, Fred L. Hartley, that Union had a "problem" with Platform A. It didn't take long for it to become known as the Problem Platform.

"Instead of facts," remembers a Santa Barbaran, "Union's P.R. people kept putting out reassurances. But more oil on already troubled waters we didn't need."

Many of the 70,000 Santa Barbarans who began that night to wonder what they were in for could be classed as upper class and upper middle class, both economically and socially. Enough of them live on trust income, the source of which goes back at least two generations, to allow them to qualify for the haughtier classification, and income for many of the others comes from retirement sources. The city had everything once, they say, but then plain middle-class others discovered its virtues—the channel and its islands, beaches, mountains, climate and, for both aging bones and blooming bodies, sun.

"It isn't that they were objectionable," a property owner with a fine view of Platform A says. "There were just too many of them."

"So we set up controls," explained his neighbor. "We knew what we had and that to keep it we'd have to protect it. Now we have zoning, master planning, architectural controls, regulations about billboards, noise and open space—even a national park and wildlife sanctuaries. All it took to keep Santa Barbara the way we like it was determination. Where there's a—"

"Except for the channel," the neighbor interrupted. "We had what it takes to handle the people, but the oil companies . . ."

He added that not even Washington was up to handling them, and that if the companies weren't up to handling the spill and damn soon, something was going to give.

"And yet," he finished, "if I hadn't done pretty well in oil shares, I couldn't afford to live here."

Many in Santa Barbara comforted themselves with the thought that at least the spill wasn't from a tanker. A well, they said, is really just a long pipe and a pipe can be closed—if not by a valve, then at least you can cap it. So this platform thing wasn't going to be another horror like that tanker off England a couple of years ago with her . . . how many million gallons of oil was it, how many thousand birds? Or even that one at San Juan the following year. Anyone who can drill in water like the channel from what is practically a skyscraper and make money doing it—well, what that kind of technology can make flow, it sure can make stop. Oil, after all, is merely a tool—a servant —and we are the master. Maybe we can't shut time off, but oil —just turn the valve, mister!

Being a mere 5½ miles offshore, the Problem Platform is clearly visible from shore, as is the ceaseless water traffic serving it and its twin, Platform B. From a distance it looks much like the bow of a giant vessel under construction, and seen from above it even appears a busy section of one, complete with cranes, racked steel pipe, deckhouses, gear, winches and a helicopter pad. At night its brilliant lights enhance the feeling of a large construcion project, even if the arcs of electric welders are missing, but whether seen by day or night, its presence is an intrusion upon a lovely shore. To many Santa Barbarans, it was an affront before the blowout. Later they realized that the danger to the environment had been underestimated at a time when there was more concern about the ugliness of the platforms.

"At least, they're not next door," one resident had said,

trying to look on the bright side of things. "The only way they can hurt us is by ruining the view."

The first day after the blowout was one of uneasiness. People tried to find out what was happening, and not having much success, wondered why whatever had happened had. Union Oil was operating on the theory that the less said, the better, until things were under control. For all the experts' technological knowledge, no one was entirely sure there had been a blowout. One thing they were sure of, though—admitting you don't know why something happened is no way to reassure the public.

"We didn't have many answers at first," a source close to Union said later. "We were a long way from the whats, let alone the whys. One thing we knew, it was going to be a P.R. challenge, and boy, was it ever!"

Inspected from the air, the Problem Platform scene was unnerving. Not only were two large areas of sea nearby alarming in the force with which they were erupting, there was something unclean about those brownish discharges from the deep. They looked not unlike two enormous wounds draining and spewing forth putrefaction. Their stain upon the sea, already a couple of miles long by one wide, was working southward, a turgid but determined mass. On the oil-drenched platform, knots of varicolored hard hats hung about idle, as if waiting for someone to come up with the answers, and nearby a couple of service vessels and a Coast Guard utility boat rolled in the swell. The passivity of the men made one wonder if they had been shocked into a deep and disabling withdrawal. The feeling was less that they had given up from exhaustion than that they didn't know where, or even how, to begin.

By the next day such was the flow of oil from the sea floor that the slick was estimated to cover 120 square miles, and it was recognized that the Ventura beaches were definitely threatened. The slick, about 8 miles long, grew by the hour, but it wasn't moving very fast, and at a conference between Union Oil and Coast Guard officials it was decided to attack it with chemical agents both by sea and air. Thus was begun the first act of a drama by now so often played typesetters of the press must have become tired of using the same words. Again, as if no lessons had been learned from previous spills, agents were applied to break up and sink the oil, and there was much talk of improved techniques. As the day wore on, thoughts on how the spill had happened were made public, together with some educated guesses as to the present state of things. It was thought that the oil was coming from the 3,000-foot level of the well, and for a while the word was that it had been sealed off by forcing down drilling mud (a clay-based substance used as a lubricant, flushing agent and to hold oil and gas under pressure in place).

"Trouble is," a drilling crew member explained, "it just went out the bottom end of the well as fast as we pumped it, then came up to the surface with the oil. Which, to this old-timer, means we got trouble—it ain't the well now, it's the sea floor what's let go."

Others from the platform were in agreement about two things —it was good to be off it, and if you haven't seen a well blowout, you'd have to take their word for it that you'd be right shook! Beyond that, they weren't saying much—some allowed they had been told not to, others recognized signs of a battle shaping up and knew which side they were on—that of their bread and butter.

"That's what this town wants too," said one, getting into his car. "But all you're going to hear is what we done to their birds and fish."

Before the disaster many Santa Barbarans had a layman's grasp of oil-drilling operations, but they were to learn the limitations of the experts' knowledge. They knew that exploratory oil drilling is done from floating rigs and that when there is reason to think there is a sufficient quantity, a producing platform is set up. They knew, too, that the Problem Platform, which is 15 stories high, has an operating deck about 125 feet square and is 40 feet above the surface, just as they knew that the rig stands on legs sunk to a depth of 180 feet of water. Some had heard that there was so much oil in the bearing sands 500 feet below the channel floor that it kept seeping around the platform legs as they were set in. While this may have had a welcome sound to Union, it didn't to those who worried about the fragility of the channel bottom—if just the legs going down could bring up oil, what would happen when they started drilling?

Theoretically, the art of drilling is so advanced that if things do get out of hand, it will not be for long, but it soon became apparent that the Problem Platform's problem was more special than the state of the art was perfect. Well A-21 began normally enough; a 13½-inch hole was drilled to the 500-foot level, then the 239 feet of surface casing (12-inch steel pipe sealed by a fast-setting cement pumped down and forced up the sides of the bore) was installed. A 12-inch drilling bit, probably the product of a company named for the father of someone who has had as much press coverage as the Problem Platform, H. R. Hughes, is then attached to the drill stem, which is inserted into the well in 30-foot lengths. This is rotated, being held by a clamp, and through it is injected the drilling mud. When the well is drilled to the designed depth, the drill stem and bit are pulled out and a steel casing of 8 inches is then put down and cemented in. The bottom of the casing is plugged, and oil, gas and water flow into the casing through perforations at the level where expected. Well A-21, after being drilled 500 feet, was angled at 15 degrees until it was down 3,500 feet and in oil sands. It was then that the bit and drill string were pulled back and oil rushed into the bottom of the well under great pressure and "kicked," in effect similar to a gusher. It was a tricky moment, but the drill string was dropped back, together with blow-out preventers (spring-loaded valves set to close off abnormal oil flow in an emergency). For the moment, it seems, the well was under control, but the increased pressure on the oil source pribably forced it upward through fissures at 600 feet to the thin cap over the channel floor. The oil then boiled up to the surface with gas and the Problem Platform entered the history books.

While well blowouts are not uncommon, it is rare that one cannot be controlled. This one was, as far as the well itself goes, but it was very much out of control in the sea floor, and control here is a very different matter from capping a well —it is more like squeezing a handful of grease and expecting to hold on to it. One theory holds that the blowout could have been prevented had Union Oil not received a waiver from the United States Geological Survey permitting a casing of a mere 239 feet, so that oil-bearing sands could be tapped there. Most wells in the channel were put down with 1,000-foot casings in recognition of the unstable condition of the sea floor due to geological faults in combination with pressures of at least 1,400 pounds. This is enough to force oil upwards through any but the heaviest drill mud mixes, 90 cubic feet of which can run as high as 80 pounds. The mud pumped down A-21 could have been dissipated by the soft strata at the bore bottom, so that it flowed away into the surrounding area, which would explain the color of the oil boiling on the surface. In any case, once the drill pipe was dropped back in and the valves slammed closed to stop the blowout, it was thought things were under control, but a little more than five minutes later and about 200 yards from the platform's northeast leg, the sea be-began to boil, rising 2 feet with the turbulence. The one possibility of control—pumping down more mud—was now out of the question. The well would have to be cleared first and this couldn't be done under conditions of a blowout.

"We thought we had it made," said a derrick man, "only that old boy had us made!"

Union wasn't giving up on trying to kill the well—various attempts were made to inject mud and outside experts were called in. Among them was a crew sent by Red Adair, famed as a well fire fighter, under the supervision of an ingenious engineer who was to plug a well out of control in Canada by using golf balls (heat and pressure compressed them to a substance which sealed off the gas). Neither Union nor the Coast Guard was admitting on the third day of the spill how badly things were out of control, nor would they estimate how long it would be before the threat was ended. At that point no one knew, but it was clear that there had better be some answers to the increasing volume of qeustions. The best Union spokesmen could do was to announce that air-spraying of chemicals was breaking up the spill, which was being carried to sea by the wind, and that there was still no oil on the beaches. Polycomplex A and Corexit were being used, shore crews were being organized and supplied with both of them and hand tools and material for making booms. In short, what began to look like a major undertaking was getting under way, and as truck and barge loads of equipment and materials arrived in Santa Barbara, people really began to worry.

"This thing is a lot bigger than just a spill," a bystander at Stearns Wharf said. "It's shaping up like a disaster."

By the end of that third day, over 30 square miles of sea were covered by heavy concentrations of oil and another 200 by light fractions. Governor Ronald Reagan offered his office's "full resources," the Interior Department expressed concern, the state asked for permission to inspect the oil platforms under the jurisdiction of the U.S.G.S., harbor masters were getting ready to close harbors and Union Oil said that it was too early to make predictions—the control operation was being played by ear. Others added that once the wind changed and the crude was on the beaches, it would be played by nose.

The possible danger to wildlife began to be more fully appreciated. The Navy was concerned for the safety of their trained porpoises, and the state Fish and Game Department began to worry about the annual migration of gray whales, their route being through the area of the slick. The Ventura Humane Society began receiving calls about oil-saturated birds on the beaches, apparently mostly sea gulls and grebes, and the Audubon Society advised that most birds affected would die, for even those that survived being cleaned would be reexposed to the oil on release, and there was also the problem of their diet, ocean fish and plankton being hard to come by in the oily waters. People were advised to bring the oiled birds they found to the Humane Society where, if not salvageable, they would be put out of their misery. The day ended with an announcement from Washington by Walter H. Hickel, who had just received Senate confirmation as Secretary of the Interior after an initiation harsher than the roughest fraternity procedures, that he was dispatching a team of experts. That Washington had taken notice meant to one reader of the *News-Press*, the dignified format, conservative view and placid style were soon to be employed in the forefront of the battle for the environment, that Santa Barbara would really have some problems.

"First they forced wells on us," he said. "Now it's experts and politicians, we'll really see what pollution is!"

Saturday, February 1, was a fine day ashore. Only the endless stream of rubberneckers blocking roads with a channel view spoke of the kind of day it was at sea. The so far uncontrolled menace was growing hourly and its stain was visible from Santa Barbara's Protestant Cemetery. This appropriate viewing stand, together with its crematory and columbrium, is such a good example of taste and landscaping one doesn't resent its being occupied by the dead. It brings a sense of peace and reassurance to visiting survivors, most of whom are female and visit in the late afternoon. They drive Lincoln Continentals instead of the Fleetwood Cadillacs they favored until, as a General Motors dealer explained, "too many of the wrong people moved here with them." Almost as fine a view of the channel may be had from the Hotel Biltmore, which, its lobby buzzing with salesmen extolling their spill products—Aquajel, Boroid, Ekoperl, Corexit—was reminiscent of the first days of the San Juan sales invasion. Representatives of firms making igniters for burning oil on the sea, such as Cabosil, were being given a hard time by their emulsifier, dispersant and sink brothers. These pointed out that between the 640-degree flash point of California crude and the amount of natural gas hanging about the Problem Platform, anyone who thought he was going to demonstrate the virtues of burning could forget it. And so it turned out, but as one igniter salesman said on his way to the airport, "The product might have had a chance if it was made by an oil company." A product, new to U.S. spill technology and which didn't need salesmen but rather agents to find enough and try to keep the price down, was straw. Hundreds of tons were soon being brought into town for distribution on beaches and at sea by broadcasting, after being chopped, and although it proved both effective and nontoxic, it was an embarrassment to the news media for a couple of days. A local and nonagrarian reporter referred to it as "hay" when it was first unloaded at Stearns Wharf, and both wire services and television reporters employed the word. The TV reaction was nationwide, but as one reporter said, the important thing was that it might turn out to be a case of straw not breaking the camel's back, but saving Union's neck.

The first oil reached the beaches that day, Rincon Point having the honor, and the Coast Guard described the slick in its main concentration as being about 4 miles wide, 12 miles long and with lighter elements now covering 80 square miles and moving about in an area of 200 square miles. The beginning of a long-term dispute arose over the quantity of oil working its way to the surface, Union estimating it at first as not more than 500 barrels a day (2,200 gallons), while others put it as 5,000 barrels (22,000 gallons). It would be a while before either side admitted that there was no way of estimating exactly, since such a spill can only be guessed at, and while guessing is more accurate now due to experience and spectroscopic examination of oil films, it is still an inexact technique and apt to remain so. To anyone flying low and often around the Problem Platform (a practice soon prohibited by the Coast Guard), it was obvious that the oil flow from the two eruptions was much heavier than a couple of thousand gallons a day, such was its turbulence, discoloration and rapid spread. Even after the experts were finished with their examination of the disaster and had gotten together on recommendations for the handling of future spills, all they could come up with was an estimate ranging from one to three million gallons.

"The best you can say," advised one of them, "is that we had a lot more oil on the loose than we knew what to do with."

The magnitude of the spill was finally admitted by Union Oil through its foremost P.R. man, Jerry Luboviski, director of corporate communications. Until then, his role had seemed to be one of shielding President Hartley from criticism by Santa "Barbarians," as they were known in some quarters. Luboviski's experience in playing down the impact of the *Torrey Canyon* disaster and making it seem that Union had barely heard of her was coming in handy. He would need all the help he could get with this disaster—not only was there enormous media coverage, but he also had the problem of the overexposed, unpredictable and very vocal President Hartley. Texaco's Captain Thorkild Rieber referred to Hartley as only a geologist during the *Torrey Canyon* disaster.

"What does he know about ships?" he asked. "He's just oil."

While there are those who say that Hartley did something of the same job for his company as Captain Rieber did for his, he is better known now for his White House in. A heavy man with an imperious manner, as a Republican party contributor he has been accused of being generous to a fault, a reference to his lending the White House one of his most able associates, Peter M. Flanigan. This expert in cover corporation funding had been chief executive officer of the Union-controlled Barracuda Tanker Corporation, which in addition to the *Torrey Canyon* owned a nonjumboized sister ship, the *Sansinena*. It was claimed in March, 1970, by Senator Joseph D. Tydings (D., Md.) that the value of this Liberian-registered vessel would be increased by $6,000,000 because of a waiver granted by the Department of Commerce permitting her, although a foreign-flag vessel, to be registered to engage in U.S. coastal trade. The intention, Senator Tydings charged, was to use her for shipping oil from Alaska to the West Coast under charter to Union, a run hard up for bottoms and highly lucrative. Flanigan denied having any part in obtaining the waiver, which was subsequently revoked, and added that he had placed his Barracuda holdings in trust when he became an aide to the President. It is said at Commerce that it is now clear why Flanigan's outfit was named Barracuda, and at Union that the honorable Senator is not a bringer of glad tidings.

The amount of oil escaping into the channel was not the only quantity in dispute, nor was it the matter many people were most concerned about. It was assumed that the flow would be halted eventually, but the toll in wildlife was both dramatic and alarming. At first Union minimized the losses, but as dead birds began washing up on Ventura County beaches, it was announced that seven scientists would serve with the state Fish and Game units. Over fifty grebes (small birds which dive for their food) were collected and, as expected, the death rate among birds cleaned was high. Union's unwillingness to accept the rule of thumb arrived at in the *Torrey Canyon* spill, which counted one bird dead at sea for each ashore, didn't soothe public feeling. Instead, there was much talk about the amount of Corexit being spread from aircraft, and although the Enjay Corporation, its manufacturer and a Standard Oil of New Jersey affiliate, continued to proclaim its nontoxicity, ornithologists were not convinced. To them the cure was worse than the disease in terms of the possible effect on the food chain, and the best agent available, one said, is time.

"We know what crude can do," he added, "but we don't know the long-term effect of chemicals. This is neither the time nor the place to find out."

Union justified their oil-slick attack by saying that if the oil were not sunk, it would reach the beaches or drift on the surface and the damage to wildlife would be far more serious than the egect of agents considered by experts to be nontoxic. In addition to selling that argument, Union had to answer a rumor that although the drill casing had been cleared of obstructions to carry drilling mud for a couple of days, it was now out of commission due to a broken valve. It was explained that this problem was being worked on, and in addition, that Union would pay all cleanup costs. An all-out attack on the spill was to be made as soon as equipment, material and manpower were ready. These promises coincided with news from the other side of the environmental battleground—formation of a new group called GOO! (GET OIL OUT!). (A suggestion that it be called GOOF—GET OIL OUT FOREVER—was not taken lightly.)

"Drilling in the channel was a goof, all right," said one of the founders, Alvin C. Weingand, who is a former state senator. "It might make it sound like we're kidding, though. And believe you me, we're not."

The Sierra Club marked the anniversary of the channel drilling lease auction by requesting Secretary Hickel to halt all channel drilling until safeguards for the environment were assured, and on Sunday, February 2, there was much talk of staging a mass demonstration at which the credit cards of oil companies, active in the channel, particularly those of Union and its partners, Gulf, Mobil and Texaco, would be burned. The day also marked the first activation of the National Pollution Contigency Plan set up by President Johnson in 1968, partly as a result of the *Ocean Eagle* disaster. It offered guidelines for procedure in the event of a major spill and it involved the departments of Interior, Transportation (which was taking over the Coast Guard), Defense, and Health, Education, and Welfare, and the Office of Emergency Planning. Kenneth Biglane, who was a witness to the *Torrey Canyon* cleanup and active in that of the *Ocean Eagle*, represented the Federal Water Pollution Control Administration, and was early on the scene. His mission was to oversee remedial and cleanup measures as well as enforcement procedures. In view of Union's all-inclusive role, the assignment was not a civil servant's dream.

"The way they act," said a F.W.P.C.A. staff member, "you'd never guess Union Oil wasn't the Federal Union."

Biglane had already taken the measure of Union experts in the matter of applying chemicals to the slick. He succeeded in having a federal order issued on Saturday to stop it, but the order was rescinded on Sunday, apparently because of Union's prediction that the seepage might not be stopped for three weeks. The intention was to drill a relief well to intersect that drilled from the platform and through which mud could be pumped to treat the substrata fissures. Although the California Department of Fish and Game joined Biglane in opposing the chemical applications, as did the Sierra Club and other concerned wild-life organizations, they lost their first battle. The measure of Union Oil had been taken and it was found almost as powerful as the Federal Union, after all.

"One of Union's P. R. types said Sierra members are for the birds," complained a Club protestor. "I told him, 'You're damn right we are.' "

The dead bird count on the beaches was up to 150 before the day was over, and an emergency wildlife center, earlier set up in the Carpinteria Beach State Park by Union, was moved to the Santa Barbara Bird Refuge near Montecito because of the traffic jams on Route 101. There the birds were dipped in a solution of Polycomplex A (about which National Audubon has reservations) in an attempt to dissolve the crude oil without cutting the feathers' natural oils, then they were rinsed in fresh water, dried and kept warm in an attempt to ward off pneumonia. The problem of ingestion of oil from feather preening was so far (and still is) unsolvable—crude is toxic, partly due to its sulphur content. Another problem was the posing of affected birds for TV exposure, and at least one elderly lady was persuaded to hold a grebe for the benefit of camera retakes until an outraged chorus of young people demanded that it be surrendered for removal to a shelter for treatment.

"These young think only of themselves," she complained on camera, shoving the victim at them.

Many hundreds of birds were collected on the beaches by what police called "hippie types"—not only were they more agile than the staid citizens of Santa Barbara, but they were also willing to get dirty. A Childs Estate bird center was doing much of the treating and doing it for long hours. As a volunteer consultant veterinary observed, one wouldn't expect such pretty girls to be so brave or work so hard. Oddly, they seemed less moved by the plight of the birds than the men, which may explain why they appeared more efficient. Onlookers were clearly appalled at the grim scene and by the very human cries of the birds—the oldsters clasped their hands as if in prayer, while the young reached out as if to help.

"What did they ever do to us?" asked an eight-year-old boy.

A Union spokesman, defensive about the rescinding of the chemical treatment prohibition, explained that the operation, which had been costing $75,000 a day, would be applied only in localized areas. He added that federal authorities had not been able to refute the nontoxicity claims by offering proof of harm to marine or wildlife. Frederick Eissler, a national director of the Sierra Club, had a ready answer—he claimed that Union had insisted on spraying and in stronger applications that recommended, in an attempt to dissipate the oil before it reached beaches and harbors to avoid claims for property damages. Union, ignoring the charge, announced that among techniques being tried, or about to be, were vacuuming the oil from the surface of the sea, containment by booms, a new type of plastic sea curtain to both contain and collect the oil, and, of course, straw.

Several groups were working to have future drilling in the channel outlawed. In addition to the efforts of the Sierra Club and GOO!, the Scenic Shoreline Preservation Conference advised the Secretary of the Army that the Corps of Engineers had the authority to suspend oil platform operations when a hazard to navigation exists or when the public interest so requires. It was pointed out that the flowing oil, whether 2,000 gallons daily or 20,000, was threat enough to the public interest, and that the navigational hazards represented by the platform were well known—not only were their buoy lights often out, but in fog both yachtsmen and commercial skippers had experienced near misses of the platforms. What, they asked, is going to happen when one of those supertankers bringing oil from Alaska's North Slope connects with a platform? The answer then, as now, was that no one knows—it hasn't happened and the hope is that it won't.

"If it does," thinks a tug skipper, "don't worry about any spill. The light from that blaze will be seen in the Gulf of Mexico!"

Santa Barbara County Supervisor George H. Clyde, chairman of the Santa Barbara Oil Advisory Committee, was angered by an exchange of telegrams with Secretary Hickel. He had wired the Secretary on Wednesday demanding the cessation of all drilling in federal waters of the channel, and received a reply saying that the Secretary shared the committee's concern and that he would keep "abreast of developments." Stopping the drilling was not mentioned, however, leading Clyde to believe that it was never considered. But conservationists in the area could comfort themselves with the knowledge that they had at least one victory to their credit—Hickel had become so concerned, he was going to make an official visit the next day, Monday, February 3.

As if in an attempt to make things look better for Hickel's visit, Union's Hartley did his utmost at a press conference to sound hopeful, saying that the flow into the channel was now predominantly natural gas. There were those who quarreled with the word "predominantly," but there was enough gas flow both to make work crews on the platform uneasy and to be smelled in inspection aircraft. Attempts to clear the jammed check valve in the well casing were still being made, Hartley said, and the drilling on the relief well 1,000 feet distant was expected to take about ten days. The basic cause of the spill, he claimed, was that "Mother nature had let us down" by letting the oil out of the drilling sands. He added that over 8,500 gallons of dispersants had been used so far and application was continuing.

Union had injured "Mother nature" enough without adding insult by blaming her for its greed in not putting down sufficient casing, said conservationists. And the only word for the use of chemicals without knowing the immediate effects and long-term results was "appalling," said Dr. Robert Holmes, an oceanographer. "With proprietary right to keep the formula of Corexit a secret," he added, "the claim that it is nontoxic is unverifiable and meaningless."

The use of chemicals in state waters by the federal government was questioned by the Sierra Club, and since the source of the pollution was in federal waters, the club argued that the state might have a right to exercise jurisdiction over them, just as it was compensated when wells in federal waters drained oil from state sources. Another attempt at drawing a hopeful picture was a statement by a Coast Guard officer at the scene: "The oil situation is under reasonable control."

As well as one could judge, the National Pollution Contingency Plan seemed to be working well, although it had not been designed to cope with the outrage of citizens in a community which includes beach front valued at $2,000 per foot. The Corps of Engineers and the Navy were locating equipment for beach restoration, the Weather Bureau had set up a local station to monitor winds and tides as an aid to slick movement prediction, U.S.G.S. inspectors were checking on platform operations to ensure that regulations were being observed (and at last without permission of or being dependent on transport provided by the operators), and the F.W.P.C.A. was keeping a careful eye on the situation (being careful, too, it was said, to keep out of Hartley's way).

The Union blowout occurred only four days after Hickel's confirmation, while he was resting up at Camp David. On Sunday he was called by an aide, who compared the disaster to the Fairbanks, Alaska, flood. This was all it took to get the green but energetic Secretary on a White House Jet Star that afternoon for Santa Barbara. En route he asked for an opinion from Interior's solicitor, Ed Weinberg, who had served under the previous Secretary, Stewart Udall, on whether he had the authority to close down the wells if he should feel it necessary. Weinberg, after some thought, opined that he would probably be on shaky ground, a condition not unfamiliar to those Santa Barbarans who remembered the 1925 earthquake and were aware of the fragility of the channel bottom. The fact was that no one on the plane knew for sure whether the new Secretary had such authority, just as no one in the apprehensive city they were approaching knew much about Hickel, with one exception —Union's Hartley. Hickel called him Fred, and their friendship was not likely to reassure those who hoped the Secretary would help save their environment.

Although Hickel had survived the Senate wringer to come through looking clean, if highly deterged, there still had to be some dirty laundry around, some thought. How could he escape it, this self-made man, once a welterweight professional, who had become governor of a brand-new last-frontier state which wanted to get going on making one of the world's major oil finds a matter of dollars instead of hopes? The fact that he was an appointee of an administration thought to be pro-oil didn't help, nor did an oft-quoted line of his to the Senators—he was not one who believed in "conservation for conservation's sake."

The unofficial and boisterous reception committee at the airport that evening must have reminded him of the Senate's early opinion of him. Hostile conservationists with protest signs were backed up by others sullen with indignation, and newsmen equipped with notebooks, cameras, microphones and skepticism were ready to shout questions. All one of them knew about Hickel, he said as the Jet Star came in for a tidy landing, was that he played his cards close to his chest and well.

"He's only got two hobbies," added another. "Cooking steak dinners, no dessert—and the *Reader's Digest*, twenty-five years of it and every word."

His press officer did hand out a news release, but the reporters were too busy throwing questions to give it much of a look. Some of their questioning sounded as if answers were expected not from Hickel but from White House press secretary Ronald Ziegler back in Washington—newsmen felt that Hickel was being kept on a short rein by the administration out of concern for his lack of tact and public relations sense, just as the naming of Russell G. Train, an earnest, private-school-tie lawyer, as Under Secretary would be seen as an attempt to give the department's executive level a more genteel gloss.

"How about a smile, Walt?" yelled a photographer.

"It's Wally," another corrected him.

A reporter in the motorcade following their quarry to a Coast Guard briefing guessed that the President hadn't given either the appointment or the appointee much thought, but that he had better get busy at both.

"It's my guess," he said, "his boy will either end up a hero for the antioilers, or in their outhouse."

At the Biltmore, Hickel and Hartley chatted animatedly, the latter playing the role of host. Although it was the beginning of another day for the disaster, his manner was breezy, even eager.

"Dig the oily bird and his worm," a girl murmured.

The press finally got a story after Hickel was flown by the Coast Guard on a channel inspection tour, although they had to wait until he conferred with his staff. All they'd had to work with so far had been his statement that his visit was to see what assistance he could offer, not to make charges. Now he said things were even worse than he had thought, that the drilling regulations needed updating, and that while Union had lived up to its obligations, he hoped to get a voluntary suspension of all channel drilling. By noon, he had been in touch with the oil companies and, according to the Biltmore press handout, had persuaded them to halt drilling operations on a temporary basis until the operations could be reviewed by federal and, perhaps, state authorities. An exception was the relief well being drilled by Union.

"This procedure will afford a breathing spell until it can be determined whether corrective measures are necessary," he said. "Our first concern at this time must be to take all possible steps to avoid a repetition of the incident I have just seen."

The announcement was a surprise and it was clear that people would have to rethink their Hickel views. He seemed a little surprised himself by the victory and he withdrew to pace a secluded hotel lawn, this stocky, hard-bellied victor. His dress was standard Administration—a fairly sharply tailored dark suit, white shirt, dark tie and shiny shoes. It was topped by receding black hair slicked back and too well annointed, and his appearance complemented his flat voice, under tight control, seeming to give nothing away. He was a hard man to get a feeling of, and even now that he was alone he was still very much Keeper of the Secret. He stopped pacing after a bit, wiped his face with a white handkerchief, then carefully removed his jacket and hung it over a garden chair. After loosening his tie and unbuttoning his collar, he sat down in an adjoining chair, and with a long sigh, turned his face up to the sun. Just as he settled himself more comfortably, a distant phone rang. He jumped up, tightening his tie and looking for his jacket. The phone stopped on the second ring and he paused, his hand grasping the jacket. He started to sit once more, but changed his mind. After loosening his tie to button the collar, he put on his jacket, giving it a downward pull by its rear flap, then walked briskly to the hotel terrace, light on his feet. The Secretary of Interior had had his time in the sun and he shut the glass door to the lobby firmly.

"What about offshore drilling at all, Mr. Secretary?" a reporter asked before he left for Washington. "Is it necessary?"

"That's not a decision for me to make," he answered, "but we always got to go forward."

The answer worried those who watched the Jet Star taxiing for takeoff. They wondered what this man was really like— where did he stand, how long would he stay with a stand, was he his own man or did his first loyalty belong to either of two presidents, the Union's or Union Oil's? It was agreed that the two presidents had more to lose than the untried Secretary— Union Oil and its partners had paid over $61,000,000 for their 5,400 acres in Lease No. 402, and the two platforms, A and B, probably ran them another $15,000,000 each, while the Federal Union expected bonuses of $300,000,000. That kind of money doesn't talk, it orders. If something has to give, it has to be the people.

"One thing," an admiring onlooker said, as the Jet Star was airborne, "with exhaust that clean, no one's going to accuse him of polluting the air."

Airborne, Hickel may have given a sigh of relief, but events in Washington would not permit him others for a while. Representative John V. Tunney (D., Calif.) asked on the Hiuse floor for a presidential board of inquiry, and the chairman of the

Senate subcommittee on Air and Water Pollution, Senator Edmund S. Muskie (D., Me.), would question both oil and Interior representatives on his Water Quality bill. At Santa Barbara, though, things were looking up. Union announced that aerial spraying had been abandoned (without any mention of continuing treatment by vessels) and that the defective check valve had been removed from the casing, permitting resumption of drilling mud application. The weather now became uncooperative, however, for as the wind picked up it turned onshore. Not only did a large area of the slick move to within 2 miles of Santa Barbara beaches, it was now trapping several hundred seals on Anacapa Island and had even reached the eastern end of Santa Cruz Island. Gray whales on their way to breeding areas off Baja California were reported surfacing in the slick, bringing renewed attacks from the Sierra Club and the Audubon Society on Union, which found it would be sued by the state of California as soon as "the amount of damage can be estimated."

"Adding money that big takes time," a GOO! member remarked, pleased.

Unofficial estimates of the polluted area now ran as high as 500 square miles, although the Coast Guard was staying with its figure of 200. Gas and oil were still boiling up in a wide area close to the Problem Platform on the east side, the bird count was growing steadily, and so were the disagreements as to its accuracy. Conservationists claimed the total was in the thousands, but Union and state sources continued to admit to no more than hundreds. The rate of survival of those birds treated was high at first, but gradually began to decrease until it was obvious that the 2 percent survival rate of the *Torrey Canyon* and *Ocean Eagle* disasters would apply. A growing mystery was the number of dead birds being brought in—was it done out of ignorance, or to emphasize the growing sense of outrage? Whatever the reason, it didn't make the work of volunteers easier, but as one self-styled expert in pulchritude noted, the larger the work load, the prettier the girls became. He singled out an Australian blonde for special mention, saying it wasn't so much her ravishing looks as the way she handled the oil-soaked birds. It turned out that she was no amateur at treating either experts or birds, being married to a scientist who had worked for the Fish and Wildlife Service.

Union Oil by now had a sizable flotilla of vessels operating from Stearns Wharf, whose restaurants were doing a lively trade with oil workers and rubberneckers. The Coast Guard tied up a couple of 80-foot patrol craft, there was a Navy oiler to receive the product of skimmers, and numerous offshore supply boats, tugs and scows chafed its pilings. Many of the latter were being used to transport chemicals, drilling mud compounds, high-pressure pumps and drill pipe to the Problem Platform. The men loading them, in spite of looking tired and carrying beer bellies, worked fast, and the drilling gangs coming ashore looked solemn. Worn down, they were having nothing to do with either newsmen or rubberneckers. It had been made clear by those who did communicate that if people would just get out of the way, they would get on with their job—oil.

"I do what I'm paid for," said one. "And it's all the same whether we're pumping the well or trying to kill it. It's oil, and that's for me."

Ashore, there was such a growing collection of supplies and equipment that the harbor area resembled a quartermaster depot. Mountains of baled straw crowded stacks of telephone poles for making booms, and nearby were piles of old carpeting to act as skirts with a jungle of steel cables to secure them. The array of mechanical equipment included cranes, loaders, straw choppers and spreaders, motor graders, dump and tank trucks, trailers, tractors, earthmovers, truck-mounted vacuum pumps, compressors and miles of hose. Chain saws and air drills were among the more sophisticated tools, while stacks of hand shovels, rakes, hoes and forks suggested the size of the army which would be called into action when the oil hit the beaches. It was coming all right, but exactly how soon and with what thickness nobody was placing any bets on. All that was sure was that at least some of it was being broken up off Stearns Wharf by tugs spraying Corexit in such a strong concentration that in gallonage it would almost seem to exceed the oil itself. Breaking up, the slick assumed a full spectrum of color and, as one observer mentioned, it seemed odd that any substance that can bring so much death should become so beautiful.

Not everyone in Santa Barbara saw the spill as a disaster, for there were those who welcomed the money that came with overtime rates and out-of-town labor. There were even those who enjoyed their "I told you so" predictions, as they pointed to how little the experts knew and how unprepared both government and industry were to handle the catastrophe.

"It's an ill spill . . ." a professor observed. "Perhaps now we'll learn how much we have to learn. Next time, instead of improvising, we might even know what works and have it available."

Although Santa Barbarans were bracing themselves for the oil's attack on their beaches and harbor that day, they might better have braced themselves for a development that Hickel was thrown by. Even before he was so advised by Hartley in a phone call, he learned that drilling had been resumed in the channel under the excuse of "maximum safety controls." The decision had been made by Interior's chief engineer on scene, and his authority appeared as valid to authorize its resumption as Hickel's had been to stop it. The latter was now convinced by the director of the U.S.G.S., Dr. William Pecora, a dry, balding, low-key man, that operations were in accordance with the existing regulations. Being for the most part fifteen years old, however, they were not designed for channel conditions, and inspection and enforcement procedures were casual. While oil was still oil, the conditions under which it was now being obtained presented new problems and increased risks. It would take time, thought and real selling to make the requirements tougher, as Hickel must have known from his Santa Barbara visit even if he had been a stranger to the world of oil, and the kind of help he would need might be hard to find. He would have to deal with the imminent expressions of outrage in Santa Barbara, and he would have to gain the cooperation of an industry that would be obliged to make a contribution not only in its interest, but actually opposed to it. The first step was to find authority to stop the drilling, which took a couple of days, the easing out of a solicitor, the aid of a solicitor general and some fine print in the leases; the Secretary could not prohibit drilling on grounds of pollution, but he could on grounds that oil was being wasted. "It goes to show how far we've come," said a F.W.P.C.A. staff member. "Once, oil was more valuable than water."

In the months to come, Hickel had more stringent regulations adopted by the U.S.G.S. and eventually he was able, aided by Union Oil's voluntary assumption of the cleanup tab, to get oil drillers to accept liability for spill costs before cause is determined. Known as "absolute liability without cause," it would also apply to tanker and terminal operations, representing an enormous advance in environmental corporate responsibility and governmental awareness. It would have come in time, undoubtedly, but not as soon or easily had it not been for the Problem Platform and its reportage in the world's news media. The corner that former welterweight Hickel found himself in and managed to fight himself out of didn't make him many friends in high places, and certainly not those he would later need. But then, he was not without seconds—they ranged from Senators to GOO!, and for all of them, it took courage and caring.

The post office in Santa Barbara had an even heavier than usual load of protesting letters to both California editors and Washington officials on Wednesday, February 5—not only was the news of the drilling resumption out, but the oil had come in at last. The beaches were deep in it, and after the failure of the telephone pole boom, it invaded the harbor. Attacks on Hickel for permitting drilling resumption came fast and they were sharp, ranging from one officeholder's "complete breach of faith" to Clyde's charge that the ban had been "tokenism in its lowest form—cold cynicism and pure hypocrisy." Official response did not help to soothe the protests, for it managed to be both evasive and obvious at the same time.

"The first order of business," said F.W.P.C.A.'s regional director, Paul DeFalco, "is to plug the hole."

Air inspection during the day for once stilled arguments about the amount of flow at the Problem Platformt—he turbulence had increased both in volume and area, and the slick was growing rapidly. Santa Barbarans were now almost unanimous in believing they were in for it. They kept saying, as they shook their heads over beaches with as much as 4 and 5 inches of crude and mousse, the worst of it was that this might be only the beginning. Some of those young given to the Bible even wondered if it could be a judgment upon them.

"Maybe we loved the place too much," said a bearded bird tender. "It's going to be hard to love anything or anybody for a while, I know that."

All that had been done, however, now proved to be but a beginning for all that had to be done. Operating on the premise that the worst had at last happened, Union announced that further pumping down of drilling mud was being suspended until they had enough to make a really massive attempt, and that in the meantime they would attack the advancing oil with an all-out effort. Indeed, with the wealth of manpower it almost seemed as if the intent were to soak up the oil with men. Not only was all available casual labor recruited, but Union employees were brought in from refineries and other company sources and over a hundred Conservation Camp inmates were trucked to the beaches. They worked well enough, first spreading straw, then, after it was oil-soaked, with fork and shovel retrieving it. They did this as if the menace had nothing to do with them—it was just another way of serving time, and they were no stranger to that.

"Do what you're told, never be bold," chanted a wildeyed black, raking to his rhythm. "That way you gonna live to be old."

Union employees, even though many were strangers to manual labor, worked with a will but with an air of embarrassment. One refinery foreman complained, as he spread straw on water from a duckboat (punt), that this was the most expensive work he'd ever done and odd in view of all his training and experience.

"I keep trying to remember the overtime," his mate replied with a Texas drawl, swinging a pitchfork full of oil-matted straw aboard. "But that still don't make it white man's work."

Between man and machine power, the near beaches were cleaned as fast as the tide went out, but there were two problems—with the amount of sand being loaded out with oiled straw and driftwood, soon there wouldn't be any beaches; and when the tide returned, more oil came with it. The contrast

between the efficiency of the cleanup operation and its useless-
ness depressed the hundreds of onlookers. They realized for the
first time, perhaps, how little we understand what we're truly
doing to ourselves. The harbor cleanup, witnessed by angered
owners of oil-stained hulls, was even more efficient. Not only was
the oil being coralled in the still water by skimmers (small flat-
bottom craft that suck up oil), but oil-soaked straw was being
herded to the launching ramp by outboards, where vacuum
trucks filled their tanks speedily, even if the water content ran
high. Boat owners had a good view of what oil can do to baitfish,
many of which died trembling in the ooze, and they also had
the opportunity to watch exhausted seabirds. These only gave up
after circling around and around in the oil, and they would pant
until their end. Eventually the boat owners were ordered from
the area because of the danger of ignition of the oil vapor (a
precaution by the book but unnecessary in that much open air),
and some were relieved not to have to witness the dying about
them. "It's hard to believe it's finally happening," one said.

"And hard to believe it won't go on forever," said another.

Many workers wore yellow foul-weather gear as protection
against the black crude, making a color contrast which to some
symbolized the good and evil forces at work, and the much-
vaunted Sea Curtain, a plastic, air-inflated boom, which, snake-
like, kept uncoiling as it was towed out to contain the Problem
Platform flow, wore the same colors. It was as much easier
to handle than log or telephone pole booms as it was to assemble,
but would it behave in a seaway any better?

"It sure looks good," an oil-smeared draughtsman for Union
said, "but my guess is that when the sea kicks up, what oil
doesn't go under it is going to go over it."

The wildlife picture was as bleak as the oil was black, and
it was no longer being denied that birds were dying by more
than the hundreds. Cormorants seemed the chief sufferers, as
they insisted on returning to the oily surf when pursued, but
gulls, loons, grebes and pelicans were also victims. Shore roamers,
such as sandpipers, were now being affected also.

"Once they swallow soil, there isn't much chance," a state
Fish and Game employee said. "I say it's shaping up to be the
biggest disaster to ever hit California's bird life."

Remedial operations on the platform had to be abandoned at one point for over five hours due to the presence of gas, and drill crews went about their duties with more caution than usual. So did their chief, Hartley, but due to another threat. He had been testifying in Washington before Senator Edmund Muskie's subcommittee on Air and Water Pollution, and it was a rather tense appearance for all its *politesse*. Muskie's lankiness, which had been compared to Lincoln's, and his seemingly easy but deliberate way of questioning the witness gave the impression he was of the people and committed to their service. Hartley's respectful yet authoritarian manner spoke of privilege— he seemed less of the people than over them. It was as if he demanded recognition of his leadership in a structure which both serves and controls people. He had no choice but to play a defensive role, and he handled it well for a man of such substance. His problem was that aside from being a stranger to the role, selling out of need isn't easy. Muskie, on the offensive, was careful not to appear aggressive, but he was determined to keep Hartley on the defensive, and he did. The onus was on the black knight defending oil's murky castle, and the white knight of God's great outdoors came out as clean and as sharp as a thistle. Each man had much to lose, but Muskie had the most to win. Hartley was already a president.

The tension in the hearing room was increased by the fact that the oil had now reached Santa Monica and Malibu in its lighter fractions. It was heavy on the beaches from Carpinteria to Goleta, its pollution had been tracked a good 40 miles offshore, and oil-smeared birds were dying as far away as Zuma. Hartley lost no time in explaining that Union had employed "resonable diligence" and had operated in conformity to federal regulations, which while not as stringent as the state's, were the conditions on which Union and its partners as tenant had been accepted in their successful bid for the tract. State experts, together with some federal officials, agreed that had the well been provided with the mandatory 1,200 feet of surface casing under state regulations, the blowout probably would not have happened, since there would have been five times the protection offered by Union's 239 feet. It would have been more expensive, not that this meant anything measured against the staggering expense caused Union by the blowout. More importantly, it would have made tapping those oil-rich upper sands more difficult. An educated guess was that the rupture occurred between the 500- and 700-foot level, leading to seepage through fissures in the strata. Thus, while Union was adamant in claiming the leak was not from the well but the fissure, it's original source was the well.

"With the benefit of hindsight," Hartley admitted, "we might have introduced additional steel casing."

He did his best to reassure committee members that even state experts accepted the fact that other parts of the channel were "vastly different" in geological formation, making it safe to drill there, and that Senator Alan Cranston (D., Calif.) need not be concerned about the resumption of drilling.

"It's clear," Senator Muskie said simply, "that you're in no better position to deal with a repetition."

Hartley, unsettled, went into much detail regarding the precautions taken. He answered the charge that Union could not have learned enough in the twenty-four-hour drilling ban to make its resumption safe by passing the responsibility on to federal officials. They had received the oil experts' views, he said, and to stop all drilling in the channel would be, as he had told Governor Reagan, just as wrong as "shutting down the whole university system because of a riot at San Francisco."

The question of the cost of restoring beaches and harbors after the cleanup was one he felt shouldn't be gone into at this time, as the main thing was to get the leak stopped.

"It's a second-order-of-magnitude problem," he said.

"Are you reserving the question of liability?" asked Muskie.

"We are trying to be prudent in our responsibility, Senator."

The combination of television lights and being pressed on the failure to control the slick led Hartley into a statement that, as reported by the *Wall Street Journal*, gave conservationists the kind of ammunition they like. It also gave Union's P.R. people what one referred to as "a real high-voltage short circuit."

"I'm amazed at the publicity for the loss of a few birds," said Hartley, in part.

In full-page ads Union protested that Hartleys' actual comment was, "I am always tremendously impressed at the publicity that the death of birds receives versus the loss of people in our country in this day and age." The *Journal* said it regretted "its inaccurate reporting," but a closing line in the ad was of more interest to Hartley's detractors: "It is well nigh impossible to say how deeply we regret this accident. We have operated at all times with procedures approved by our partners and the Federal Regulatory authorities." The point, said Hartley knockers, was well taken—no one did know how sorry Union was. All they knew was the company kept passing the buck to the federal government, anl as to the birds, Hartley had nothing against them except that they don't buy oil. His employees, however, were admiring for the most part: "A driver but he'll square with you," "Nothing too food for Union," "Got a lot of stick," "Better not get in his or Union's way," "Right man for a hard game," "Always took care of us in a strike," and "He's what Union is all about."

A remark by Hartley at the hearing was to stay with him longer and bother his communications staff more than his bird gaffe. He was attempting to direct attention to the bright side by pointing out a virtue of channel drilling.

"During an earthquake something could rupture," he said. "By taking the pressure off, maybe we'll eliminate trouble in years to come."

The reaction was immediate. It ranged from an inference that Union thought Santa Barbara should pay the company for taking the oil in order to save them, to "Would an earthquake be worse than another spill?" Independent experts pointed out that if the only safeguards possible were those already in use, such as storm chokes (spring-loaded valves set to close on abnormal flow or pressure), things were dark indeed. Supervisor Clyde's strong words reinforced this view.

"As early as 1966," he said, "everyone in the Interior Department was hell-bent to get oil leasing in this area. It scares the bejesus out of me to think that the breakaway Union Oil Company well is only the fourth of 180 wells planned by that firm."

He went on to say that while he couldn't swear that Interior was influenced by the oil companies, "In a matter of minutes after we said something to the Department, the oil industry knew what we had said verbatim." State Assembly leader Jesse

M. Unruh (D., Calif.), even more sharply critical, said that "Hickel is treating the giant oil companies as if they were totally without blame—as if they were the injured party." It was a dark day on which Union people looked hard to find good news to hand out, and the best they could come up with was that the relief well was now down 650 feet. Even that, however, was diluted by the fact that it would still take ten days to two weeks to complete it. Dow Jones wasn't reassuring to Union either—it quoted Union stock at $54.50, a drop of over 13 percent in a fairly stable market.

"The market price of Union Oil shares," said a GOO! collector of torn Union credit cards, "is a lot higher than our evaluation."

February 7 was a day of storm in both Washington and Santa Barbara, the former being of a political nature while the latter was of natural origin. Hickel, after consulting with President Nixon and Attorney General John Mitchell, reimposed his ban on channel drilling with an announcement that there would be no further leasing in the channel either. This created a storm which Hickel not only survived, but came out of looking more a victor than the about-to-be victim some at the eye of the storm had thought him. President Nixon voiced approval of his Interior Secretary's handling of the emergency, going so far as to tell Congressman Charles M. Teague (R., Calif.) that federal troops would be supplied if needed and that, as a Californian who had given thought to vacationing in Santa Barbara, he had "more than a passing interest" in the area's plight. Mitchell "strongly concurred" in the action taken by Hickel, who said it was based on "a lack of sufficient knowledge of this particular geological area." This "lack of knowledge" item had come up the day before when a witness, Dr. Spencer M. Smith, of the Citizens Committee on Natural Resources, was being questioned. He said that concern had been expressed about the possibility of leakage from a fault in the channel strata in the fifties, when drilling was first being considered seriously.

"I find it rather incredible that those involved called it an unknown risk," Muskie replied. "While it is to the national interest to discover new reserves of oil, the question is whether other interests have been considered."

"Other values have not been considered in the process," the witness stated.

"I agree," Muskie said.

Santa Barbara's storm brought winds up to 35 miles per hour, swells of 15 feet sweeping under the Problem Platform and 10-foot breakers coming over the harbor jetty. Even though heavy with oil, the seas made delivering drilling mud and equipment too dangerous, although, as one skipper pointed out, it would have made a good test of what the platform could take by way of collision. Mud pumping was again suspended, and in compensation it was announced that 7,000 barrels had been used in the effort, some of it at 3,700 pounds per square inch. That is a lot of mud and a lot of pressure, but it still hadn't plugged the flow and even Union's experts were sounding nervous. Booms had proven ineffective, skimmers were pumping up too much water to be practical for the amount of oil collected, as was the case with truck-mounted vacuum pumps, and straw was presenting a problem in disposal—burning meant enormous air pollution even with flamethrowers, and suitable dumping areas were in short supply.

"There are no pat answers," explained the Eleventh Coast Guard District Chief of Staff, Captain Benjamin Chiswell (echoing Captain Thompson's words at San Juan), to Lee Dye, of the Los Angeles *Times.* "To my knowledge, the company has not failed to do anything that has been suggested. But, frankly, I just don't have any more ideas."

The bird count continued to rise and there were reports of birds diving through the heavier areas of the slick and failing to surface. The fishing industry was suffering also, the 800-square-mile slick meaning polluted catches and fouled nets and gear.

"The oil has ruined our plastic buoys and it turns nets into soggy sponges," fishermen complained.

The effect on the food chain in which larger fish eat oil-contaminated smaller fish was another unknown and a big one. Equally unknown was how long it would take channel marine life to recover, but there was some comfort in the fact this spill was of crude oil, not diesel oil or other more refined products. They are known to be more toxic to marine organisms than crude, the effect of which is more one of smothering and strangling. The Woods Hole Blumer report states:

Biological damage occurs at the very moment of the accident. Water currents will immediately spread the toxic plume of dissolved oil components and, if the accident occurs in inshore water, the whole water column will be poisoned even if the bulk of the oil floats on the surface. Where oil can be detected in the sediments there has been a kill of animal life; in the most polluted areas the kill has been almost total.

A massive assault with drilling mud was pushed during the night, coinciding with a visit by Muskie, Cranston and Unruh on February 8, and since mud again appeared in the flow on the surface, Hartley was optimistic.

"There's a 75 percent chance of the operation succeeding," he said, "and if that fails we're almost certain to stop it with the relief well."

People wanted to believe it and there was no reaction of cynicism, but another line of Hartley's had such repercussions that it overshadowed the expressions of dismay by the official visitors, strong as they were. In his own way, Hartley got the idea across that the spill should not be called a disaster.

"I think of a disaster in terms of people being killed," he explained.

There was a major change in both the weather and the mood of Santa Barbara on Saturday. The wind turned to offshore and the day was bright with both sunlight and the news that Union Well A-21 was killed at last. A plug of concrete had finally set up in the bottom of the 3,500-foot well and the quick-drying concrete level in the well rose during the morning until it was sealed. It brought weary smiles to the more than 1,000 workers on cleanup crews, who assumed that the tides would no longer be bringing oil to foul the oft-recleaned beaches. It was estimated that another three weeks of intensive effort would be needed to finish the job, and with an end in sight, costs to wildlife were looked at. Eighteen species of birds had been affected, and of the almost 800 in collection centers, about half had died or were dying. Acute damage to marine life was estimated officially at 1 percent, a figure criticized as meaningless, and 700 boat owners were being besieged by detergent salesmen. Oiled straw still afloat in the harbor was being shepherded by propeller action of boats, and Governor Reagan declared the city a disaster area. This made it eligible for federal aid, but it was pointed out that Union's responsibility was no more lessened than was the validity of actions being brought against it. These had been multiplying to a total no one could even estimate. The general air of relief was mirrored by the lack of reaction to a statement by President Nixon, saying that if drillers would "make the necessary expenditures in setting up their wells offshore, there is a minimal danger of this kind of activity."

"Money," said a dour geologist, "isn't going to stabilize the channel any better than drilling mud will plug the fissure. All that's plugged now is the well."

The warning was echoed by a letter to Hickel from Congressman Teague, saying that all drilling in the channel should be immediately and permanently stopped, no matter what the cost to the federal government. This attitude was seconded by former Interior Secretary Stewart Udall, who was considered a champion of environmental causes. Saying that he was sickened and saddened by the spill, he accepted responsibility for the letting of leases. Although the geological conditions in the channel were known to be unstable, he said, department experts had made no dissent. The experience of twelve years of drilling in the Gulf of Mexico had not led to any big spills, they claimed, yet others charged that spills were so frequent in the Gulf that the press didn't bother to report them. Informed Washington opinion puts the lease decision down to Budget Bureau pressure during the Johnson administration. This view holds that in the end Udall had no more choice in such matters than Hickel in the Nixon administration—even if the latter hadn't found this out yet.

This same source feels that Hickel may not have had much control over departmental appointments either. Otherwise, he asked, having survived his Senate workout how could Hickel have gotten caught with a former Chamber of Commerce lobbyist as his special assistant for oil policies, The latter had been instrumental in blocking the water pollution control bill, according to Senator William Proxmire (D., Wis.). This possible conflict of interest was compared in Santa Barbara to the presence of a top Union Oil officer on the California Water Resources Board, and it was offered as one reason the board had been unable to stop oil pollution of Los Angeles harbor. However murky these surmises, a cleaner atmosphere was promised by the F.W.P.C.A.'s area director, DeFalco, who was thinking about using steam cleaners to get the oil off shoreline rocks. He was not, apparently, thinking much about the surviving flora and fauna attached to them.

GOO! called for an end to offshore operations in the area in a petition signed by nearly 30 percent of the residents, who were urged to mail samples of the oil to their representatives in Congress.

"We sent out petitions with spaces for 5,000 signatures," a spokesman said. "But now we are getting requests from all over the country."

By the end of the week Union faced some new public relations problems, having shrugged off news of approximately 800 lawsuits and that the bird count was now officially over 1,000. Fresh oil had appeared in volume not unlike the original spill at the Problem Platform, and the resulting slick was described as being about 3 miles long with an onshore wind moving it toward the beaches. It was announced by Union that this was merely a "bleeding off" from oil-bearing sands and that it would have to work itself out, but reaction was so strong that before the day was ended, the press was advised that "remedial work is being attempted." State officials estimated the flow at 50 barrels a day, Hartley countering with a figure between 3 and 5. In any case, equipment was being cranked up for more beach cleaning and people's anger and fear was such that DeFalco made a statement reported in the Los Angeles *Times*.

"It may be oil that was not bled off before," he said, "or it may be something else."

Feb. 9, 1969, Buzzards Bay, Mass.
The tanker Algol *carrying a cargo of #6 fuel oil grounded and began leaking oil, which continued for several days and formed numerous slicks. Loss to marine and wildlife undertermined.*

A two-man submarine dove on the new spill source on Thursday, February 13, and turned in a report of gas and oil seepage from the shallow sand beds. It was explained that with the plugging of the well most of the strata seepage was natural gas, but that when an oil pool is opened, gas comes first, and as it is exhausted, the gas left in the solution sends it up under pressure. It was now at this stage, experts thought, but to play safe, booms were being readied. One was a new design—sawdust-filled gunnysacks secured to plastic floats.

This second pollution event gave leverage to adherents of making the channel an oil reserve to be tapped only in a national emergency. It was an even better reason than the recent oil discoveries on Alaska's North Slope, which no matter how large, wouldn't compensate for forbidding the tapping of channel sources. According to *The New York Times,* Mayor Allan R. Coates of Carpinteria didn't impress a House subcommittee with his pleas for a moratorium, and Congressman Ed Edmondson (D., Okla.) even asked Mayor Gerald Firestone of Santa Barbara if he thought local people would be willing to make up the loss to the federal treasury if drilling were halted.

"Mr. Congressman, I think the people of Santa Barbara have already paid enough," Mayor Firestone replied.

Union, which cannot be accused of refusing to try new techniques, announced that it planned to set a large inverted funnel on the channel floor to try to catch the oil welling up at the Problem Platform. This venture was welcomed as an earnest attempt on Union's part, and with the new slick, said by the Coast Guard on Wednesday, February 18, to be 8 miles long, Union received permission to go into production as a means of relieving pressure. It was planned to unplug a previously capped well by explosives, then tap the 250-foot level where oil was thought to be seeping. The furor this resumption set off coincided with the filing of over $1 billion in claims against Union. The regional oil and gas supervisor came out with an ill-timed defense of federal regulations and supervision, denying that their lack of stringency caused the blowout. "Accidents happen," was his unoriginal comment, and, he added, "Mother nature let us down," a reminder of Hartley's reference to her.

"Pretty soon, we'll be hearing Father Time will take care of things for us," a University of California at Santa Barbara student commented.

Four days later it was reported that Union's Platform B, which is set on the same fault line as the Problem Platform, was the source of another new slick. It took some time to clear the matter up, but it was finally announced that B was neither leaking nor in production. The slick had been caused by a service craft carrying the slick to B's area.

"Which gives an idea of just how thick the oil is out there," said a GOO! member.

While divers worked to plug the seepage near the northeast corner of the Problem Platform, other discharges were reported on both its east and west sides. Whether accurate or not, before long Interior authorized the use of all five of the producing wells on the Problem Platform in order, it was explained, to relieve the pressure on the shallow sands. The theory, disputed by some engineers, was that drilling cessation had permitted the pressure to build. This resulted in the discharges, rather as a boil might suppurate if not drained, and with less pressure there would be less flow. Conservationists argued that since it was still unknown what caused the new discharge, the thinking sounded more financial than therapeutic—the discharge was worth money, and instead of referring to a boil suppurating, the simile should have been a pot of gold running over. The fact that the official bird count was now over 1,500 troubled many, and that the survival rate was called "extremely slight" angered others.

"Straight talk would say the death rate was extremely large," said an ornithologist.

It reminded him, he added, of a quote from an article in *The Oil and Gas Journal*:

The hysteria whipped up over the Santa Barbara Channel blowout is beyond belief. A disaster, it wasn't—no lives were lost, no extensive damage to property occurred. A regrettable mess, yes— expensive, very. The prizes of offshore are well worth the potential dangers.

"The hitch is, of course," the ornithologist added, "that we don't know the potential dangers."

On February 26, Hickel announced that additional personnel

were being dispatched to aid in controlling the new leak. It was from Well A-41, the original having been caused by A-21, and this was news. So was Union's statement that the flow from this leak was not as large as the original, but larger than the discharge of 2,000 to 4,000 gallons a day which had been coming from the oil-rich sands since A-21 was plugged. The guess was that both were caused by faults in the channel floor allowing deep reserves to work their way upward, and it was also made clear that this well would probably have to be plugged too. Hopefully, there would not be the delays caused by lack of mud and equipment on hand as on A-21, but an officer of the California State Lands Committee charged that neither Union nor the government had prepared a disaster plan in advance. It was also disclosed that neither well had been inspected by the U.S.G.S. after drilling had begun, which was ammunition for conservationists. It strengthened their case against further drilling and Hickel was pressed through various contacts to make the temporary ban permanent. The result was an announcement that he hadn't decided when to permit resumption of well operations, but that when he did, production wells would get the go-ahead first, because there was less danger with them than there might be in new drilling. By way of reassurance, it was pointed out that California had not suspended operations on any wells under its jurisdiction. It was well known, however, that although their drilling had been fought both on grounds of environmental safety and as a threat to scenic values, they were not in an area as unstable as that of the Union wells. April 1 might be the day for production resumption, it was intimated, and it was a choice that GOO! found appropriate.

After his eagerly awaited appearance before the Muskie subcommittee on February 27 Hickel was more of an enigma than ever. The hearing was full of surprises, the most notable being that he called for even stronger antipollution measures than were contained in the Muskie bill. Hickel recommended that both oil well and tanker operators accept unlimited liability for spill cleanup instead of the $15,000,000 limit in the bill (the bill's provision had drawn strong protests from both the industry and underwriters). Hickel further recommended that it apply not only to oil but also to other environmentally harmful substances. He urged that a federal revolving fund to cover first costs be set up and he proposed that the Secretaries of Interior and Transportation (which embraces the Coast Guard) be authorized to decide when a ship and/or cargo should be destroyed in event of a major spill. He saw the reinterpreted regulations covering cleanups in the present leases as valid, but he expected court action by a drilling group headed by Pauley Petroleum, Inc. His suggestions left the Senators to at least some degree speechless, an unusual condition for them, and when they recovered from their surprise it was with paeans of commendation. Hickel and his five aides, including Russell Train and Director Pecora, smiled gratefully but not without at least a little surprise.

At first Hickel had seemed uneasy in the glare of the television lights on this his first appearance before a Senate body since his initiation, and he did considerable consulting with his aides, who also appeared a little apprehensive. Once he got on the question of liability he gained assurance, saying that his thinking did not exclude acts of God.

"Do you consider the Santa Barbara spill an act of God?" Muskie asked.

"An accidental act of God," he answered, smiling.

He handled the touchy question of federal authority being extended to the 3-mile limit now controlled by the states. The extent of offshore drilling was suggested by the fact that 15,000 wells have been drilled, of which 4,000 are state-controlled. He argued that overall authority for cleanups should rest with Interior rather than with the Coast Guard, causing a captain of that service to look up in surprise from his note taking.

"At Santa Barbara," asked Muskie, "isn't the authority split? Who is in charge?"

"Right or wrong, I took charge," said Hickel. "I—"

"Actually," interrupted Train, his voice sounding like a cautious New York Mayor John Lindsay's, "the on-site Coast Guard commander is."

Muskie recounted the number of federal agencies involved, implying a struggle among them to be top dog, and Hickel with a chuckle admitted there had been an occasional "lack of communication." The mood changed to one of concern with the testimony of Dr. Pecora on the matter of risk and whether an earthquake-prone area could be considered as an undue risk. It was developed that his U.S.G.S. judgments were based on findings supplied by the drilling companies, which spurred Hickel to ask that the Survey be given additional funds and personnel. The general agreement was that, as Senator Cranston put it, "we don't really *know* much." It was also agreed that there is no guarantee against a well blowout.

"Amen," someone murmured.

As February passed, the second leak seemed to be smaller but the original continued. More encouraging for Santa Barbarans was the revocation by the state Lands Commission of all offshore oil exploration permits. It was decided to defer the opening of bids on a 5,000-acre tract of tidal lands off Santa Barbara pending a review of state regulations, which was expected to take several months.

"I keep thinking of our losses in this tragedy," said a beach property owner. "But then, a decision like this comes along and I know we have a chance to control our future."

The Coast Guard reinforced this note of optimism with its report that the oil leakage from the new seep was down to about 1,000 gallons per day and that the weathered slick from the first spill was now stationary about 10 miles off Santa Barbara. Commercial fishing was said to be off as much as 90 percent, but some blamed the recent heavy rains with resulting silting for the poor catches. There were even rumors that the oil companies were so discouraged by their drilling finds, to say nothing of public relations problems, that they were ready to talk to Interior about trading their leases for others, perhaps at Alaska's North Slope. Most of those opposed to channel operations, who were being called antioilers, said mistrustfully that the oil companies didn't get where they are with that kind of thinking —it took more than a few dry holes and public outrage for them to call it a day.

"Besides," asked one, "without Hartley, what would we do for laughs?"

In line with the optimism was word of a Hickel plan to set aside a 15,000-acre sanctuary in the Santa Barbara Channel in which leasing would be barred, and to make the existing buffer zone of 21,000 acres on federal offshore lands permanent. It was believed that most of the companies currently holding leases would be permitted to resume operations once their procedures were approved, but that Union would have to convince Interior's experts that its operations (other than relief drilling) could be done without further risk. Considering the recent events, it was as "heavy a burden of proof as burdens come." Moreover, the Santa Barbara City Council, if it went along with some people's demands, would insist that the oil companies be penalized by fines of $10,000 for each bird, fish or mammal killed by spills. Such a provision might be enough to discourage even a Hartley, one antioiler said, particularly if, as rumored, there had been no more than two definite finds out of the forty-five wells drilled on a total of seventeen leases at over $1,000,000 each.

The experiment with inverted funnels was less encouraging, though—during the first week of March Union lost the one on the sea floor under the Problem Platform. It was no sooner in proper position that it was damaged by underwater turbulence during heavy weather. Plans were being made to try a more rugged version, but one of the difficulties to be overcome is that seeps are not stationary. They ooze from varying fissures almost as if determined to outfox the engineers trying to position the funnel. As to the second leak, drilling mud was still being pumped in, and while the oil flow was less, there was still no forecast of when it would subside.

"One thing about the channel," a Union engineer said wearily, "it can sure teach you a lot."

Ashore, however, it was difficult to learn what was going on and there were those who found it equally difficult to believe what they were told was going on. Too often the announcements sounded more like reassurances than statements of fact. It was as if, said one angered property owner, the natives wouldn't become restless if they didn't know much. One of the troublesome unknowns was that not even the experts could agree on the damage to marine and wildlife, let alone what to do about it. As Dr. N. H. Sanders of U.C.S.B. wrote in the *News-Press*, the most obvious losses were of birds and mammals living normally near the water surface, but there were also losses of intertidal and superficial life forms which inhabit the beaches and kelp beds. One dead dolphin with an oil-blocked breathing hole was a victim, as were a pair of seals being treated at the Childs Estate, but Dr. Sanders felt it was the intertidal losses that would have the most serious long-term effects, since the destruction of these forms meant food chains were broken and the ecological balance disturbed. Authorities agreed that while the lack of knowledge regarding inshore kills was disturbing, even less was known about losses at sea. It could only be assumed that since by mid-March the beaches in the San Diego area were being assaulted by a black tide believed to have originated with the first spill, a lot could have happened to marine and wildlife on the 200-mile trip of this tide, which took six weeks.

There was no shortage of thoughts on how to deal with the spill—the F.W.P.C.A. was obliged to set up a program to process the more than 3,000 ideas submitted by the public. How many, if indeed any, would prove worth pursuing was unknown, but for once the experts were welcoming the ideas of laymen.

"With us right now," said a staff member, "no idea is so far out it can't be in."

In Washington there was an air of optimism during March. It was becoming clear to both Senators and Representatives that the environment's loudest trumpeter, Senator Muskie, had found a political vehicle that might carry him far. Many hurried to climb aboard, for all that they hadn't abandoned their "it'll never fly" thinking. Environmental concern was an issue that could offend no one except those who already had a black eye, such as Union Oil. The race would go to him who would be first over the line with the environmental mostest, but how to keep Muskie's mostest newest was a problem for the Senator's staff. His message was being seized on by so many politicos, there wasn't much new left to come up with, and he was going to need a new vehicle. "There is a danger in looking and sounding too clean too long," said an aide.

He had environmental competition from the oil industry too, which responded with what it has most of—money. The Western Oil and Gas Association announced a $240,000 wildlife research program and the American Petroleum Institute came up with elaborate plans for oil-spill control centers. They were not designed for major spills, however, because the techniques and equipment for these were in the future. The U.N.'s Intergovernmental Maritime Consultive Organization (I.M.C.O.) proceeded at an accelerated rate on development of a clean seas program, and individual oil companies shifted P.R. gears to sell the public on how much they were doing for what they were threatening—sanctuaries were being set up, both wildlife and visual ("Is it a sequoia or an oil derrick?").

Hickel, as his congressional hearing appearances became more polished, began to look more and more like a champion of the environment, at least to those who had decided which was the real Wally. He was even generous enough to be sympathetic toward Stewart Udall, who in his appearance before Muskie's subcommittee set what may well be two records—drinking the largest amount of potable water and trading the least amount of political water. He described his approval of the channel leases as an "ecological Bay of Pigs," a good line, and he came through looking both innocent and ineffective. In this he was not alone among witnesses before the subcommittee, but none looked more uncomfortable than the industry representatives. It was said that their high color was not the result of either expense account entertaining or the great outdoors, but their assumption that oil was less a national resource than the industry's. The succession of those "a few birds" disasters began to have an impact as major on the home screen as another unplanned and unwelcomed tragedy, Vietnam.

"Oil always meant the good things of life," complained a senior P.R. director, "and we were the good guys because that's us. Now we're the bad guys, but there still wouldn't be the American Way without us. Only, who's going to buy that?"

As March drew to a close there was something else being bought—the "Hickel package" gave signs of becoming a reality and probably not even he had expected it would be so easy. It consisted of the enlarged sanctuary, stiffer regulations affecting casing, blowout preventers and their testing, mud-pumping control systems, readily available spill-control devices, and more complete exploratory drilling information (formerly looked upon as a proprietory asset in a competitive business). As to the awkward compensation question, the thought was that there would be some form of repayment for those companies that surrendered their leases. Union and its partners had $72,000,000 in theirs, aside from the leases. It was a matter not included in the Hickel developmental costs.

"Compensation is a something else," a staff member said. "Call it a grab bag, and a big one."

In Santa Barbara things didn't look quite as rosy to those faced with daily evidence of pollution—beaches kept becoming fouled in spite of vigorous and frequent cleaning by Union's crews; dead shellfish were being encountered with increasing frequency; congealed straw was said to be coating the channel floor, as well as residues from binding materials sprayed on the slicks to make them easier to recover and the discharges themselves continued at a steady rate. The Hickel package was welcome enough and a lot of previous attitudes toward him were being amended, but the trouble was that current Washington thinking seemed devoted to the future. Santa Barbara was faced by the present, poisonous, foul-smelling and despairing. The people were looking for answers to the question of how to turn off the oil. No one was coming up with them, and there was a good reason—except for more drilling, no one had any.

The companies permitted to resume operations were Phillips Petroleum, Mobile and Humble, the Union partners already performing "remedial" drilling and production. Promptly, Santa Barbara County filed a suit seeking an injunction to prevent resumption on the basis that the new regulations were too vague and would not have prevented the Union spill. Although not unexpected because of the intense antidrilling pressure in the area, it was something of a setback to the new pro-birds-and-fishes Hickel. On top of that, instead of the $600,000,000 appropriation he had tried so hard to get for his clean-water programs, the Budget Bureau cut it to $214,000,000, in spite of congressional authorization for $1 billion.

"This kind of money," said an aide, "is about enough to take care of Capitol Hill's Potomac effluent."

The New York Times came up with an accolade for Hickel, having watched him long enough to become convinced of his environmental sincerity. It took exception, however, to what was seen as appointments being made on political rather than professional grounds. The *Times* concluded that if Hickel could learn "to say no" to White House pressure as well as he had learned sensitivity to conservation values, he would enjoy a much happier and more successful tenure. The paper's William M. Blair wrote about the Hickel watchers who were unconvinced that there was a new Wally, while others no longer feared that "he was running for President of the Sierra Club." Blair described one White House source as being concerned both about Hickel's bad press and his outspokenness.

"His trouble," the source is quoted as saying, "is that he docsn't have a filter between his brain and his mouth."

Featured in the news on April 6 was the refutation of a report that thousands of seals were endangered by the oil slicks. Government biologists claimed that only six dying or dead seals had been found on the rocks and nine more on the beaches of San Miguel Island. No one knew how many might have died at sea nor how many more would be caught in the oil as they left the island. The Coast Guard didn't bring much reassurance to those worried by the drilling resumption, and indeed, there wasn't much to bring. The rate of flow from the seeps had not lessened, they said, and there was no sign that it would.

"At least, we don't get any more bottom growths," said a boat owned.

> *April 7, 1969, New Orleans.*
> *The 7,301-ton freighter* Union Faith *was in collision with a barge loaded with 9,000 gallons of crude today. "Now I know what it would be like riding through hell," said a witness of the resulting fire. One crewman missing.*

As he expected, Hickel faced a suit brought by a group of oil companies headed by Pauley Petroleum protesting that had they known they would face unlimited liability for spills, they would not have bid. The petition states as clearly as any environmentalist's charge that the government knew, or should have known, that the leases "are in a known area of faulting which is subjected to earthquakes and tidal waves and that the drilling requires operations which reach to the presently known limits of the relevant technology." The phrasing is in contrast to that of the National Petroleum Council, which said that in ten years drilling would be done in depths of 6,000 feet and that the process "is limited primarily by economic attractiveness rather than by technical ability."

"Maybe, it ought to be limited by environmental hazards," said an antioiler.

April saw increased activity by GOO! and other concerned groups, among them some city and county agencies which had begun to look upon channel drilling as constituting a public nuisance. Stearns Wharf, a supply base for the platforms, was frequently picketed, weights of trucks serving it were checked for violations, and in other ways the drilling operators began to feel the weight of public disapproval. As regularly as oil came ashore it was cleaned up, and attempts to plug the seeps continued along with cement dusting of the surface (to the concern of ecologists worried about bottom pollution).

A new worry for those who saw their fight as an example to environmentalists everywhere turned up in the past-tense phrasing coming out of Washington. Announcements referred to the spill as "recent" instead of "present," and the continuing problem of the leaks as being solved with the result that much of country viewed the disaster as over instead of possibly endless. Supervisor Clyde picked April 27, the ninetieth day of the spill, to attack such past-tense phrasing, saying there was new oil on the beaches every day, that it would continue until the seeps were plugged and that all efforts had been unsuccessful. Senator Cranston added to the confusion by saying that some veterinarians from the Wildlife Health Foundation had inspected the seals and sea lions of San Miguel Island and found them neither dying nor suffering from the effects of the spill, as had been reported. They reported that although the animal's lethargy might make them look dead to a layman, they had taken their temperatures and found them normal.

"They should have taken ours," said a GOO! officer, "boiling over."

Those human temperatures rose even further on news of a statement in the *Wall Street Journal* by a Union vice president, who said that "we are capturing most of the escaping oil by means of hoods . . . chemical devices . . . chemical dispersants.

. . ." Hartley reiterated the claim that oil seepage had occurred long before the blowout, and that by taking more oil out, pressures are reduced. In twenty-five years, he said, the oil might be gone and the platforms with them.

"So now after drowning us in oil, Union is going to save us by taking what's left," said a picketing Union credit card holder, who wore it mutilated on the sign he was carrying.

April 4, 1969, Liverpool Bay, U.K.
Tanker Hamilton Trader spilled nearly one half million gallons of heavy fuel, polluting 50 miles of shoreline and killing several thousand birds.

By early May GOO! had 100,000 signatures on a petition asking President Nixon to halt all Santa Barbara oil operations. Concern was expressed that Alaskan North Slope development might be discouraged by GOO! environmental muscle—if oil had to be had, better there than here went the thinking.

Continuing worry for antioilers was the unreliability of reports of damage to mammals and wildlife. Two whales were declared by F.W.P.C.A. examiners to have died of natural causes in spite of being oil-covered, and a report of 150 sea lion pups dead on San Miguel Island gave rise to predictions that nothing out of officialdom, whether government or industry, would be believed until the oil flow was stopped. Gladwin Hill in *The New York Times* at the end of May described how tensions were building in the community with three civic groups on one side—"the conservatively disposed conservation minded, moderate militants as in GOO!, and a fringe of radicals"—parading with black armbands and mutilated credit cards, and the government and industry on the other. Boats carrying citizens' groups to the Problem Platform had been attacked by firehoses, federal and state officials were letting increasingly less news out, commercial employees were warned not to become involved with the environmentalists with the reminder that the oil companies were customers, and it was discovered that an advertising campaign to lure tourists with the slogan "Santa Barbara is as enjoyable today as it was last year" was paid for by the oil companies.

Damage estimates to the ecology continued to vary widely, and the only reason many were not called lies instead of inaccuracies was that there was little proof on either side. The U.S.G.S. put the seepage at 30 barrels a day, others at 100 barrels and the sea life toll was estimated at 10 percent by Biglane, who claimed things would be back to normal in a few years, while others put it at disaster proportions from which the ecological balance would not recover for a half-century. Beaches were said to be again pure, yet others claimed an overlay of sand was being attacked by an oil layer 2 feet under which would keep rising indefinitely.

> May 31, 1969, Trelleborg, Sweden.
> Tanker Benedicte *spilled over one half million gallons of crude oil after damage to her tanks. Pollution of tidewater and shoreline resulted.*

The battle lines were drawn clearer in early June with the release of findings by a White House advisory panel directed by White House science adviser, Dr. Lee A. DuBridge. The panel recommended that the current program of oil extraction be continued in order to drain the channel areas. Supervisor Clyde called it "a premature, cheap solution," GOO!'s Weingand said it favored oil production "over the people's welfare," the Sierra Club's Eissler said that there was no guarantee that the wells could be pumped dry, and Senator Cranston objected to the panel's composition, saying that most members were those who had recommended drilling in the first place. Pecora explained that while Union was trapping as much oil as it could from the seeps with eight inverted funnels, as much as 50 barrels a day were escaping. This he put at ten times the natural seep rate, and for the first time it was revealed that Union's production from its wells was 4,000 barrels a day. Estimates on how long it would take to drain the oil field varied from two years to twenty, another reminder that the experts were better at guessing than knowing. On hearing Pecora's opinion that Union's five wells just couldn't do the job and the panel's suggestion that it would take fifty, even a federal geologist was appalled.

"This isn't the first time that good crude oil has made bad blood," he said, "but there's never been an oil issue about which both sides knew so little."

The report itself was not released and the environmentalists' anger was not assuaged by the discovery that the panel had held only one meeting and that the only presentations made were by oil interests and the U.S.G.S. Most of its members were in one way or another connected with the industry, upon which, according to Under Secretary Train, Interior was dependent for drilling data due to insufficient funds for geophysical and geological surveys of its own. Those who considered the possibility of selling Hickel on the Alaskan North Slope as an alternative source of crude, permitting him to do his former constituents a favor as well as pointing up Udall's error in approving channel leases, were not encouraged by a piece in the *Wall Street Journal*. After pointing out Hickel's annoyance with Udall for attempting the role of ecology's innocent, he was quoted as saying that there was more to the job of Interior Secretary "than climbing mountains and paddling canoes."

"I can't be bothered with details," Hickel said. "I like to sit up there in my office and get the big picture."

The big picture, most Santa Barbarans felt, is always composed of details, among which are the effects of the oil spills on fisheries. The receipts at Santa Barbara Fisheries, Inc., for the first six months of the year were 185 pounds of halibut compared to the previous year's 9,050, 46 of bonita compared to 14,779, and sea bass was down from 2,072 pounds to 864, according to Charles Ireland in the *News-Press*. One view held that the disappearance of anchovies in the channel following the blowout might be a cause, and that now "there was no anchovy, no plankton, no halibut—nothing." The skeptics didn't see Hickel making room in his big picture for the seal controversy either. Interior claimed that there was no evidence that any seals or sea lions at San Miguel Island had died due to the oil, or that the animals' food supply had been affected. It was possible, Interior's experts admitted, that the pups might be more susceptible to oil, just as it is that oil might have been ingested while nursing, and even that the smell of the oil could prevent mothers from identifying their young. Other sources insisted that this was the reason mothers were denying their young nourishment through ignoring them, and that more than a hundred pups were lying dead and oil-soaked. The behavior of seals on clean beaches, it was said, and that of those on the polluted ones was radically different.

The month of June ended in Santa Barbara with a suggestion by two California Republicans, Murphy and Teague, that the channel leases be traded for rights in the Elk Hills Naval Oil Reserve, which contains over one billion barrels of oil and has been held by the Navy since 1912. It was an example of imaginative thinking, and because it originated with members of the administration's party, there were those who thought it might have a chance. It was even pointed out that by decreasing chances of more spills, it would lessen the threat to the Navy's dolphins at Point Magu. (They were used for experiments in underwater communication and control systems, and it was said that they had been found to have a better sense of direction and humor than either oil or environmental leaders.)

"They think more," said a psychologist, "and talk less."

The July 4 weekend was not without fireworks of a nonchemical nature. Senator Cranston asked Hickel if he could see the DuBridge report, which recommended expanded channel drilling. Cranston was also concerned by a report that there were now twelve oil-collection devices under the Problem Platform and that only half the flow was being captured. A further concern was that a plastic sea curtain for which good things had been predicted in containing surface oil at the platform had failed in its tests, parts of it breaking away. Other tensions came from the discovery that many beaches from Ventura County to Santa Barbara had received a new coating of oil. What was needed, some said, was not a July 4 observance of the War for Independence but a War for Environmental Rights. Initial skirmishing had begun already. In the opinion of some, faculty members at the University of California at Santa Barbara were showing signs of reluctance to back the drive for a permanent ban on drilling because of hints received of the leverage the oil companies could exert not only in funding programs but in employment of students. It was not a shot heard around the world, as had been the blowout, but it was heard in enough academic areas to make the hearers wish it hadn't been fired.

At mid-month the American Civil Liberties Union filed a suit on behalf of others which asked for a prohibition on drilling in the channel, the most prominent plaintiff being GOO!'s Weingand. Its basis was a denial of constitutional rights which included enjoyment of an environment free from improvident or negligent pollution, and it charged that drilling was resumed both without a public hearing and based on evidence still kept secret. The implications were far larger than the channel question, and the action was a reminder to others concerned with threats to their environment that the battleground offered by the Problem Platform was national in its potential—those Santa Barbarans who had taken up such an extraordinary veriety of arms against Interior and industry were fighting not only for their environment, but everyone's. The newest weapon in the arsenal was a GOO! sail-in, in which boat owners circled the Union platforms as a form of protest.

"Unless you include anger," said a professor, "the operation's pollution was minimal."

While not readily accepted as such by some environmentalists, the Problem Platform was servings something of a problem solver in offshore operations. An example is the use of the inverted tents or funnels, designed by Richard R. Headrick and manufactured by a Firestone subsidiary, which channel the oil forced upward by natural gas to peaks, connected to a storage source. While the cost is modest, running under $10,000 each, the placing is both expensive and tricky. They are reasonably efficient in their area of operation (about a 65-foot diameter), but movement of the seeps remained a problem. This could be due to the fact that as discharge back pressure is increased in the area which is tent-covered, the seep moves to the nearest point of least resistance.

"Of course, if you covered the entire channel bottom you'd have it licked," an engineer said, "but not even Union is about to try that."

The Sierra Club, which had also been pushing for a look at the panel's report, was advised by the White House that the information is privileged, as was the state attorney general by Hickel. It was explained that parts of the report were based on information supplied by Union and, as such, is its property. Director Pecora added that geological and geophysical data are collected by an oil company at great expense, and that it is offered to the government for consideration with the priviso that it remain confidential. But demand for release of the report developed a steady pressure similar to that of the channel's natural gas, and by the end of the month Union agreed to its release by the government. The U.S.G.S. then announced it would publish the report with all pertinent Union material in a month or so, raising a new question—since Union had agreed to the release, why should it take so long? To some it sounded as if the government in its wisdom wished tensions to ease first, but instead, as one outraged citizen protested, "we natives are just getting more restless." Oddly enough, Union's acquiescence coincided with the appearance of a slick so large some compared it to that of the original spill.

The six-month anniversary of the Union blowout was marked by Senator Cranston's reading into the *Congressional Record* a summary of the present situation, including the continuing leakage which was fouling beaches and the sea to the depredation of marine, wild and human life. He added that experts were predicting a 100 percent certainty that California would be rocked by quakes in the future. He once again made a plea for passage of his bill, now amended, which would ban future channel drilling. The state, by way of backing him up, refused to lift its ban on both drilling in its channel bottom and the granting of new leases.

"We don't know enough to authorize drilling with safety," a state spokesman said.

As if oblivious of the state's desires, Hickel a day later announced approval of drilling by Union for another eight wells below the 1,000-foot level, saying that the nine wells authorized in June had so lowered pressure that the leak had been reduced from 30 barrels a day to 15. The new authorization, together with the granting of permission to the Sun Oil Company to erect a platform off Carpinteria between Union Platforms A and B and two belonging to Phillips Petroleum, made conservationists wonder which Hickel they were dealing with. His response to oil industry demands later in the month strengthened their doubts—not only did he ease the penalties against those responsible for spills by removing the clause calling for reparations for damage to third parties, but he withdrew a provision which would have permitted release of oil company geological data filed as part of its application. Without such information, the public can hardly know whether operations can be pursued safely, and this defeat for environmentalists left them outraged and at a loss as to what to make of such an unpredictable man. One opinion held that although he could be touched by wildlife deaths, he was best reached by oil interests.

Government response to the A.C.L.U. suit didn't allay doubts. It saw the action as seeking special privileges and, as "an uncontested suit against the United States," inadmissible. To the defense that the outer Continental Shelf Act does not require public hearings as to the effect on public interests, the A.C.L.U. answered that since under the act the oil companies are granted hearings to protect themselves, so should be the public. The kind of evidence which, though inadmissible, would be provocative appeared at the end of the month. It was a new slick, and it reinforced public concern. This one, near ARCO's platform west of Goleta, turned out to be leakage not from that source but presumably from old core holes drilled in past geological investigations. The specter of a multitude of these cores beginning to seep made no one happy, including the oil interests.

November 6, 1969, Boston, Mass.
The Liberian tanker Keo carrying 210,000 barrels of #6 fuel oil sent an S.O.S. today on breaking in half during a northeaster 240 miles off the coast. Coast Guard predicts possible loss of 36 crewmen and major pollution threat.

By November, some Santa Barbarans realized that they were letting their anger at the Problem Platform become almost a way of life, but contemplation of the fact that the Sun Oil Company was about ready to install a new platform base in the channel was no diversion, nor was the denial by a federal judge of a motion that would have prevented the Corps of Engineers from granting further drilling permits or platform installations without public hearings. The plaintiffs insisted that public hearings should not be denied, as they represent due process, but the bench maintained that the Corps is not obliged to hold such hearings. Had they been held, they might well have stopped Sun—its projected platform was to be in the same area as Union's and thus would be faced with the same hazards. This would have given litigational comfort to the plaintiffs, who could have used some, but it turned out the industry was comforted by the decision. Rewarded is a more accurate word, perhaps, for they had worked hard and in high places to end the possibility of public hearings each time leases are up for bid. The antioilers' theory was that if you can keep them talking, they won't be drilling, and the oil companies knew that there was a lot of validity in this, but no oil. On the way down from their high places, the companies touched base with Hickel, taking with them a line they are said to be more fond of than he is. The President, it goes, was asked whom he wished for Secretary of Interior. The answer: "Oh, any Hick'l do."

During November neither industry nor government was saying more than they were maneuvered into, and when they did speak, it was said, their voices were indistinguishable. It was thought that Union had thirteen wells in production in August, but it was impossible to find out how many were being drilled or contemplated. Union's director of communications would communicate only that drilling rigs were in constant operation. Phillips wasn't communicating much either, and from Humble came word that rich finds were present in depths of 1,000 feet. The implications of blowouts at that depth and in that bottom made knowledgeable citizens pale. Nor did another realization cheer them—at least one Shell tract impinged on sea-lanes, and while it was argued that their width of 1 mile was ample, retired tankermen didn't agree. Industry statements on this topic were scarce, and reporters redefined the press conference as a way of communicating in which nothing is communicated unless its communication benefits the communicator.

"When oil's the game," recited a writer, "mum's the word."

"For mum, read mummy," corrected another.

This reminded them how often spelling is influenced by point of view, and the name give the Sun platform was cited as an example. At first it was understood to be Platform Milhaus, but then the unlikelihood of an oil company calling a platform by the middle name of a politician, particularly if he is a President, was raised. When the name was checked, it was found to read Hillhouse. The origin of Hillhouse was lost in the excitement of a Sun announcement that they had their permit and would exercise it shortly by moving Platform Hillhouse on site.

While some antioil people took comfort that the total of actions being brought against Union amounted to $1 billion, presumably Union's communications people took their comfort in the company's estimated expenditure of $2 million to $3 million for spill cleanups. It was, after all, a voluntary undertaking even if it wouldn't be in the future, and if nothing else it could be called a major investment in public relations (if we can't stop the oil, we'll get rid of it). But the conservationists were increasingly discouraged at the lack of success they were having in getting various congressional bills affecting the channel out of committee. Current Washington thinking held that the cure for the oil threat was to produce more of the same—if you pump it all out, it can't seep. Thus, the ecology is saved, the ruffled lobbyists are soothed and a seat may be salved. The hitch, of course, is the danger of the drilling and extraction, and just how dangerous the Problem Platform had demonstrated.

"It's a question of leverage," a GOO! leader said. "We get sympathy—lots of it—but sympathy can't turn off the oil. Only the lawmakers can do that, and right now they're too well oiled themselves to be able to hold on to the spigot. And yet, you can't pin oil on them—it's too slippery."

Laymen were able to understand that if you pump all the oil from under the channel none will remain to seep, however technical and obscure the language employed to sell this approach was. What they didn't understand was what replaces the oil in the enormous underground space created. If it is left empty, as official silence on the question suggested to some it would be, what would prevent the channel floor from collapsing? And if that happens, can it affect the shoreline by triggering slides, earthquakes and such? To some experts the question seemed so childlike it hardly deserved an answer. But as with many simple questions that have simple answers, professional response tended to be complicated. This has been explained as being due not so much to the professional's inability to think and express himself simply as to his fear of being robbed of his technical mystique, leaving him naked and indistinguishable from the layman.

One professional bothered by childlike questions to which there are only childlike answers, and for this simplicity the more unnerving, is Dr. Sanders. An assistant professor of geography and the husband of the pretty Australian blonde bird therapist, Dr. Sanders was aware that all-out drilling could cause sinking and consequent cracking of the channel floor with the attendant risk of earthquakes. There were risks as great in attempting to replace the oil with a filler, and a member of the White House panel told him that to think the purpose of drilling was to deplete the pressure was a misconception. The object was not to deplete pressure but the oil, and he added that there was no gas drive in the field in question. Hydrostatic pressure, which must be maintained, could be provided by seawater injection, this authority felt, a technique which according to one U.S.G.S. source is so hazardous that it may well be preferable to risk cracking of the sea floor. That fluid injection is gaining wider support because it is helpful to the oil producer in extracting his product more completely does not negate the hazards presented. In Dr. Sanders' view, substantiated by a U.S.G.S. report, early pressures greater than hydrostatic were created in the deeper structures of the Union tract, uniting with the upper structures at the time of the blowout. He felt that these pressures had now been reduced to below normal, so that Hickel's excuse for drilling resumption—to lower pressure—was inaccurate. It seemed apparent that the intent of the remedial program was not to lower pressure in order to stop the seeps, but simply to get the oil out. And if such an approach were to be followed to its effective end—the point at which even with water injection oil can no longer be produced—the area could be in for at least thirty years of operations. No one can predict what might happen during such a period, but a guess can be made oil would still find its way from lower zones to upper fissures, and through them to the surface, to marine life and seabirds, to beaches, to . . .

"Perhaps, the most troubling burden we have to bear in this dreadful time," said an elderly resident, "is all the not knowing. And in this, by far the worst is not knowing what and whom to believe. With neither knowledge nor trust, we are as helpless as the poor creatures dying in the oil."

Part of the ignorance was the result of deliberate withholding of information on such grounds as proprietary value, litigation and "protecting the equanimity" of the public. A larger part, however, stemmed from both the limitations of experts and the brand new challenge offered by the Problem Platform—there just had never been anything like it, and even the most educated guesses had an eerie way of looking like a retarded form of coin tossing. While there had been considerable experience with oil spills affecting wildlife, as in the *Torrey Canyon, Ocean Eagle* and *General C.* disasters, many conclusions remained hard to come by. This was because so little was known of conditions before the events, and because of the rather peripheral nature of the studies themselves. Predictions, therefore, had little to go on—a count made after an occurrence without equivalent before figures have little meaning—and this was true of attempts to predict both the long-term and the immediate effects on channel marine and wildlife. The only study of magnitude was initiated by Dr. Dale Straughan, an Australian ecologist at U.C.S.B. Her study team was large enough to cover considerable ground, being financed by that $240,000 grant from the Western Oil and Gas Association. The underwriting source, naturally enough, made the project suspect in some eyes even before it was in operation, but the general feeling was that a scientist as young and attractive as she was in her press pictures should at least be given a fair hearing. A statement by her reinforced the attitude of patience: "The important factor is the chronic effect and the long-term impact—whether genetic damage poses a serious danger to some species."

One reason conservation leaders were being careful in assessing Dr. Straughan's study is what became known as the Problem Platform's *Life* magazine problem. In its June 13 issue *Life* came out with a heart-rending spread on the damage to sea mammals at San Miguel, the expert camera work making the dead pups look more than usually appealing. The Department of Interior was fast in replying with a well-documented denial that the deaths were due to the oil. The department was joined by the Coast Guard and later supported by some state officials.

There was no denying the impact of the pictures, though—they included sea lions and seals oil-covered and lying helpless on oil-drenched rocks. Later, the local view was expressed that possibly the lowered fish population was responsible for the erratic behavior of the mothers in the pupping season, and this with other factors did imply that the oil could at least have contributed to the abnormal pup deaths. Feelings ran high on both sides, and it was a good example of the danger of not knowing what to believe—do you believe the experts or the editors of *Life*? One might even end up by not believing directors of communications.

In mid-November the Problem Platform leakage once again increased and the resulting slick extended as far west as Naples. with a slick off Point Mugu 3 miles long and 1-2 mile wide. This was countered by some good news, called a genuine break-through in a *News-Press* editorial. The U.S. Court of Appeals issued a temporary restraining order on the Corps of Engineers, denying issuance of permits for channel operations for ten days. It was called by counsel for plaintiffs "the first judicial ray of light piercing through a dark and foul oil slick" (phraseology that some felt could hardly be indicative of the quality of the brief). Ten days, as one of the victors admitted, was no lifetime, but the order did mean that the efforts of conservationists wer being taken seriously at last.

The determination of Sun Oil to proceed with setting up Platform Hillhouse prompted the leaders of GOO! to organize a protest fleet of boats for a fish-in. Their operations, it was hoped, would inconvenience those of Sun, and their intention was to "have everything out there that can drop a fish hook." The plan was to delay the platform placing for twenty-eight hours, symbolizing the January 28 blowout, and participating boat owners were asked to form a cortege behind the platform base while it was under way and to fly upside down brooms at their mastheads. This would symbolize sweeping oil activity from the channel, but as an ex-naval officer objected, the inverted broom usually means complete victory. He thought such a claim, to judge by the size of the flotilla compared to Sun Oil and Platform Hillhouse, might be just a little premature.

The timing of placing Platform Hillhouse became tricky, due

to an awaited ruling on an appeal to block it before a U.S. Supreme Court Justice. The A.C.L.U. was getting used to close timing in channel actions, however. On November 3 the Federal District Court had ruled against a plea for a restraining order on the Corps of Engineers' approval of eight drilling permits and a platform, but plaintiffs weren't told until November 6. The Corps of Engineers issued their approval in the interim, producing plaintiff charges of "stratagems and ploys" in a matter of utmost importance to the public. It was regarded as a small try, and a particularly unsuitable one in the case of a 260-foot-high platform with capability of a sixty-well installation. On the other hand, Sun's executive vice president didn't think much of GOO!'s fish-in, calling it "a public relations stunt of enormous disservice to the public," according to the *News-Press*. The thinking and wording was reminiscent of Hartley, and the paper asked editorially if he had "any conception of the dedication and durability of the thousands of citizens who have democratically signed petitions and staged protests against oil exploitation of this environmentally special Channel region?"

The answer to the question came in the form of a rumor that Sun would seek an injunction against the fish-in, but with the appearance of the flotilla at the battle site on Friday, November 21, there was still no evidence of it. As the oil source said cheerily, it was hardly needed—the flotilla consisted of only half a dozen boats and a helicopter carrying GOO!'s Mrs. Sidenberg, who lowered a lawn sprinkler on a cable as a fishing lure. There was little sign of combat, except for one boat being assaulted by a paintbrush thrown from the Problem Platform, but the picketers did take credit for having forced the enemy's tug and its tow, consisting of a large barge carrying the platform base, to divert course. Sun Oil spokesmen estimated that it would take about a day to prepare and place the base, which was to be done by tipping it from the barge. This was an operation which GOO!'s people were looking forward to, for some in the trade had described it as hairy—success depended on the proper balancing of the structure. It was said that experts had so carefully figured the weight distribution that nothing could go wrong. As members of the opposing factions waited for Operation Big Tip, they had something in common—both were keeping their fingers crossed.

Sun P.R. men were generous in their handouts about Platform Hillhouse. Called "a showcase of pollution control technology," it was described as a design specially suited to channel conditions, loaded with fail-safe devices, a wide range of alarm systems to indicate malfunctions and the latest electronic controls. It was painted blue to make it less conspicuous, and it was, said a P.R. staffer, "so foolproof, even an earthquake could hardly throw it," an allusion particularly unsuitable for that geological area. ("Ouch!" said a brother P.R. man.)

The expression was soon repeated, for as the base was being tipped from the barge, it became obvious that the expert calculations were off. The 15,000-ton structure flipped and went to the bottom upside down before reaching the site of installation. Conservationists were delighted by the fiasco, and better still, by the chance that it might not be recovered and put into its proper location before the Supreme Court, to which the plea had been referred, handed down its decision. This decision, scheduled for Monday, was two days away, and Sun lost no time in sending down divers to have a look at what was already being called "the Problem Base." GOO! members talked hopefully of the problems faced by Humpty-Dumpty, but before dawn a heavy-duty barge-mounted crane was moved in and preparations were under way to attempt righting the structure. The base was resting in 190 feet of water, presumably neither damaged nor snagged, and the intention was to tow it to the site on its side. It made an unsettling image, its eight enormous legs reaching for the sky, and both GOO! members and Sun employees recalled superstitiously that it was the thirteenth channel well. One GOO! member, on being told by a Sun man that the fish-in was a failure, replied that no action that resulted in so much of the country witnessing a fail-safe disaster could be called anything but a success.

"One might even call it an upset," he told the critic.

The fish-in protestors wired Nixon on Sunday that the platform accident was another example of the hazards of channel drilling, and this action helped to overcome their disappointment at the success of the effort to right the rig. A couple of GOO! craft were anchored at the erection site with the intention of blocking the rig, and although the Coast Guard was patrolling the area, it kept out of the way both navigationally and legally. The question of who would give way presented a nautical nicety interesting enough to warm the heort of any admiralty lawyer worth his brief, but the confrontation was yet to come. Somehow, the platform again slipped out of control and was once more bottoms-up to the delight of "fish-iners." The Supreme Court, in considering the appeal and faced by a two-week adjournment, accepted affidavits disputing a Sun claim that Hillhouse had been in place since the previous Friday. Even as the evidence was being presented, the rig was still about a mile and a half from the site which had been checked and rechecked by the GOO! boats occupying it.

In the end the Court rejected the original plea and did not grant a temporary injunction. The rig was moved to its site in what must have been one of the nicest bits of tug handling ever— the GOO! position, it turned out, was off, but not so far that the great structure and barge didn't have to be shoehorned past them to the site 100 feet away. The reasoning by GOO!, as the skippers agreed, was better than their plotting, but they comforted themselves that even the plotting was more professional than the rejection of the U.S.G.S. regional supervisor, Donald Solanas, who (from a Coast Guard craft) warned the fish-inners away. The Coast Guard said that the GOO! boats were not violating any rules of the road by their presence, but Solanas took the names of the protestors, saying that he would forward them to the Department of Justice. The request by GOO! officials for an investigation of possible conflict of interest Solanas might have in supervising drilling operations had no connection with his threat, it was said. It was merely a reflection of their concern that Interior and the Corps of Engineers might be representing special interests.

As the month drew to a close, it looked as if Platform Hillhouse might down its first well on the blowout anniversary. January 28. And as if for a Christmas present, a company spokesman referred to Santa Barbarans, according to *The Los Angeles Times*, as "chronic bitchers." GOO! members, who had been picketing Stearns Wharf, were heartened when the weight of a crane snapped some steel framing, thus adding a safety factor to their arguments that the wharf should not be used for oil activities. Union helped the cause by coming up with charges of its own for once. The claim was that there had been a breach of contract with its drilling contractor, who allegedly had violated drilling regulations and whose negligence cost the oil partners $25,000,000. This admission that there had been negligence at the Problem Platform, let alone willful disregard of federal and state regulations, brought smiles to antioilers.

"Mother Nature may have let Union down," they said, "but Lady Luck hasn't let us down."

Secretary Hickel came up with an idea in early December which is a good example of accommodation thinking—he suggested the possibility of underwater production rigs to eliminate environmentalists' objections to channel platforms. To most environmentalists, however, this was merely a gimmick that evaded the issue, for the major objection to channel drilling was not its unsightliness but its threat to the environment of the area. Besides, antioilers pointed out, underwater installations would still need adjacent surface facilities, operational risks would almost have to be greater, and the technology required put the possibility far in the future. A Humble Oil official classed such an undertaking as "extremely difficult"; nevertheless, Hickel said that he had consulted potential manufacturers of such a system and would continue to explore the possibility.

"It may be good for Hickel's image, but the problem is not what we have to look at in the channel, but what we face in living," a Sierra Club member commented. "Putting the oil menace under water doesn't get rid of it, it only hides it."

A more heartening prospect for Santa Barbarans was agreement of Union and its partners to pay damages in joint actions brought on behalf of several thousand people, most of them property owners. The pleas were to be heard by a panel of retired judges and it was agreed that establishment of liability or negligence would be waived, a precedent of importance. It meant that in other actions, and there were many, it would not be necessary to go through the machinery of fault-finding. The strength of the people was beginning to be felt, conservationists

recognized, and this awareness extended far beyond the law—
it would make spills even more expensive, and the more a spill
costs, the less chance there is of there being one. Some antioilers believed it might lead to eventual cessation of all channel
operations, and although this would take a while, it was something to look forward to. Indeed, so seriously were spills now
viewed, there was a hand-lettered warning on a platform supply
vessel: "NO SPILL NEVER." The message, double negative or not,
was getting across.

> *December 17, 1969, Dakar.*
> *The 207,000 ton Shell tanker* Marpessa *has exploded and*
> *sunk 50 miles off shore. The largest tanker lost to date,*
> *she had discharged cargo and was steaming in ballast. Had*
> *she been loaded, her spill would have been almost half*
> *again that of the* Torrey Canyon's.

The Problem Platform's next contribution to public outrage
took place on Thursday, December 18, in the form of a new
slick. It was about 10 miles long and 5 miles wide, its brown
color suggested that it might have been chemically treated,
and antioilers speculated about what they would be told this
time. As it happened, U.S.G.S. inspectors were on the platform
at its first appearance, Tuesday afternoon, but it took divers
over eight hours to discover the source, which was a rip in a pipe
at the platform base at a weld. At once the Platform's sixteen
wells were shut down, soon to be followed by fourteen more on
Platform B. The immediate question asked both on the platform
and ashore was, why hadn't the leak been taken care of by the
automatic shutoff revices required in the new, stiffer regulations
on the basis of which resumption of operations had been
authorized? Even as investigation was begun, Supervisor Clyde
and others were sending protests to Hickel, and with publicizing
of the new spill, outrage grew. The leak had not been immediately corrected by automatic shutoff, it was explained, because
it was too small to activate the valves. The antioil reaction was
loud and clear—"If a spill this big is too small, what's the use
of all these new controls?" This spill, called "almost impossible,"
was put by the Coast Guard as high as 12,000 gallons. That "almost" had become a reality in spite of the pipe having been

"coated to prevent corrosion, protected against electrolysis and inspected periodically," and it suggested a new area of environmental danger. The *News-Press* warned editorially: "There are more than 100 miles of oil and gas pipelines on the channel floor. . . ."

Taking advantage of the new spill, Senator Cranston referred to the panel's recommendation that unstable underwater fields be set up as reserve resources, aptly quoting the report's view that as yet safety devices had not been perfected to the point of guaranteeing against fractures in pipes and containing equipment. By Saturday, what appeared to be still another leak showed up between the Problem Platform and its neighbor, Hillhouse. Union disputed this, saying that conditions were as they had been for several weeks, except for Tuesday's pipe failure. The slick caused by the latter was still in the area, though working seaward. Union took another view on Sunday, an official reporting that the platform leak had increased, and the Coast Guard spoke of a new slick a mile and a half off Rincon. Union advised that the increased seepage had been apparent since the wells were shut down Tuesday night, but would subside with the resumption of operations as pressure was reduced. The statement alarmed the more experienced conservationists because of its implication—channel operations must continue, for if they don't, seepage begins and slicks are formed. It seemed such clear industry vindication that some even wondered if the Tuesday pipe failure had been deliberate in order to make a telling, if fouling, point.

Oil came ashore at Rincon and Carpinteria and along a 10-mile stretch almost as far as Venture. Heavy pools formed in the rocks, sea and shore birds were again ingesting oil through preening, and it looked as if a familiar story was about to be told. However, a new fact emerged—in announcing that Union had resumed production, Solanas put it at "the normal rate of 22,000 barrels a day." This was the first time the figure had been released and it gave the antioil group an idea of what they were up against in output. The input consisted of, as one observed, "pollution for profit's sake."

"We now have firsthand evidence, much to my disappointment," the Associate Press quoted Solanas as saying, "that the only way these seeps are going to be contained is to increase production."

He put the leakage increase at 500 barrels per day during the well shutdown, saying on Tuesday that it was back to its normal "10 to 15 barrels." A Union spokesman, asked by Steven V. Roberts of *The New York Times* how the new seep could occur in the light of government and industry assurances, sounded weary.

"We don't have the answer to that," he said. "There's not a great deal we can say because it did happen again."

The year ended for Santa Barbara with almost as many unknowns as there were when Platform A became a problem and entered history. In a erport to the Audubon Society, the curator of ornithology and mammalogy at the Santa Barbara Museum of Natural History, Waldo Abbot, spoke of the difficulty in getting accurate bird counts, and predicted that the effect of the original spill would be seen in the fall and winter, as the flights returned. It was obvious that the diving varieties suffered the greatest losses, and he felt it was lucky that with several thousand birds affected, none of the twelve species were on the rare list. The *News-Press* quoted him as saying:

> In the case of Western Grebes, there have annually been 4,000 in the Rincon area, which is sort of an ancestral hunting ground. These great rafts of birds have been observed for years.
> Suddenly, they have been reduced to a handful. It will take a long, long time before the original population is restored, if ever.

Just as the first month of 1969 had brought the Union blowout, the first day of 1970 began with a bang from Union's president. His company, Hartley said, would install another platform in the channel "as soon as possible." Interior, thrown by this awkward start for the new year, explained that it had not authorized such a platform and that it would be some time before it did. This, instead of calming down Santa Barbarans, exasperated them. They saw an implication that a third platform would be approved eventually, and heads already registering the effects of New Year's Eve toasts to an environmentally safer year became even more fractured. The only answer to the question of why Hartley came out with such an enraging statement so soon after the newest leak at the Problem Platform was that it might have been his way of serving notice on Interior to get with it, it being the permit.

"Like putting pressure on them to let him reduce pressure on the oil sands," was the way a startled U.S.G.S. staff member put it.

"You could call it Hartley's New Year resolution," a GOO! leader said, "but ours is simpler—never!"

"A third platform? Over our dead body!" said a Sierra member.

"His," corrected the member's wife. "And not even then."

In authorizing the Sun installation, Hickel referred to the need for remedial drilling, a view in which Hartley joined. The latter made an offer which Sierra Club officials called "a lure with a deadly hook"—he suggested that 24 percent of the bonus and royalties from the federal leases be given to communities adjacent to the area of operations."

"It is equivalent to paying someone to help with your suicide," remarked one of the officials.

"Our sense of environmental responsibility is not for sale," said a Santa Barbara official.

The threat of another Union platform intensified antioilers' efforts to reach President Nixon, and GOO!'s Mrs. Sidenberg made an attempt at contacting him at San Clemente. News of the formation of another White House advisory group, this one to be called the Council on Environmental Quality, was construed by Santa Barbarans as merely recognition of the political importance of environmental concern, not as an action that would stop channel operations. This, it was beginning to be realized, was something that Santa Barbarans might have to learn to live with, no matter how much oil was pumped out. Still, antioilers weren't giving up. Congressman Teague requested that the channel crisis be put at the top of the Council's list and Governor Reagan came through at last with a plea to Washington that all drilling be banned in areas outside the Problem Platform location until adequate safeguards were devised. It was a strong demand and one that took courage for a governor of an oil-producing state, and this may have given Reagan reason for saying that it could not be ignored. Senator Cranston also was active that first week of the new year, protesting to Nixon that the Corps of Engineers was quietly proceeding to amend its regulations so that public hearings need not be held for the granting of drilling permits. This, he said, would eliminate the last chance Santa Barbara had to register its objection to further operations. As if in answer, a U.S.G.S. statement from Washington summarized its findings of the blowout effect by way of a year-end report, calling the leakage at the Problem Platform "completely under control." The basis for this conclusion appeared to be that while it was admitted 10 barrels a day were still leaking, this was now considered "normal activity." The reaction to this curious view was that one could just as well call the limited effectiveness of oil-retaining devices at the platform, such as booms, tents, hoods and skimmers, a "normal activity." A biologist at U.S.G.S. commented that while such seepage might be considered a normal activity by industry since it could afford it, it was abnormal to those who couldn't. And these, he added, included the ecology.

The new year also brought new lawsuits, that of District Attorney David Minier being of special interest. He filed in Santa Barbara's municipal court in an attempt to avoid the one-year statute of limitations that had been applied on his attempt to sue after the blowout. The oil companies had obtained a federal injunction against him, but his brief maintained that events in federal waters affected state and county waters, and so were within his jurisdiction.

"I could no longer in good conscience refrain from prosecuting merely because the oil companies were holding the threat of jail over my head," the *News-Press*'s Robert H. Sollen quoted him as saying.

The oil companies were served with papers ordering their appearance in municipal court. In answer, they refused to waive the one-year statute of limitations against Minier. He, too, fell back on the threat of jail, but this time it was being applied to company officials in event of their failure to appear. The legal implications of this action, it appeared, would be small compared to the potential problems with the removal of oil installations from the channel. Aside from the enormous financial reimbursement which would have to be picked up if leases were canceled, there was the issue of what to do with the rigs themselves. An industry plan for their disposition caused numerous shudders, since it called for removing all the equipment and fixtures above the waterline, then cutting off the legs and towing the rig out to sea for scuttling. It was not a matter of immediacy, since off-shore wells can produce for as long as forty years, but it did present hazards new in terms of possible pollution through damage to submerged pipelines. The very concept of contributing to further ocean dumping worried some, and it was a reminder that even if the industry was obliged to operate under new and stiffer regulations, their thinking hadn't changed—it was still "drill, pump, and dump."

A voice that spoke with a fresh note in the new year was that of U.S.G.S.'s Director Pecora, who implied that while there was no plan to authorize Union's third platform, it was doubtful that in the projected location it wolld contribute to the remedial drilling plan. He added that all applications would be looked at carefully and that he had no objection to public hearings. The response to this ostensibly encouraging view was that it didn't sound like the Interior Santa Barbarans knew—could it be that Hickel was in such a bind that he had to stick with oil interests, but that a lower-echelon type was free to make conciliatory motions for him? Or, wondered others, was Pecora being groomed for better things? The answer, it seemed, might be known only in the White House.

Other voices spoke in January, but they did little to reassure Santa Barbarans. Sherwin D. Smith in *The New York Times Magazine*, writing about California's vulnerability to earthquakes, stated that according to the U.S.G.S. National Center for Earthquake Research in Menlo Park, California, the area's tremors are being recorded at 10 per day and that before the end of the century they will total 100,000, of which 100 will be strong enough to feel, 10 will be damaging and at least 1 will be major. He goes on to point out that the San Andreas fault, which contributes to the quake-prone fragility of the channel, is building up with underlying tensions and must be taken into account as an area of special hazard. A good example of how not to treat the area is illustrated by the Rangely Oil field in Colorado, where the water-injection technique was applied to wells to facilitate extraction of remaining oil. The resultant small earthquakes, it is thought, were caused by the subsequent reduction of fault-line resistance. A voice of attempted reassurance was that of a Western Oil and Gas Association witness testifying before the Senate Interior and Insular Affairs Committee. He stated that "We have no record of any pollution to the surface from sub-surface damage to an oil well from an earthquake," but this statement was soon to be contradicted—U.S.G.S. stated that "both onshore and offshore oil wells have been damaged by sub-surface faulting during earthquakes." A recent example was the finding that in the 1964 earthquake at Seward, Alaska, a submarine land slide was followed by seismic sea waves which resulted in oil spills and fires, both there and as far away as Crescent City, California. Indeed, those Santa Barbarans who were tempted to believe that Hartley might just have something in his claim that further oil extraction meant there would be less oil to spill, would do well not to remind themselves that it was the abnormal pressure built up by fluid injection that led to the Los Angeles Baldwin Hills dam break. And if that were not enough to make them more anxious than they were already, they could turn to another U.S.G.S statement, this one of unusual candor:

The numerous complex interrelated variables that determine whether or not subsidence occurs when core fluids are withdrawn from a reservoir are understood so poorly that accurate prediction beforehand of the amount of subsidence is difficult, if not impossible.

January 13, 1970, Sabine Pass, Texas.
An Atlantic Richfield Oil Co. offshore well blew out today.
One man was killed, four were injured and the resulting
fire raged for three hours. Drilling was at the 10,700 foot
level in soft shale, which collapsed and fell back in the
well cutting off the fire.

A delegation of Santa Barbarans, who won a meeting in Washington with Hickel and Pecora to try to achieve a clearer understanding and better rapport, were told by the latter that drilling and production procedures are more important factors in pollution hazards than the geology of the ocean bottom. Members of the delegation were troubled, believing that the channel, as an unstable formation, was both potentially and actually hazardous, and that the latest techniques left a lot to be desired. They were somewhat mollified by Pecora's offer to divulge the data on which remedial drilling was based, but they didn't get far with Hickel—he refused to grant either a ban on drilling or a two-week pumping moratorium to test the validity of remedial drilling, and added that he "felt compelled" to grant drilling permits without public hearings unless there were unusual circumstances. As an example he cited drilling at depths of 1,000 feet, in spite of having authorized two permits for Humble to drill at such a depth without public hearings. Moreover, according to his own U.S.G.S., nearly two-thirds of blowouts occur in deep wells, and engineers agree that the deeper the well, the greater the pressure and the larger the control problem.

The effectiveness of GOO!'s boycott of Union products was demonstrated by the closing of at least one Union gas station in January, and others indicated a drop in business. There was, however, some unfavorable reaction—many felt it was unfair that small businessmen should have to suffer for the alleged misdeeds of a giant, and even the *News-Press* printed an editorial regretting the situation and saying that it had never favored the boycott. GOO!'s executive committee, disturbed by the reaction to the suffering of Union dealers, was reconsidering the wisdom of the boycott, and some people were puzzled by the silence of Hartley on the topic. They wondered if he, as was said to be the case with Hickel, was at last listening to his P.R. people. If so, the antioilers would miss the ammunition he had supplied. The campaign to burn Union credit cards continued and one holder discovered an added incentive—if you burn it, you can't lose it.

Some big guns were enlisted in the Battle of the Channel as the Problem Platform's anniversary neared, among them Senators Muskie, Nelson, Cranston and Tunney. Proposals included demands that the federal government take back the leases with due compensation, remove the platforms as seepages subsided, set the area up as a national oil reserve and, on the basis of a predicted one major offshore spill a year, defer further production on the outer continental shelf until safeguards were both developed and proven. It was finally recognized that such major action could not be taken by the Secretary of Interior who, sympathetic or not, was powerless. His out was that he had inherited the situation (the same excuse used by two administrations about Vietnam), but this limitation of guilt by inheritance did not go down well with Udall. He was said to be ruffled still by Hickel's failure to acknowledge his note of good wishes on the latter's taking office, but as a Washington observer comments, between Hickel's roughing up by the Senate and the Union blowout, there wasn't time for niceties then and it was too late now—there had been too much oil over the water.

The blowout's noise in the world press many felt made a major contribution to environmental awareness, even to the extent of outweighing damage to the ecology locally. The Union wells were thought to be bringing in $100,000 a day, which, even if the cleanup cost amounted to $5,000,000, was still a paying proposition. As an employee admitted, however, it hadn't been easy money and due to the growing impact of the blowout it was getting harder.

"It's almost as if core samples have been replaced by public opinion samples," he said. "And the latter has sure gotten easy to come by."

On the blowout's anniversary, Weingand of GOO! said that "from a minor political issue antipollution concern has developed to the hottest issue of our time, excluding war and peace." (Observers felt he had a right to be proud, even if he might have added to his hottest issues pot and the Pill). Another GOO! official, Marvin H. Stuart, said that "environment has replaced motherhood in the politician's lexicon, but rather than curse the late bloomers for how far they have to go, I'd bless them for how far they've come." A Wilderness Society official pointed out that however great was their concern with the channel, the North Slope presented even greater hazards to the environment. It was thanks to the fight put up by Santa Barbara, he went on, that the fight there would be easier and, hopefully, even winnable.

"And until the oil industry relearns that it is dependent on us, who are dependent on a healthy environment," an ecologist concluded, "they're going to have what happens when there's no snow—tough sledding."

The release of the U.S.G.S.'s report justifying remedial drilling raised a new issue at the end of January—the information was far less complete than had been supposed, and was insufficient for outsioe experts to make a jurgment on the recommendation. One geologist guessed that only 10 percent of the available facts were contained in the report, but others felt that it did clear up the cause of the blowout. This was seen as insufficient casing, and although that used had been approved by the U.S.G.S., it was still a serious error of judgment. While recognizing that wells could be damaged by earthquakes, a far more likely cause of major pollution was seen in fractured pipelines and storage facilities, a prospect that didn't make Santa Barbarans feel any happier about channel operations on the anniversary of the blowout, which was marked by an environmental conference. Clyde and other heroes of the environmental battle were honored, there was much speechmaking, and warnings were given that politicians had done so much ecology and environment mouthing, the words were becoming both meaningless and a bore. It was cautioned that progress should not be taken for granted.

"We must produce oil," said a participant at the Stearns Wharf sit-down, which closed the day's activities, "but we must protect life. It's that simple and that hard."

> February 10, 1970, Venice, La.
> The Chevron Oil Company Platform Charlie caught fire today. By March 31, when the last well fire would be put out, it would have leaked over 27,000 barrels of crude into the Gulf of Mexico and created a slick of 52 square miles. Total Chevron offshore drilling violations put at 347.

The February announcement by Humble that it would relinquish its lease on a 9-square-mile drilling tract south of Union's was the month's first surprise. The company spokesman was careful to explain that the decision was not due to any possibility of unsafe geological conditions, but to a disappointing show of oil as a return on its $45,000,000 investment. The news was welcomed by antioilers, whatever the reason. Had it been made by Union, one would have wondered if public relations problems had played a part. Humble's P.R., however, has generally been responsible, just as statements by its executives are usually mature. With the unknowns of strata flow behavior, some wondered if Union with its production of 30,000 barrels per day wasn't drawing on the Humble tract and might be planning to eventually pay a royalty. In any case, while environmentalists couldn't claim a victory, they could hail a step forward for their side, which was a stride backward for the enemy.

"By giving in," said one, "Humble has at last justified its name."

Environmentalists were heartened shortly by a Los Angeles City Council resolution calling unanimously for total elimination of all channel drilling and production activities in both state tidelands and federal waters. It did except Union's production program, called now by antioilers "remedial for cleanup cost sickness," but it was a major stand for a civic body to take in an oil-industry-dependent area such as Los Angeles. One of the reasons for urgency, the Council said, was that oil from channel spills had reached that city, which is Union's headquarters. If nothing else, it spurred Santa Barbarans to put more pressure on their own Council to take over Stearns Wharf so that its oil operations could be ended, and a new committee was set up for the purpose. In its first statement, it accused various branches of the city government of lack of action in enforcing existing statutes applying to oil operations, which pleased antioilers almost as much as an oil company's answer to a brief pleading for hearings amused them. It argued that "hearings would only have inflamed the already heated atmosphere attendant to drilling in the Channel." The antis began to feel a little heady on reading Sollen in the *News-Press*, who reported that Hartley had let it be known that Union would be "glad to get out of the Channel" if adequately reimbursed by the federal government. Although this change in Hartley's views coincided with an announcement by GOO! that its membership had doubled, not even GOO!'s vocal president claimed credit for the revised corporation thinking. It was recognized that much would depend on what would be considered "adequate" compensation. If Hartley was ready to follow Humble, said antioilers, there must be a hitch, probably a big one.

February 14, 1970, Arichat, Nova Scotia.
The 16,000 ton Liberian Tanker Arrow, owned by Imperial Oil Co., grounded on Cerberus Rock in Chedabucto Bay. She carried 3.8 million gallons of bunker oil, and on breaking up spilled almost two million gallons. Slick extended 110 miles out.

February 16, 1970, St. Petersburg, Fla.
The Greek tanker Delian Appolon, under charter to Humble Oil Co., grounded today and broached her tanks, spilling refined oil. Polluted area extended 100 square miles, including 20 miles of shoreline. Thousands of wildfowl killed, bayou marine life damaged.

February 20, 1970, Eureka, Calif.
A barge collided with a Humboldt Bay jetty today, spilling 84,000 gallons of its 2.5 million gallon cargo of petroleum products most of which was contained.

February 27, 1970, Jacksonville, Fla.
The Bahamian freighter Merc Buccaneer and the oil barge Eastpet were in collision today, spilling 7,000 gallons of bunker fuel into St. John's River. Slick extended 8 miles, polluting 3½ miles of river bank, threatening St. Marks Wildlife Refuge.

March 3, 1970, Sydney, Australia.
The 58,000 ton Liberian tanker Oceanic Grandeur was holed on rocks in the Torres Strait today. Spill formed, 45 square miles. Oyster beds, cray fishing and nesting areas of sea birds endangered.

On March 10 Humble began to sound once again less like its name. According to the *News-Press*, it had had an application pending for exploratory channel drilling on two more tracts since September 19. Interior had approved them (unannounced) on February 20 and permits were now before the Corps of Engineers for consideration of national security and navigational factors only. The environmental aspects had already been passed on by Interior and without public hearings. In contrast to the quiet approval, the reaction to it was very loud. Senator Cranston, appearing at a Santa Barbara Senate subcommittee hearing on minerals, materials and fuels, again asked Nixon for a moratorium on offshore drilling. Next, a GOO! official recounted a near-miss between the S.S. *Lurline* and a drilling vessel operated for Humble, then cited that while by Coast Guard definition navigation is hazardous for a 2-mile area around a drilling operation, Interior was authorizing drilling in 1-mile-wide shipping lanes. Other testimony included that of Dr. Sanders, who pointed out that Humble proposed to drill in 600 feet of water, despite its being an untried depth. He went on to illustrate that the remedial procedures had failed to reduce the seepage, noting that although the number of producing wells had doubled, the flow appeared about the same. GOO!'s Weingand called for a congressional investigation of Interior because of its "public be damned policies" and close relationship to the oil industry, and an official of Atlantic Oil enlivened the hearings inadvertently. He said that while his company was not a part of channel activity, his office window's "view of the oil wells was evidence of the goodness of the land."

"And the more of them there are, the less goodness of this land will we have," grumbled a member of the audience.

The operations of Humble, more rumored than stated, made people increasingly uneasy. The guess was that they were drilling in water of more than 1,000 feet and the certainty was that they had found oil. Another certainty appeared in an *Oil and Gas Journal* article which stated that production of oil in 100 feet of water costs about three times more than shore operations, while working in 1,000 feet of water could be twelve times as much. It wasn't the expense that bothered antioilers, it was implication of difficulty of operation, which would have to include hazards. Humble did say that it had no immediate plans for production at these new depths, but it was mentioned that the problems involved were not primarily technological but financial. This was a worry to antioilers, for while the industry may not always find a way, they are never short on means. Union, as illustrated by its remedial drillings, was able to find both. Real estate appraisers, busy with the growing number of claims, now put the depreciation in property values as high as 50 percent because of the reluctance of customers to buy. This was not of serious concern to Union, nor was Representative Teague, who as the month ended disclosed a report to the effect that the Navy was looking favorably upon relinquishing the Elk Hills reserve area in exchange for the channel tracts. That still spelled oil, and besides, there would be compensation, even if Nixon had before him for signing the Water Quality Improvement Act. This had been passed by both houses with such large majorities that it was clear the environment issue was in and was going to stay. Among items for protection of the public, it provided in cases of accidental spills limitation of liability of up to $14,000,000, and where there was negligence or carelessness there would be no limitation of liability. As one who had worked hard to get the bill through said, it would make spills expensive instead of just embarrassing.

By early April Humble was seeking approval of fifteen drilling applications, having already been granted thirteen. Union's platforms were said to be producing 40,000 barrels a day at close to $3, and the seepage remained about 10 barrels a day. Estimates as to how much oil was being caught by the submerged tents varied from 25 percent to 60 percent, and all that was certain was that both platforms stood in an ever-present slick. Phillips and California Standard, operating off Carpinteria, were producing 35,000 barrels, and according to *Offshore*, an oil publication, the channel was about to become California's fifth largest oil field. There may have been Santa Barbarans who took civic pride in their area being so ranked, but more of them worried about the shortage of U.S.G.S. inspectors available. Rowland Evans and Robert Novak in their syndicated column put the problem down to the Budget Bureau's refusal to grant an Interior funding request for additional personnel. Budget claimed that Interior's intimacy with oil interests was responsible for laxity in enforcement procedures and that more inspectors would be of no benefit. It insisted on stiffer procedures before granting further funds, and this curious interdepartmental strife suggested to one observer that Hickel, busy with the Arctic pipeline problems threatening his attempt at image-building as the alligators' friend, had better start minding his Washington store.

"Budget," maintained this source, "always forks up when the right Washington or San Clemente call comes in.

According to Sollen in the *News-Press*, as April ended Platform Hillhouse with its sixty platforms was all set to go, but advanced technology was not able to overcome one drilling obstacle. The state Lands Commission refused to let Sun pipe oil through state waters to Ventura County, and Santa Barbara County wouldn't issue a permit either. Sun next pulled a switch by arranging to utilize Union's pipelines, but by then permission to start drilling was withheld and all that could be done with Hillhouse was to continue to admire it. This was fine with GOO!, whose members were about to celebrate Earth Day with a petition of 200,000 signatures. It was a good omen that this latest advance in drilling had been rendered useless, but the problem with Earth Day, as Morgan Bulkeley pointed out in his *Berkshire Eagle* (Pittsfield, Mass.) column, was that after society was "purged with righteousness," it could "slump like a hog back into the luxurious wallow of over-population, pollution and desecration of the environment. At least it can be said that the hog has stirred, even though he does not appear to be reformed."

May began on a Hickel note, and for him not a happy one. As if he didn't have enough troubles with the Alaskan pipeline controversy, antioilers in Santa Barbara were claiming that the channel leases he was thinking of canceling with reimbursement covered tracts on which no oil had been found, and on top of that he was stuck with what to do about the GOO! petition sent to him from the White House with no comment. Soon to come and far worse was the *Washington Post* disclosure of his historic letter to the President, which was quoted verbatim before the recipient had even seen it. Hickel's pickle, a U.S.G.S. employee said, wasn't Kosher, but sour. On June 5, 1970, those who were his critics began to wonder if they wouldn't miss him. At a press briefing at the White House on the canceling of oil and gas leases in the channel for which he had fought, it was plain, to quote James Doyle in the *Washington Evening Star*, that "White House annoyance with Hickel's public dissent has been no secret. The signals now seem clear—Hickel was disinvited from the briefing."

According to Hickel's Book of Job, *Who Owns America?*, not only had he already briefed reporters, but White House press secretary Ron Ziegler explained his absence by saying that it "was pretty technical stuff and so Pecora briefed on it," without mentioning a White House staffer's call to Hickel that tried to explain that it had been decided to give Senator Murphy and Representative Teague exposure, as they were up for reelection. Asked if the disinvitation meant that the White House would be happy if Hickel stayed on as Secretary, Hickel says Ziegler replied, "How could I answer that without getting into trouble?" Clearly it was eulogy time, and Jack Anderson inaugurated it in his column by quoting Lloyd Tupling of the Sierra Club, who said that "although I've always felt that the reason for his appointment was oil and Alaska, I think he's done a generally constructive job." He might have added that although Hickel had much experience in Alaskan construction, in Washington you have to be more than a builder.

By mid-June, after almost eighteen months of continuing oil pollution from the Problem Platform area, some conclusions were being drawn as to ecological damage. A U.C.S.B. team found that barnacles, limpets and intertidal algae were affected by successive waves of oil coatings and that intertidal rocks were becoming tar-coated with a resultant loss of floral cover and attachment potential. Feeding was made impossible for marine organisms, but kelp and the intertidal anemone proved resistant to the oil. The team made no attempt to predict the larger, long-term effects of the disruption to the food chain, and as one marine biologist pointed out, there just wasn't anything to say except that it won't be beneficial. All authorities agreed that the greatest loss was suffered by wildfowl, the latest count being 3,587 birds, but they did not agree on the ratio of actual count to overall kill, though many accepted the two-to-one ratio. Most were unable to say how the ecology is affected when there is such a large loss among the bird population. As to the fish loss, there was even less agreement on the count—it was guesswork and the guesses varied as widely as fish swim.

The state Lands Commission found itself making a contribution to the art of oil-spill containment by its insistence that control techniques must be effective before further permits are granted. Although Standard Oil of California had developed a massive boom for use at its Platform Hope, as with all booms the question was how it would operate in a turbulent sea condition.

The American Petroleum Institute, paralleling the report of the recently established President's Council on Environmental Quality and its prediction of a three-year wait until a spill of *Torrey Canyon* size can be handled, forecast details of the next massive spill—source will be a tanker, cargo crude, amount more than 5,000 barrels, location close to shore and pollution period more than five days. Oddly enough, cause was not predicted, but it doesn't take a computer to figure the odds on its being human error.

The odds were no less hard to figure on Senator Cranston's bill to set up a channel sanctuary, even though it did receive *New York Times* editorial support. It was compared to Hickel's proposal, which has become more and more a White House product, but Cranston's bill would cancel all leases in the channel (except for Union's) until remedial drilling is complete, not just the twenty proposed in the White House request. Of the fifty-one that would remain, forty-eight were not in production, and the *Times*, recognizing that the channel is especially vulnerable to earthquakes and has only a shallow capping layer over the oil formation, said that "we would prefer to have a comprehensive plan to restrict, if not prohibit, offshore drilling near any shoreline in America found to be rich in those qualities that please the eye and relax the spirit of man." It is a good line, that one, and one that many Santa Barbarans wished could have immediate application to them. The specter of an American shoreline drilling sanctuary must have shaken many an oil man, and it goes to show what a long shadow the Problem Platform had cast.

Representative Teague, discouraged by the prospects for passage of a sanctuary bill, in August started planning an alternative one. This would put a moratorium on further drilling offshore until underwater techniques were perfected enough so that all phases of the operation could be undertaken safely. Clearly, development of such a technology would take some time, a delay that would not be displeasing to antioilers, and although Lockheed Offshore Petroleum Service was already testing an oil-company-financed underwater production rig off Vancouver, it's a long way from that to practical underwater exploratory and drilling techniques. Teague seemed to feel that resistance to passage of lease cancellation legislation was less oil company objections, which were strong enough, than the intransigence of antioilers. It appeared to some that they wanted all or nothing, leaving no room for compromise, but accommodation is as sacred to Congress as the franking privilege. The intransigents argued that the wheels of Congress are still "too well oiled" to do anything else but run on the power source provided by the petrochemical lobbies.

November 9, 1970, Torquay, England.
The tanker Pacific Glory *is moored three miles off shore with 7 vessels equipped for detergent spraying standing by. The 42,000 ton* Pacific Glory *was in collision with the tanker* Allegro *on Oct. 4, spilling much of the 20,000 ton crude oil cargo.*

The indefatigable GOO! president, Mrs. Sidenberg, decided to take on the Corps of Engineers shortly before Christmas. She asked for an investigation of it by the Joint Chiefs of Staff and the Department of Interior because the Corps, which had earlier abandoned the practice of environmental hearings before granting permits, allegedly also ignored written objections on grounds of navigational hazards and drilling at untried depths. It was "riding roughshod over the legitimate rights of a community," she complained. A couple of days later at a National Science Symposium in Santa Barbara, antioilers were startled to hear one who at least a few of them had begun to think might be their champion, Dr. Pecora, endorse oil industry plans for further channel development. A member of the Federal Council on Environmental Quality, Dr. Gordon J. McDonald, admitted that agreement had not been reached with either Interior or the Engineers on advance assessment of the environmental impact of all contemplated projects, making his hearers wonder exactly how much counseling the Council would be permitted. And Humble's president, Thomas D. Barrow, in light of Dr. Pecora's industry-supportive role, didn't do much to lift spirits by resurrecting the view that channel oil should be pumped "both because it was there and needed." It looked as if the Christmas stockings of those Santa Barbarans who feared for their environment would not be very full and' as one remarked, they might not even be hung.

The new Pecora look puzzled many at the year's end, and according to Robert H. Sollen in his Sunday piece, the symposium "illustrated the gap between the new generation and the industrial and bureaucratic establishment." He saw Pecora as chastising the community for not backing administration efforts to get a small part of the channel set up as a sanctuary, and it was because too much had been demanded that full channel development would now proceed. Pecora said that while he would recommend holding public hearings, the government had decided that more platforms were inevitable, and therefore hearings would be meaningless. Since Pecora didn't have the authority to make such major and basic decisions any more than had Hickel or, perhaps, his successor, Rogers Morton, antioilers felt such stands must have originated at the White House. It seemed hardly possible that the 16 percent royalty accruing to the federal government was the determining factor in this new hard line, and Pecora's apologetic use of the inheritance syndrome—being stuck with a bind not of his making—didn't clarify the matter.

"What's behind it," said an angered Santa Barbara official, "is high-level politics. Or, rather, the financing thereof."

> December 29, 1970, New York.
> Hope was still held out today for 21 missing crewmen of the 19,000 ton Panamanian tanker, Chryssi. She sank 270 miles south west of Bermuda en route from Venezuela to Salem, Mass., after breaking in half and spilling her full cargo of crude oil.
> The Coast Guard announced that it had suspended the search for the master and crewmen of the Finnish tanker Ragny, which broke in two without warning 600 miles southeast of New York.

The Los Angeles Times started the new year with an editorial containing an October, 1968, quotation of President Nixon: "Are we doomed by some inexorable thing called progress to give to our children a land devoid of beauty, empty of scenes of grandeur, filled with gadgets and gimmicks, but lost forever to the wonder and inspiration of nature?" To this rather Moynihanian question of unknown ghostmanship, the Times editorial reply can be summarized by the line, "The nation is still awaiting an answer."

An answer of a kind was delivered about a week later in Santa Barbara at a Department of Interior hearing. This pertained to applications for drilling platforms from Union for its Platform C adjacent to A and B, and from Sun Oil for its Platform Henry 5½ miles offshore between Summerland and Carpinteria. Interior had decided in advance of the hearings to grant the applications, it seemed clear, and nothing said by its officials gave any impression to the contrary. Between their warnings to the audience against "applause or any form of outcries or demonstrations" and the reminder that the department was "not required by law or regulations" to consult the public, not even a bone was thrown to the antioilers. The only constructive element that came out of the hearings, in the view of conservationists, was the announced intention of Senator Henry M. Jackson (D., Wash.), chairman of the Senate Interior Committee, to hold hearings on the hearings. He was concerned about the lack of public notice and statements by Interior people regarding the advance decisions of approval, although he intended also to inquire into the state of the art of offshore drilling and production. (An antioiler defined the art of offshore oil extraction as consisting of little conscience and much drilling mud.)

January 18, 1971, San Francisco, Calif.
The tankers Arizona Standard *and* Oregon Standard *were in collision today ¼ mile west of Golden Gate Bridge in fog, resulting in a major pollution crisis. About 840,000 gallons of Bunker C oil would be spilled, slicks would cover a 60 mile area, bird loss would reach 6,000, cleanup costs more than $4,000,000.*

January 25, 1971, New Haven, Conn.
The 23,000 ton tanker Esso Gettysburg *grounded at the harbor entrance today. Spill would amount to almost 400,000 gallons of domestic heating oil, forming a 12 mile slick. A 30% bird loss was forecast and the recently formed Federal Environmental Protection Agency compared the spill to the September, 1969, one at Buzzards Bay in which marine and wildlife were still affected one year later.*

The mood in Santa Barbara on the second anniversary of the Union blowout was quite different than on the first, which had produced much outraged vocalizing and energetic picketing. Now there was a quieter, more meaningful approach—people had learned how to live with the menace and the limitation it put on their freedom to determine the nature of their environment. It was clear to them that this privilege, seemingly guaranteed in the American way of life, was not to be theirs without continuing struggles. It was also generally recognized that the struggle involved more than the immediate area—it would have an effect on all communities threatened by pollution. The recognition that they weren't alone in their battle heartened many of the fighters and made it possible for them to accept the distance between environmental hope and political reality, such as the introduction of legislation by Senators Cranston and Tunney, together with Congressman Teague. This would revoke thirty-eight leases in the channel and apply a five-year moratorium on twenty others, but on the basis of Pecora's warning at the anniversary symposium that Santa Barbarans might as well get used to the idea of continuing oil operations, no one was counting on its passage. After all, the oil companies' total investment in the channel amounted to $1 billion, exactly the amount of lawsuits pending against them, and so the real issue was between a community's way of life and the demands of a national industrial-political complex.

Union was said to feel that it had gotten off lightly with clean-up and indirect costs of $16,000,000, and in comparison, GOO!'s annual budget of $25,000 is laughable. But the latter figure, agreed those who heard Mrs. Sidenberg at the symposium, represents full value.

"What happened here could happen to almost any community in the country in different kinds of environmental damage," she said. "No place will be safe until we can get some sensible policies in government."

A boatload of GOO! members took advantage of the fine weather on the anniversary to pay the Problem Platform a visit and to collect samples of the continuing seep. They encountered a slick in the vicinity which looked as if it had been treated chemically, and they suspected that a supply vessel was doing its best to churn up the surface in an attempt to dissipate the slick. Crew members on that craft took pictures of the GOO! group, but whether these were to be forwarded to the Justice Department, as DeFalco had announced he would forward the names taken of those picketers in a previous GOO! action, was uncertain. What was certain is that the group was successful in collecting samples of the oil to send to the White House as a reminder that after two years it was still leaking. As reported in the San Francisco *Examiner*, the day was also marked by the state Lands Commission approving a drilling permit for Standard Oil of California to drill off Orange County. Its chairman, however, warned that the action did not imply that mass drilling would be resumed.

"This particular well and this particular circumstance," he said, "meets the criteria of the policy of the Commission with regard to safety."

Since the state requirements had so often been touted by antioilers as being more stringent than those of the U.S.G.S., they regretted the authorization but there was little they could do about it. There wasn't much they could do about the issuance of a preliminary draft of an Interior environmental impact statement in late February either. It recommended further exploratory drilling in the channel, saying that such action would present no "serious environmental problems." Its issuance was to provoke comment from other federal, state and local agencies, as well as from the public, as represented by conservation-minded groups.

"It was sort of where we had come in, only all over again," commented a member of one of them. "Some of us are beginning to wonder how much of the environment will be left by the time they let us try to save it."

The March, 1971, issue of *Proceedings* of the Marine Safety Council summarizes in an article by Commander Daniel B. Charter, Jr., U.S.C.G., the role of the Goast Guard in oil spills, as established by the Water Quality Improvement Act of April, 1970. Under it the Coast Guard provides the on-scene commander who coordinates federal efforts and provides equipment and personnel, but there are some problems, as illustrated by this quote:

Unfortunately, the present technology for cleaning up oil spills is sadly inadequate. Even for small spills, the cleanup methods now used are almost totally ineffective except in very calm and sheltered waters. Very little is known about how to cope with spills, or about the variety of chemical products being shipped in bulk for the first time. Many oil slick containment booms, or fences, are now being sold commercially, but none tried at the Gulf of Mexico oil well incident last March were able to hold the oil slick against the forces of the sea.

Chemical dispersants and sinking agents often do more harm than good, and unfortunately oil does more harm to fish and other marine life when it mixes with the water than when it remains on the surface. Compounds which stick to oil and sink it to the bottom have similar disadvantages in that they bring the oil into contact with shell fish and other bottom life. They also tend to release oil to the surface after a period of time.

Conservationists who shook their heads over this discouraging summation of the state of the art of spill control found an additional reason to be depressed. In spite of all there was to be researched, the Coast Guard received a mere $4,000,000 per annum for this purpose, together with development of techniques and equipment. It is true, as those who have attended congressional hearings at which Coast Guard requests for funding are considered know, that the organization is humble indeed. Legislators sometimes go out of their way to encourage modest commandants to ask for more but such a practice is not always productive. While it is curious to find a federal agency asking for too little instead of too much, the reason is natural enough—the Coast Guard has been a stepchild too long. In wartime it comes under the Navy. In peacetime it has served under the Treasury Department, and is now under the Department of Transportation. Even as the Navy submarine force has been called the silent service, the Coast Guard has tried so hard to be inconspicuous to avoid disfavor that it is known as the "hide and sneak service." Both mariners who have been rescued by it and those who fear for the environment hope now that it has greatly increased responsibility (the Navy having even handed over to it its icebreakers), it will speak with a louder voice. As has been suggested, having its own uniform instead of the Navy's might help (look what its own uniform did the wild blue yonders of the Air Force).

In March, contrary to the reassurances given at the January Sumposium by Dr. Pecora that offshore exploratory drilling was safer than production drilling, there was an exploratory drilling explosion in the Gulf of Mexico. In spite of the fact that exploratory work is usually done from floating rigs instead of the more stable stationary platform, Pecora's view had been seconded in the February environmental impact statement by Interior. While the opinion of those who didn't agree had been received politely enough, it was with an air that said the U.S.G.S. experts were *the* experts, whereas the public was merely the . . . well, the people. The statement had claimd that in the drilling of over 5,000 offshore wells there had only been four pollution-causing blowouts when a high-pressure oil-and-gas reservoir was tapped. The Gulf blowout, a Sun gas well, made it five, and it was one remarkably similar to that of the Problem Platform. Said the *Oil and Gas Journal*: "After the blowout preventers were closed, gas bubbled up through the ocean floor about 50 yards from the rig unloading mud, and a relief well may be needed to kill it."

Casing was down to 1,100 feet under the new, supposedly safer requirements, the drill was at 4,000 feet, and it was assumed that the seepage originated below the 1,000-foot depth. One observer of experience believes that the persence of mud indicated loss of drilling control—insufficient weight of mud permitted the gas to exert upward pressure. What gave the lie to Pecora's reassurances of exploratory safety, this source said, was that the floating drilling rig shifted about 200 feet from the well after the blowout, so that it was out of contact with the well, which was then uncontrolled.

"In other words," he said, "all of a sudden the well was on its own, and had it been oil instead of gas, it would be a case of another Fred Hartley having some new Union suits to try on for size."

The month of March was notable in environmental circles for the pollution report by Dr. Dale Straughan, and the findings were both unexpected and, to some, immediately suspect. According to a *Time* magazine story, the report found "damage to beaches, flora and fauna was less than predicted and the area is recovering well." Factors of interest contained in the report include the assertion that the government and industry estimate of the spill total as 3,000,000 gallons was too low, and that the heaviest rains in forty years had caused silting which settled on the bottom of the channel, taking with it much of the oil and complicating the study. The study estimates the seabird loss at 4,000 out of an assumed 12,000 population and mentions the loss of one barnacle variety. The low animal count is explained by Dr. Straughan (described in the media as a "pretty 31-year-old Aussie with gray eyes glued to her microscope") as being due to the fact that toxins are the lightest components of oil and therefore evaporate on the surface rapidly. Dr. Max Blumer, of the Woods Hole Oceanographic Institute, disputed this, saying that on the basis of his studies of a refined oil spill at West Falmouth, Mass., in 1969, the most toxic elements of oil are the most persistent. In her rebuttal, Dr. Straughan claims that the Union spill was so close to shore, there was no chance for dissipation of toxins before marine life was already contaminated.

Other critics of the study, their numbers perhaps increased by suspicions as to its impartiality in view of the funding source, point to the loss of a sea worm species and that of intertidal fauna. Still others criticize the study on the basis of its technique being insufficiently sensitive to pick up anything other than massive changes. Dr. Blumer objects to the incompleteness of the study, its limited use of gas chromatography and spectometery, and the failure to analyze the oil itself. By contrast to Dr. Straughan's optimistic evaluation of the Union spill, the Woods Hole investigation of the West Falmouth one found that "the oil decimated offshore marine life" and that in the following months the oil on the bottom retained its toxicity so "that 8 months later bacterial degradation was not far advanced." The controversy over Dr. Straughan's study has become so widespread and vituperative, a sociologist observed that "it looks as if more tempers have been lost than marine life."

An elegant color-illustrated folder distributed by the American Petroleum Institute lays down a barrage of fire, using a P. R. range-finder to defend Dr. Straughan's study by aiming at GOO!'s Mrs. Sidenberg. It described her as "at the age of 68 tearing around town in a wheezy old Pontiac when, with her money, she could afford a Bentley. Her favorite sports are sailing, tennis, foxhunting and, above all, squaring off against oil executives." The folder goes on to quote Mrs. Sidenberg's story about herself:

"The *Washington Post* once quoted me as saying about the oil platforms," she recalls, "that we ought to go out there and *burn* the goddam things *down*. I didn't say that. What I actually said was we ought to go out there and *blow* the goddam things *up!*"

The A.P.I. folder in further defending the findings of Dr. Straughan, whom it describes as "cutting a most attractive figure in mini and boots and going 80 m.p.h. in her Fiat 850," quotes the manager of a Santa Barbara barge-mounted aquarium. The latter states that although its marine life is dependent on water circulated from the harbor where "at times the oil lay on the surface six inches thick, our loss of life was no greater than we normally have in an aquarium where animals of all kinds feed on one another. The oil floated on top and didn't seem to poison anything below." Obviously, oil cannot poison directly that which it cannot reach, and since the seawater suction lines to the aquarium are of necessity more than 6 inches below the harbor surface, the oil was not pumped into the tanks and the inhabitants were not exposed to it. Dr. Straughan's thoughts on the study reflect a more straight approach, as quoted in the folder.

"I do feel good about the study," she says. "The team got along better than most. We had our limitations of money, of boat time, of people available on short notice. But there are gaps. I'm somewhat critical of certain aspects—yet that's inevitable when people are working freely."

Her husband, Dr. Ian Straughan, professor of biology at U.S.C. and also Australian, defends both her and the study ably:

Considering the rush and difficulty in organizing a team of experts on the spot, she did a damn fine job.

Myself, I'm certain I'd have gone about it differently. Women tend to follow intuition and we men are more systematic. But all some people want is heat and not light; they discredit findings of honest scientists with the most sweeping, insulting intimations.

Why the hell they are that way is a mystery to us Aussies. Maybe, it's because we're not up to our bloody necks in graft and corruption.

March 29, 1971, Portsmouth, Va.
The Coast Guard patrolled through a massive oil slick 100 miles square today, searching for 28 survivors of the tanker Texaco Oklahoma, *which broke in half 120 miles north-east of Cape Hatteras, N.C., and went down with her cargo of 220,000 barrels of heavy sulphur fuel oil.*

April 9, 1971, London, England.
The British tanker Hullgate *was in collision with a Danish vessel, the* Ida Hoyer *today, forming an initial spill over a mile long. Said the Hoyer's master, "In these matters the human element is so often involved."*

April 12, 1971, New Orleans, La.
The last of 12 offshore well fires was put out today on a Shell platform in the Gulf of Mexico's Bay Marchand area. Only 10 of the platform's 22 wells shut down automatically when the first blast occurred. Fires raged out of control 133 days, were allowed to burn while relief wells were drilled to kill them by mud to avoid pollution spread. Four men killed. Losses to Shell, $3,000,000.

At Interior's May hearing in Santa Barbara conducted by the U.S.G.S. in connection with the application for additional oil platforms, all area speakers opposed the application. A new show of unanimity in the history of public hearings, it was almost as unusual as a preference by the U.S.G.S. to the aesthetic value of these 200-foot high structures which most Santa Barbarans regard as a scenic blight. It was asserted that since they serve as an attraction to fish, they have a recreation value in addition to their economic contribution to the community, and that they act as an aid to navigation. Speakers were unanimous in rebutting these claims, some of which were viewed as laughable, and it was pointed out that not only are fishermen warned away from the platforms by employees, but the Coast Guard advises their being given a wide berth.

A controversy between Sun Oil and Phillips Petroleum about the possibility that the latter was draining oil from the lease of the former provided a lighter moment in the otherwise depressed atmosphere of the hearing, but it was pointed out that it was at the environment's expense, since it was one of the reasons Sun wanted Platform Henry.

"We know what happened to Henry VIII," said a historically minded observer, "and this Henry will have even more wells than he had wives. Maybe, there'll be a reformation in environmental concern—instead of money coming first, it will be people."

To the surprise of some antioilers, and quite possibly to ex-Secretary Hickel, Rogers Morton turned down the applications for Sun's Henry and Union's C. The victory was looked upon merely as a step forward—the threat of oil operations would remain until legislation was passed to make the channel a sanctuary and this, in view of the twenty-five congressional bills stuck in committee or already forgotten, was going to take a while. Along with the platform decision came word that Morton had reinstated fourteen drilling permits earlier suspended, pending environmental hearings. The area involved was largely south of Ventura County and east of the sanctuary. At least antioilers could see a partial victory in the fact that thirty-five other leases suspended would remain so until 1973. That, as one of the battlers for the ban on channel operations admitted, is not a long time, but a lot had been accomplished in two and a half years. On the whole, antioilers were favorably impressed by what they saw as Morton's reasonableness, and some even went so far as to applaud the new Federal Environmental Protection Agency for its recommendation that pumping be increased from existing wells, rather than drill new ones.

"I never would have thought I'd be for increased production," an antioiler said, "But if it's a choice between that and more wells, pumping is for me."

Charles M. Seeger, writing in *Environmental Quality* magazine, pleaded for the bill introduced by Congressman Teague, which would terminate the leases seaward of Santa Barbara and around the channel island, where no oil has been discovered. He explains that one reason no bills affecting the channel have managed to get anywhere is the problem of reimbursement—can the Congress pay Humble $3 per barrel for the several billion barrels under the bottom just to let it lie there? But the areas covered by Teague's bill possibly could be withdrawn for merely the price they brought—$210,000,000. That is a pretty large "merely," perhaps, but oil thinking only comes king-size. As Seeger mentions, Hickel's solution to the money problem was to exchange twenty or so channel leases for Elk Hills tracts. Navy admirals allowed before a Senate Interior Committee hearing that they had no objection.

"Then, figuratively speaking," says Seeger, "the admirals slipped around to the back door of the House Armed Services Committee, which has jurisdiction over naval petroleum reserves, and conveyed their strong opposition to Chairman Mendel Rivers."

Seeger offers no explanation of what prompted the admirals to follow such a devious course, but as the expert navigators they must be to have attained such exalted rank, it was clear to one observer that the course they chose might be less concerned with the oil reserves than with sea conditions encountered in some uncharted and dangerous political waters, as Hickel may have discovered too late to avoid foundering. In any case, the committee chairman being dead and the former Secretary done for, the plan has now been revived by Morton, and with an additional fifteen leases as proposed in Teague's bill, it might stand a chance of passing. Should this occur, it will go to show that where there is enough public will there is a legislative way, even if opposed by petrochemical means.

Santa Barbara and its struggle registered with the White House to such an extent that it was used as one of the reasons a Department of Natural Resources is urgenly needed, as reported by Gladwin Hill in *The New York Times*. The legislation backed by the administration would have such a department take over some of the responsibilities of six agencies—Interior, Agriculture, Defense, Commerce, Transportation and the Atomic Energy Commission. At Santa Barbara, not only were two Interior agencies involved—the U.S.G.S. and the Bureau of Land Management—but also the F.W.P.C.A.

"After a quick look at the bureaucrats on the scene and at the mess," says Hill, "the water pollution control people bowed out under departmental instructions."

The summer White House in San Clemente was about to

take notice of oil spill realities too. In late August, the Navy fleet oiler, USS *Manatee*, spilled an estimated 10,000 gallons of bunker oil after refueling the carrier *Ticonderoga*. The resulting slick, 5 miles long, threatened 30 miles of beaches, including that of the summer White House, and was attacked vigorously. The Navy's information officers avoided mention of their embarrassment at having threatened the beach of the Commander-in-Chief, who is protected from every other conceivable hazard including jellyfish. Instead, there was considerable information about a new substance to contain oil, Mono-Cleat, and the work of a device attached to a Navy yard oiler. This consisted of two steel arms 75 feet long placed at an angle on the bow, so that oil is funneled into a vacuum head for pumping into holding tanks aboard. Floating booms were employed to protect the Mission Bay Harbor and 100 men and loaders worked on the beaches from Carlsbad to the Torrey Pines Park. "Torrey" suggested to many the way pollution history has of repeating itself, Union's tanker, the *Torrey Canyon*, being of such spill fame it is only equaled by Union's Platform A. The cause of the Navy spill was also familiar—human error.

The President might have found firsthand experience of a spill helpful in his role as final court of appeal in environmental matters. For instance, the U.S.G.S. had urged approval of the Union and Shell platforms in opposition to the Environmental Protection Agency (F P.A.) recommendations, but Secretary Morton refused to go along because it would be incompatible with the concept of the federal sanctuary, proposed by the administration (and thought up by Hickel). Morton's stand, according to Senator Cranston, was the first "show of sanity" since the Union blowout, and it also illustrated that at least sometimes appeals by congressional voices, such as Tunney's and Teague's, do have some influence if conditions are right. One such condition is illustrated in a *News-Press* story by Paul Veblen, who was with the President at Portland, Oregon, at the end of that September. Veblen quotes the President as saying that "I made the decision, but he (Morton) made the announcement."

"It's good to give the secretaries a chance—it really is," the

President said. "They take a lot of heat. So I told Morton, 'Rog, you go out there and make the announcement.' But I, of course, made the decision."

Some of those on this scene had come quite a way since Morton's predecessor was "disinvited" from the White House announcement of the sanctuary, and so had the cause of environmental concern. A study was begun in October of the channel natural oil seeps off Coal Oil Point, those ancient guides for mariners, under a small federal grant. Divers had been plotting their sources and flow, in addition to taking samples for identification and study. Some antioilers, however, found themselves frowning on the project, as did the oil companies. The former didn't relish publicity on the natural seeps out of fear that it would divert attention from pollution caused by drilling, and the oil companies were said to fear that elimination of the seeps would mean the loss of a hook to hang their own spills on—it's known as the other-guy excuse.

As the end of the year neared, an ancient controversy was entered into by Senator Cranston, who found it necessary to defend environmental interests under attack by an assistant secretary in the Interior Department. The latter had testified that the Senator wished to "delegate to the State of California responsibility for management of a national resource," according to the *San Francisco Examiner & Chronicle*, quoted in a Washington dispatch by Sydney Kossen.

"The administration has chosen to resurrect the red herring of federal jurisdiction," Cranston said. "No amount of bureaucratic double-talk can disguise the Interior Department's obvious unwillinbness to give any consideration to environmental values when they conflict with the production of oil."

It was a reminder once more that in spite of some victories, Santa Barbara's battle for the environment was yet to be won. However, there were those who saw in a Humble drilling plan both a retreat by oil interests and at the same time a distinct technological advance. Humble, according to *The New York Times*, would seek "step by step" approval of a unitized program for oil and gas extraction in the northwestern Santa Barbara Channel 25 miles west of the city. The system included a deepwater platform 775 feet high with a submerged production system equipped with safety and antipollution components. One advantage of the plan would be a reduction in the number of drilling platforms required, and this together with the location and the employment of submerged production installations, said an important word to those involved in channel oil, both pro and con, who had sensitive hearing. The word was compromise.

It would not accommodate the hard-liners, but it would have appeal for reasonable men. It is such men, after all, who both made possible the life style which Santa Barbara had for so long enjoyed and also produced the oil on which so much of our living is based. At last, perhaps, and thanks to the Problem Platform, it might be possible to produce offshore oil without threatening those for whom it is intended.

CHAPTER 5

CONCLUSION

Antigods and Stillers of the Sea

THE NEWS ON the Problem Platform's third anniversary, January 28, 1972, was less of the Santa Barbara Channel than it was of what the Union blowout had done to help others determine the future of their environment. The pluses for the channel cause amounted to a growing list of bills affecting drilling and production operations, six federal and five state, stuck in committee. Most Santa Barbarans were more interested in the burdens they bore, chief of which was that they were still denied the right to an environment of their choosing. The Problem Platform was still a problem—the sea floor continued to leak oil in spite of production having doubled—and a decision handed down in a local action was so astonishing it received national attention.

The presiding judge dismissed 342 counts charging Union and its partners with pollution and found them guilty on one count each, for which they were fined $500. The court deemed that the defendants had "suffered sufficiently" in the light of civil damage suits brought against them, leaving the Santa Barbara District Attorney David Minier and many others speechless. When he found both voice and sense of control, he announced his determination to appeal.

"This is a case in which justice itself is held in contempt," said a court observer. Some Santa Barbarans perceived that the more people elsewhere who become involved in saving their environments, the better were the chances for the channel (there is not only safety in numbers, but muscle), and they had watched the Alaskan pipeline controversy closely. The possibly 100 billion or more barrels of crude awaiting extraction in the North Slope area is of enormous significance to Alaska and, indeed, to the nation. This last wilderness is threatened not only by oil spills from tankers and pipelines, but also by something new on land—thermal pollution. What oil at 180 degrees being pumped through hundreds of miles of 40-inch-diameter buried steel pipe can do to the frozen tundra of Alaska is an unknown, as is what degradation of the tundra can do to area ecology. North Slope oil development is vital to Alaska, as Governor William A. Egan has pointed out. He speaks of the human miseries of his state in contrast to its natural resources, saying that one can help the other. The mayor of Fairbanks, Julian Rice, agrees.

"God placed these things (oil and minerals) beneath the surface for a purpose, for us to use," *The New York Times* quotes him as saying, "To say that we shouldn't use them is to be anti-god."

Theology aside, there can be no question but that development of one of the world's largest oil pools will disturb this wilderness; yet the oil will be taken—the nation needs it, overseas sources can be uncertain and industry's investment and the area's desire is already too great. Still, a *New York Times* dispatch from Anchorage by Steven V. Roberts quotes a minister who lives near the Brooks Range and is at odds with Mayor Rice and his deity thinking:

Who will speak for those who will have no place left in the world uncontaminated by their predecessors' self-righteous need to convert everything, including beauty and solitude, into dollars? I say that all the oil in Alaska is not worth the loss of this last great wilderness.

At hearings held as required by the Environmental Policy Act assessing the environmental impact of the pipeline applied for by the Alyeska Pipeline Service Company, a partnership of seven oil companies, it developed that the pipeline would stretch almost 800 miles from Prudhoe Bay to the year-round port of Valdez, on Prince William Sound, from where tankers would carry the oil to the West Coast of the United States. The original cost estimate, $600,000,000, would have even then made it the biggest private construction job in history and today's price tag is around $3.5 billion, making its eventual output of 2,000,000 barrels of crude a day run about $1.27 each. Allowing for the cost of shipping by tanker to the West Coast at 75 cents a barrel, the price is getting near enough to today's market price of $3.45 to make some question whether North Slope oil wells will prove the gold mines they dreamed of. What there is room for, and lots of it, is the dispute over the ecological dangers involved. Wallace H. Norenberg, state commissioner of fish and game, is quoted in *The New York Times* as saying that "the fact is that there are serious voids in our information on the entire Arctic eco-system, and to arrive at the conclusion that, based on what we know, impacts will not be unduly great is unfounded." This opinion is at odds with the urgency contained in a speech by Secretary of Commerce Maurice H. Stans, in which he asked that programs to halt pollution be weighed, carefully and slowly, to determine if they will be too costly or ineffective.

"Are we so afraid of what might happen to the Alaskan environment," the *Times*' James M. Naughton quotes Secretary Stans as saying, "That we will sacrifice the enormous new sources of oil which we need for our homes and our cars and our jobs and our country? The time has come to stop overheating the view that we are killing ourselves."

From the environmentalist standpoint, there is more to fear from the pipeline than "overheating." In addition to the hazards of thermal pollution, there is the effect on wildlife of those sections above ground, and of the access roads required to build and service the lines. This has been compared to the railroads' opening of that other frontier, the West, by a Sierra Club vice president, Dr. Edgar Wayburn. Another problem, and little mentioned in the furor over the pipeline itself, is the spill hazard present in tanker traffic, Prince William Sound being one of Alaska's most important fisheries. The Coast Guard in the summer of 1971 used its biggest icebreaker, the USS *Glacier*, to carry scientists for an investigation of the Western Beaufort Sea, adjacent to the North Slope, to assess the biological, chemical, geological and physical variables of the marine environment. It is vital, says the Coast Guard, that we record what the environment is like in its unpolluted state before investigations of actual pollution are undertaken, since the area is one "In which the likelihood of future pollution is great." It is also one in which we may experience the impact of a major spill in subzero temperatures. The possibility offered here for new cleanup techniques excites at least one expert, who isn't sure how the solidified oil would be handled but guesses it's always safe to start with bulldozers and work up from there (down, if the ice isn't thick enough).

"One worry we won't have," he adds, "is losing pump suction —ice picks don't need it!"

The Coast Guard estimates spillage by tankers in the Valdez West Coast trade would run 392 barrels a day. It doesn't mention the hazard present in as much as thirty *Torrey Canyon*s of crude stored at quake-prone Valdez with the possibility of, as in the 1964 quake, waves of 170 feet in the harbor. The prospect is made more grim by the fact that not only is Prince William Sound one of the world's roughest areas in winter with winds of 100 miles per hour, but millions of water fowl favor it, being one-half of northern Canada's and Alaska's population. They congregate also at southeastern Alaska and British Columbia waters adjacent to the tanker route, and 95 percent of the world's pink salmon spawn there. The Gulf of Alaska is said to be suffering pollution already from tankers at Cook Inlet, as evidenced in February and March of 1970 when there was a bird kill estimated at 100,000.

Approval of the pipeline permits has been held up by actions brought by the Environmental Defense Fund, Wilderness Society and Friends of the Earth, and Secretary Morton expresses himself as "deeply, bitterly disappointed." Interior was required to suggest alternative sources of energy and to submit them to government departments for comment, and it was the failure to do so that gave environmentalists their chance. Observers see the case going on appeal to the Supreme Court, but no one is predicting when.

Alternatives to the Alaskan pipeline have been given little attention, and one study, done by Resources for the Future (financed by the Ford Foundation), finds that a trans-Canadian pipeline would provide more benefits than the Alaskan project and would not endanger the environment to the same extent. It calls the trans-Alaskan route the least inviting of several possibilities, saying the trans-Canadian route would be cheaper and would eliminate the possibility of tanker spills and of an active earthquake area to be crossed. Other observers, puzzled by U.S. insistence, have supposed that the trans-Alaskan route was favored because of the benefit in construction income to Alaska. However, a state Housing Authority study reveals that instead of supplying steady income for Alaskans, only 7,500 men might be required for three years of construction and a mere 300 would be permanent. Other reasons offered for U.S. insistence on the trans-Alaskan route is that Alyeska's investment is already so large that there will be the question of compensation if it is not utilized, and a more sinister rumor has it that much of the North Slope product has always been meant for Japan. If so, it knocks out the industry argument that we need more domestic oil.

The trans-Canada route would be slightly over twice as long as the trans-Alaskan, according to the *Wall Street Journal,* reaching from Prudhoe Bay in a southeasterly direction across the Canadian border to the MacKenzie River Valley down to Edmunton, Alberta, from where it would go to U.S. West Coast and Midwest markets by existing pipelines. While this makes for a lot of mileage, there would be one major saving, both economically and in terms of pollution hazards—a minimum of forty-eight supertankers would be not needed.

The delay in pipeline approval is said to be costing the oil companies $100,000 a day, but what may be of even more concern to them is the existence of two reports in opposition to the trans-Alaskan route, revealed by Jack Anderson in his syndicated column. He had earlier discovered that the views of some of Interior's leading ecologists were excluded from the department's favorable impact statement, and through sources at the Pentagon he learned that the Alaska District of the Army Engineers took a highly critical view of Interior's report, but that the fact was hushed up.

The draft statement [by Interior] is deficient because it fails to comply with the letter and spirit of the Environmental Policy Act. . . . It contains limited detailed analysis of the proposed construction and operation of the pipeline. . . . Conclusions on environmental effects appear to be unsupported opinions.

Anderson also says that a secret Canadian study "flatly" disputes the administration's claim that the cleanest, cheapest way to transport Alaskan oil to the United States is across Alaska. Whether cheaper or not, there would still be another high-priced pipeline across Canada, at a cost said to be by one observer of a cool $5 billion because of Arctic conditions. This would be a natural gas line to move the product at almost $1 per 1,000 cubic feet, but it wouldn't be in operation until the Alyeska pipeline is flowing, as the gas is a production by product. It will be expensive fuel, and while the consumer will pick up that tab, the problem of financing is a tough one.

"Call it a real gas," says a Canadian engineer.

More interesting to him were the archaeological reports on the trans-Alaskan route—artifacts dating back 10,000 years have been uncovered, leading to speculation that further finds might throw light on the New World's first men. It was already apparent from the digs that the climate of Alaska 10,000 years ago was better than now, and life, thanks to ample big game, might have been easier. One unknown, but perhaps not for long unless bulldozers destroy the finds, is whether Eskimos and Indians may have shared the same culture. There is some evidence of this, if not as much as there is of the present Eskimo population being an obstacle to the pipeline. Another Canadian observer feels that for Eskimos past and present, life may have more to offer than ours. The civilizing influence of the pipeline, he suspects, might not be considered much of a stride forward.

"Who knows?" he asked. "Now we've found early man thanks to oil maybe someday they'll dig up the last man because of what we let oil do to us."

Another alternative to the trans-Alaskan pipeline has been checked out at an expense of $50,000,000 by Humble, an Alyeska partner, and this is shipment by tanker direct from Prudhoe Bay. The *Manhattan*, the biggest U.S. tanker, was converted for icebreaking in 1969 and dispatched on an experimental voyage in late summer to try the Northwest Passage for size. As the first merchant vessel to make it, she satisfied a 500-year ambition, but her accomplishment was not done without difficulties. Displacing 150,000 tons and 1,000 feet long, the *Manhattan* steamed through over 800 miles of ice. Some icebergs were 100 feet high and floes were as much as 10 feet thick. The speed was slow, being 2 or 3 knots at throttle settings designed to move her at a good 14, and there were times when she stuck altogether and had to be assisted by an escorting Canadian icebreaker. Among the lessons learned were that while she had 42,000 shaft horsepower she could have used a lot more, she lacked sufficient reversing capability, and in spite of a special overhung bow and ice girdle, her hull contour could stand improvement. She ventured 120 miles into McClure Straits, where she was defeated by polar ridges and a "compression field," her escort being damaged. However, it is clear that vessels designed for such work would be able to handle the route, and eventually, they might not only be tankers. Ore carriers of similar design have been contemplated, but as with tankers, the basic question is not one of technical possibility but of financial return. Until recently, when cost estimates of the pipeline were revised, tanker haulage didn't look like too good a bet, but the disparity between tankers and the pipeline costs of moving oil may now be evening out. A lot was learned from the *Manhattan's* voyage, including a lesson in what happens when an oil tanker takes on a cargo of wheat. She loaded 65,000 tons of it for Pakistan, and while it showed her versatility, it brought loud complaints from other ship operators who saw in it unfair competition. Humble's response, now that the Arctic was out of season, if not out forever, was that something had to be done with her. If she hadn't made history already, she would have as the first, and undoubtedly the last, icebreaker to enter the grain trade in the Indian Ocean.

Some thinking almost as imaginative as that which had gone into her turned up at the Electric Boat Division of General Dynamics in July, 1971. It was to provide giant submarines to serve as tankers, thus eliminating the pipeline. It was claimed that this would please both the oil industry and environmentalists, since submarines wouldn't offer the pollution hazards common to surface tankers. The submerged hazards they could offer, however, might exceed even those of the tankers. Still, a research submarine for polar investigation of ice movements is now being developed, representing not only a research departure, but evidence that Arctic shipping isn't dead yet—it may just be waiting for some technical thaws.

In the meantime, a study by the Massachusetts Institute of Technology puts annual accumulation of oil spills at 5,000,000 tons, the E.P.A. estimates the number in U.S. waters alone at 7,500, the Coast Guard projects that annually one out of every fifteen ships will be in a collision, with a rate increase between 1964 and 1968 of more than 20 percent, and the Battelle Institute predicts that U.S. Navy tankers will average one 6,750,000-gallon spill and ten 750,000-gallon ones each year. The majority of the more than 2,500 vessel casualties from July 1, 1970, to June 30, 1971, were the result of personnel faults, according to Coast Guard figures, and of these a small minority were by harbor pilots. The next largest cause, 524, is equipment failure. The majority of the vessels were less than ten years old, they were tankships, and suffered their casualties in daylight and close to, or in, a port. However accurate the figures, it is still not easy to ascertain the basic cause—what caused the personnel faults? And what was *really* wrong with the masters of the *Torrey Canyon, Ocean Eagle* and *General C.?* Even equipment failure is not easy to pinpoint—if a tanker was lost at sea by breaking in half, was it the sea condition, metal fatigue, design, loading, improper handling, or maintenance?

Since most vessel casualties are the fault of the master, it is prudent to take a close look at him and this has been done to some extent. He is about to receive more thorough training, be examined more closely, and when under way, he will soon be able to command his vessel with far less reliance on guesswork as to the moves of the other fellow—traffic patterns are being set up at many port approaches and, even more important, he will have far better and more constant communication with other traffic and traffic controllers. There are other areas in which he can be helped, and most important is a change in command philosophy—that way of life and duty stemming from the days of sail. Then the captain had to be master of all he surveyed, but thanks to electronics, communications and vessel speeds, he can now survey far more than he can command. In terms of tonnage and what his cargo can do to the ecology, what he can master has decreased in ratio.

His job can be made easier, and his ship safer, if he is given more frequent leaves ashore, even if of shorter duration than is now customary, to break the almost rhythmic dynamics of steady duty; his junior officers should be encouraged to speak up in operational matters (had the *Torrey Canyon*'s chief officer been listened to, the disaster could have been avoided, just as could that of the *General C.*, had anyone had the courage to point out the proximity to shore); a more efficient and convenient arrangement of the pilothouse should be provided so that he could do more than one thing at a time (try monitoring radar while listening for another vessel's whistle); and his employers can free him from what has been called chronometer pressure—the time bind that demands a tight schedule and judges or rewards him accordingly. It is less expensive to miss a tide than cause a spill or lose a vessel. Also to be examined might be his traditional role of supreme authority; while he would still be responsible for his ship, there are decisions that might be made by the owners, such as when to sail and dock in hazardous weather or unsuitable conditions. His chief officer, as with airline co-pilots, might spell him in command responsibility both as a backup system and for experience. And fitness reports on masters might be written up by their junior officers.

An innovation more threatening, probably, comes under the heading of licensing, or license renewal—the master should be examined by psychological testing to determine his emotional fitness to command. Too many casualties found to be error on the part of the master have a look of aberration about them, and some suggest a more obvious possibility, particularly in the case of foreign flag vessels. Wine consumption on most of these vessels is as regular as the changing of watches at sea, and it is capable of inducing rather more euphoria. Masters, it has been said, should keep their spirits up, but their consumption down. Lastly, all masters sailing U.S. waters should be bound by and meet the requirements of Coast Guard licensing and regulations.

Tanker tonnage in 1969 increased by 14 percent, according to a Sun Oil survey, 101 vessels being new. The next year the number of new tankers was 213 and their average size was larger. Those now under construction are still larger, averaging 116,000 tons deadweight, and of these many are over 200,000. In 1971, tanker construction amounted to almost 25,000,000 tons, with seventy-two ships more than 100,000 DWT. There are several tankers now in service over 325,000 DWT, two 477,-000-tonners are under contract and at least one of 500,000 is projected. Some big thinkers of the tanker world claim that only one factor holds up design of a million-tonner—ports and dry docks. The industry claims that a smaller number of mammoths are safer than a multitude of the old 16,000-tonners, and there are design improvements which, if adopted, would reduce both the chances of casualty and the size of spills resulting. Aside from hull cracks, which almost all tankers are heir to and which can be remedied by "adding meat" either after launching or during surveys, new tankers can be accepted as inherently sea-worthy due to underwriters' and governmental requirements and inspections. Maintenance is generally adequate, but there is a tendency for aging vessels to break up in heavy seas. This problem might be overcome through more intensive checking for metal fatigue and care in ballasting and the taking on of cargo. As with us, metal comes and goes according to its vicissitudes, but eventually it keeps on going and with a tanker that's apt to mean down, way down.

Maneuverability and ease of control are areas that can stand much improvement in tanker design, and it is almost inconceivable that instruments of such huge destructive potential can be so helpless—even sailing vessels had more flexibility under way in turning and stopping. Becalmed, of course, they were helpless, but tankers can lose power, too. As a starter, thought might be given to requiring all tankers over 100,000 tons to be twin-screw, independently powered. This would provide both greater maneuverability and reliability, and directional bow thrusters would afford much more flexibility in docking, turning and stopping. It is inconceivable to many, even some in the world of shipping, that these giants of the sea need as much as four miles and perhaps fifteen minutes to stop in an emergency; after all, the victim they menace could be a sister ship. Among radical design innovations to be considered are variable pitch and directional propellors with 180-degree radius, submerged braking jets, retractable hull flaps, drogues (sea drags), and stern-mounted, vertical gravity panels.

"It's really weird up there on the bridge with all that time to brace yourself for collison," says a merchant marine midshipman. "I mean, with anything else you can slam the brakes on, or tramp down on it and get the hell out of there.

The amount of spill in a grounding or collision could be reduced if smaller tanks were used, however regressive it may be to think "small" in the tanker world. When today's tanks open up, it usually means a major spill—they are so large, one authority complains, they "can create their own thunderstorms." Smaller tanks, meaning fewer eggs in the basket (in docking, tanker hulls can seem as fragile as eggshells), should be installed as breakaways. Such a design would utilize a tanker's forebody to serve as a framework to carry cargo tanks, which serve now not only as containers but as hull. If they were double-bulk-headed, the space provided within could be used for ballasting or tank washings in service, and under salvage conditions they could be employed as reservoirs for compressed air to improve buoyancy. Another advantage of breakaway tanks would be the elimination of off-loading, usually performed under the most difficult and pollutionally hazardous conditions—why heat the cargo, pump it into receivers, then move it out, when the breakaway cargo tank could simply be released and towed away?

All these recommendations put the price of the vessel up, which puts the price of oil up. But many consumers complain not about the direct price they pay for the product, but the indirect price— the dollar cost due to import quotas and depletion allowances. The cost of quotas is estimated at $100 for each family of four annually, and that for depletion varies so much the figures are meaningless. As was observed in the early days of the allowance by an I. F. Stone admirer, "These aren't pennies from Heaven—they're dollars from our underground wealth which others are being paid to take from us, then process and sell back to us as theirs."

Tankers are going to get in trouble no matter how ingenious their design and no matter how diligent their navigation and watchkeeping (even if their bridges had deadman controls as used on locomotives so that the watch stander would be there, is he awake?). A tale, perhaps apocryphal, of an English Channel encounter between two vessels appears in *Oceanography International*:

> The only sign of life that could be observed aboard the Greek ship was a big, black dog. On seeing that collision was imminent, he began barking furiously. The barking brought a man in a boiler suit onto the bridge. He put the wheel over just in time to avoid collision, patted the dog and went below.

Once the tanker is in trouble—aground, in collision, afire, or drifting as a dead ship—it is usually in big trouble. The salvage world is not as limited by the traditional way of doing things as is tanker design, but what it does offer in imaginative thinking, such as filling a hull with styrofoam to raise it, it lacks in tools to work with. As with a fire, the plight of a vessel in a hazardous situation grows in seriousness as time passes, and so does the pollution risk. To appear on the scene quickly for most salvors is out of the question—days may go by, at the end of which not only is it apt to be too late for the vessel, now a DTL (declared total loss), but it may be too late for the area ecology too. A solution is to set up emergency salvage stations along the major tanker sea-lanes, maintained with trained crews and suitable equipment for salvage, spill containment and cleanups. The latter would include a self-propelled floating salvage base with suitable accommodations, machine tools and gear (an obsolete vessel, such as a Liberty or Victory ship, could be adapted), a pair of salvage tugs with beach gear, substantial towing equipment and derricks, a few heavy-duty lighters and seaworthy air tanks. Most important, of course, are receiving containers for the cargo, and while various plastic reservoirs are now being developed for this purpose, the air tanks could double as oil receivers. A more practical and larger container exists in the multitude of overage tankers now being scrapped, such as the Second World War T-2's. While they need not be self-propelled, they can be provided with enough boiler capacity to feed a wreck's cargo-heating coils, and they are cheap.

The major source of oil pollution of the sea is not the big spill—the tanker, offshore rig, or submerged pipeline—it is the product of daily operations in shipping, producing, refining, loading and discharging of oil and its refined elements. The oil terminal and refining spills are usually easily contained and prevented, since they are in protected waters, and with the stepped-up operations of the Coast Guard and U.S.G.S., offshore spills are no longer looked upon as a necessary evil of oil extraction. Tankers, together with oil barges, are the chief agents of ocean oil spills, but cargo is far from being the only oil spilled there. All modern vessels have the capacity for spilling some, even the atom-powered freighter *Savannah* (on which more was spent and less learned than with the *Manhattan*). She is equipped with oil-fired auxiliary boilers, and for all her modernity and grace of hull line, she is heir to a much overlooked contributor to pollution of the sea—bilges. This retainer of seepage, not only of sea water but lubricating oil and bunkers, is pumped over the hundred gallons, it can run heavy with oil. Instead, it could be put through a centrifuge and the separated oil content would be held in holding tanks for shoreside discharge, the water being permitted to rejoin the sea. Although industry sources claim that a bilge generates so little product it is ridiculous to consider containment, with the thousands of ships steaming night and day, the year round, the residue would fill even one of those half-million-tonners.

There are two sources of oil pollution that not even the tanker industry claims are minor, and both can be eliminated. The first is a by-product of ballasting vessels which have discharged cargo—their buoyancy is such that they simply are not seaworthy, being prone to capsizing and acting rather as a leaf blown at the will of the wind. A few tankers now have tanks for ballast only, but the normal practice is to flood the required cargo tanks with seawater, and on nearing port this ballast is discharged over the side. Oily residues go with it, however, and these are not inconsiderable—they can run as high as 2 percent of cargo. In part through Standard Oil of New Jersey's clean seas program, a load on top (LOT) technique was developed in which saltwater ballast, being heavier than oil, is allowed to settle. It is later pumped over the side until the level of oil is reached, and this residue is discharged into shore receivers. The system is not foolproof, though—sea conditions can agitate the levels so that they mix, and proper pumping requires a fine eye to know when to shut off and a quick hand to do it. In addition, some residues, particularly the more volatile and toxic elements of crude, may be carried over the side. While an improvement, LOT does not match the cleanliness of tanks used solely for ballast.

Tank cleaning at sea is the other preventable source of pollution, by limiting the chore to port duty and discharging the residues into shoreside reservoirs. A few tankers even have separators for use at sea, and the hope is that they will include bilge product in their processing. The company most likely to attempt such a program is Jersey Standard, being environmentally aware and concerned about public relations. So P.R.-minded are they that Mobil, a subsidiary, is currently advertising a philosophy of want instead of plenty: "Oil is precious. Let's not waste it." The copy mentions the use of "double bottom tankers—a Mobile development—as more protection against wasteful spills." Such a bottom does not offer much protection against high-energy strandings, in which a vessel grounds under way (as the casualties reported herein illustrate), and many a seasoned seafarer must smile at Mobil's claim for its development. Double bottoms have been around almost as long as oil has been used as bunkers (fuel), where the latter often is carried, and that predates the seafarers' first hearing of the word "ecology." Still, at today's prices, no one is going to deny that oil is precious—both to buy and to clean up.

A principal hazard faced by the more than 4,000 tankers in service is maritime traffic. The rate for the English Channel, supplied by Wesley Marx in his concise Sierra Club book *oilspill*, puts the traffic at 300,000 ships per year, running at right angles to 100 ferries a day, and adds that of the 30 ships per hour passing "through the Straits of Dover, radar indicates that 20 per cent of them disregard recommended traffic patterns." He goes on:

The type of seamanship tolerated in some maritime circles enhances collision probabilities. A recent example: two ships collided in the English Channel. The next day another ship steamed directly into their wreckage and sank, despite the wreckage having been well marked. A fourth ship then steamed into this wreckage, and it sank, too. Typical wreckage marking has been increased from one lightship and five buoys to two lightships and fourteen buoys, but this seems not to be enough.

One of the items considered by the U.N. Conference in Stockholm was the question of tanker routes, and it is hoped that both this question and other safety agreements affecting tanker operation can be worked out through Intergovernmental Maritime Consultive Organization meetings. However, I.M.C.O. agreements are merely resolutions, and as Captain Edward Oliver, U.S.C.G., an expert in marine operations and personnel licensing, asks in a recent issue of the U.S. Navy *Proceedings,* "Is the international maritime legal machinery too cumbersome to cope with the changing needs of the 20th Century?"

The answer, one hopes, is negative. The nations have been getting together lately more effectively on pollution agreements, seventy-five of them having agreed to certain standards designed to reduce the size of spills. These deal with tank size and arrangement, and another recent agreement governs the increase in compensation payment for oil-pollution damage caused by a ship. It has been doubled to $30,000,000 with total liability of $60,000,000, a figure that gets up into Union Oil damage levels, be it a *Torrey Canyon* or Problem Platform. The financing is provided by oil importers in the nations adhering, according to Reuters. Rear Admiral Halert C. Shepheard, U.S.C.G. (Ret.), of the American Merchant Marine Institute, who is deeply involved with I.M.C.O. affairs, writes in a letter of the numerous projects under way:

There is so much under consideration by IMCO regarding spill prevention, control and cleanup developments I just do not know where to begin. I am spending full time on the subject and am truly confused trying to keep up with the many projects under way.

Until that day when there won't be any operational spills by tankers, the Coast Guard will be busy trying to detect who is responsible for slicks and going through the motions of prosecuting them. It is felt that the most effective punitive action for domestic polluters may be public opprobrium through news media exposure, but that doesn't solve the detection problem. *The New York Times* estimates that spills run as high as 10,000 annually, meaning that visual sightings alone will take some doing. The question of which ship in a busy sea-lane is responsible will take even more, particularly since those polluting discharges that are deliberate usually take place at night, if for no other reason than surveillance is being practiced. Of the detection devices being tried, one, a microwave radiometer, is not unlike a radar-style sensor used for vessel-sighting in the dark—plane-borne at 2,000 feet, it can detect almost miniscule slicks. While both the oil industry and the Coast Guard are researching various methods of spill surveillance and detection, the largest number of projects is being funded by the E.P.A. Included are techniques such as utilization of carbon isotope ratios, polynuclear aromatics, chromatographic, infrared methodology, ultraviolet fluorescence emissions and aerial-mapping cameras in a multiband array.

"We anticipate it will take us about five years to get enough data so monitoring and surveillance networks can be developed," the Coast Guard Commandant, Admiral Chester Bender, said recently. "It is necessary to know first what to measure and where to place sensors before installing an extensive system for pollutants."

Federal regulations prohibit harmful discharges of oil that cause a film or sheen upon or discoloration of the water, which gives rise to some fine points on word meanings and film analyzing. As pointed out by a chemical engineer at E.P.A.'s Edison Water Quality Laboratory, Bernard Hornstein, the term "sheen" is defined as "an iridescent appearance on the surface of the water," and the legal criterion of "harmful" is being visible to the human eye unassisted by instrumental techniques." His investigations cover film thickness and establishment of levels of visibility, and laboratory experiments, along with use of 35-mm. color photography, and may lead to practical standards. In the opinion of some, as prosecution of polluters grows, there will be a lot of very busy expert witnesses.

One observer of the sea pollution scene, Cyrus Adler, president of Offshore/Sea Development Corporation of New York, is so little concerned by oil spills that he claims for them biological virtue. He points out in a letter to *The New York Times* that there isn't a U.S. port which can be used by 100,000 DWT tankers, or larger, and offers as a solution offshore terminals away from the littoral. He mentions that single-point moorings are not used off our shores, in part due to:

politicians, who fear that an SPM might spill some oil near their summer homes, and ill-informed environmentalists.

Oil spilled on the 98% of the ocean that is a relative biological desert can be beneficial, bacteria breaks down the oil droplets and zooplankton eat the products, which are nutrients. It is only in enclosed nearshore areas and estuaries that oil spills become deleterious.

This thinking fits in nicely with a theory that claims the only problem is to keep oil slicks from reaching such areas, which can be done by proper emulsifying. The followers of this approach avoid the high cost of emulsifying agents by recommending mechanical emulsifiers, both to break down spills and for tank washings and bilge-pumping product.

"This is the kind of reasoning which reminds me of the American Indian's trust in crude as a cure-all," says a zoologist. "If it didn't work, it was the medicine man's fault."

"Oil and biota do not mix," write Dr. Royal J. Nadeau and Thomas H. Roush of the Edison Laboratory, explaining that dead animals exhibit the acute and direct toxic effects of petrochemicals by suffocation, narcois and necrosis:

Death occurs when the organisms are coated by a layer of oil that interferes with their mechanisms for obtaining oxygen and the creatures die of suffocation.

In narcosis and necrosis, organisms may exhibit the narcotic effects of soluble oil fractions in the water column. These soluble components are absorbed into the tissues of the animals, directly killing or weakening them.

They go on to say that the chronic effects include the accumulation of compounds in the tissues of commercially important organisms and that this can lead to tainting, off flavors and human health hazards. Accumulation of chemicals from a sublethal concentration in the water can lead to a lethal concentration in the animal, which through behavioral changes can result in an adverse effect on a population of animals. While these scientists see the ultimate desirable fate of oil from a spill as a breakdown to carbon dioxide and water, they admit that some oil will enter the food chain as unmetabolized hydrocarbons. They have hope for bacterial seeding of oil spills with commercially prepared cultures to encourage the bacteria's growth as a means of effective cleanup, but warn that the cultures of oil-degrading bacteria may contain human pathogens, thereby presenting a health hazard.

This concern was echoed by Dr. Max Blumer, of the Woods Hole Oceanographic Institute, who was joined in a sensational assertion last February by Donald G. Comb, a former Harvard biochemist and presently a research director. They testified before a special Massachusetts Commission on Marine Boundaries and Resources in Boston which was holding hearings on projected East Coast offshore drilling.

"Many compounds in oil are carcinogenic (cancer-causing) and come to shore with an oil spill," Dr. Comb said, according to Karl Grossman in the *Long Island Press*.

"The link between petroleum and cancer is established," Dr. Blumer said, adding that the link between oil and cancer had been fully established by tests going back to the late fifties:

The results are indisputable—the carcinogens in oil were isolated and petroleum was shown in animal experiments to cause cancer. This is common chemical knowledge that pre-dates the present concern involving oil pollution, and when oil hydro-carbons are taken up by marine organisms and oil-contaminated seafood is eaten, the carcinogenic compounds can be transferred to man.

The persistence of oil seemed to worry Dr. Blumer almost as much as its toxicity, and he stated that oil from the 1969 Falmouth, Massachusetts, spill not only is still there, but it is decreasing at such a slow rate the area stands a good chance of being contaminated for forty years. He explained that oil is uncontrollable once spilled into the environment—since it is water-soluble it combines with the sea unless it is totally cleaned up on spilling, a task yet to be achieved. The carcinogens are present in both crude and refined products, he went on, and even the lumps of oil and finely dispersed elements which wash up on recreational beaches present a hazard because prolonged skin contact can absorb the carcinogenic agents. Sunbathers and swimmers, of course, lack the protection afforded refinery workers, who are clothed and gloved, and in some cases equipped with special protective designs and respirators. One critic of the Straughan study of the Problem Platform spill, whose testimony received applause at the hearing, was Dr. Norman K. Sanders, U.C.S.B. geologist. He commented, "I come from California with a message. Leave your oil where it is."

Industry representatives were present at the Boston hearings as "monitors to insure veracity" of testimony, but although invited to comment, none volunteered, according to Grossman. U.S. Representative Otis G. Pike (D., N.Y.), however, attacked the industry for its deleterious effect on the economic health of the citizen. He maintained that the House Ways and Means Committee is "loaded in favor of the industry," a new spoke in the wheel circling the inaction of Congress on environmental bills. He charged that the allegiance of Congressmen is gained through campaign contributions from the industry, which it can well afford thanks to the depreciation allowance. According to Grossman, Pike noted that the "average American laborer pays 20$ of his income for taxes," and that "Standard Oil of New Jersey with a net income of almost 2 1-2 billion dollars paid only 10.8$ per cent in 1970 taxes, Texaco with just over a billion only 6.4$ and Gulf, with earnings just under that figure, a mere 1.2%."

"The oil industry," Grossman quotes Pike as saying, "will argue very vehemently that there's nothing wrong with the oil depletion allowance. . . . There are some great inequities in our tax laws and just their fantastic size and wealth shows we give them too much allowance."

Conclusion 265

Pike also spoke of his efforts to have the import quota system abolished, saying that without it there would be no need for offshore operations, and that because of the artificial need it created, oil sold in the Northeast was at the highest prices in the country. Representative Les Aspin (D., Wis.) told the hearing that the policy was costing the U.S. consumer an "extra 46.5 billion a year." A spokesman for the American Petroleum Institute, Wilsone Laird, came out with a unique reason for retaining the import quotas: "We don't care what happens to the poor Arabs," Laird, who had headed Interior's Oil and Gas Division, said he joined the A.P.I. because "frankly, the money was better." He might be called an exemplar of what Representative Aspin classified as the "oil industry's truly remarkable public relations network," and is something of a switch on those in the U.S.G.S., which Dr. Sanders accused of being part of "a wholly owned subsidiary of the oil industry."

"All its people are oil people who go back to the industry after they're through," Grossman quotes Sanders as saying. "It's like having the fox watch over the chickens."

The methods used in the effort to hold up research drilling off Long Island and Massachusetts were based in part on the experience gathered from the Problem Platform fight, and many Santa Barbarans must have remembered Union President Hartley's suggestion of paying shore communities a royalty when the read Secretary Morton's suggestion of funneling some of the income from East Coast operations to the states.

"It's where we came in," said one, "and if Long Islanders stay with it, it's where maybe the oil boys will leave for easier pickings."

Surprisingly, the thought was followed by a suitable action a week later with the Independent Petroleum Association of America's announcement that it would try to get more money for crude to encourage oil exploration within the continental United States. Soon after, Hollis M. Dole, an Assistant Secretary of Interior, announced that a Deputy Assistant Secretary for Mineral Resources, Gene Morrell, would produce a report on the best way to encourage oil and gas exploration on federal lands. Areas where little exploratory drilling has been done include the eastern edge of the Rockies, the Denver Basin and Montana.

"All of which means that if we can control offshore drilling here, the encounter is going to shift west to the Forest Service and the Federal Parks system," says an East Coeast conservationist. "Tension, they say, is necessary to support life, oil to reduce friction, and hope to encourage it. With me, I just get plain tired."

This weary observer will not be encouraged by hearing that oil demand in 1970 increased by more than a billion barrels, the United States, the largest consumer, increasing its share by 4.2 percent, aceording to *Petroleum Press*. While threats of immediate natural gas shortages in the United States wouldn't encourage him either, a Morton statement to the effect that our supply of coal is sufficient for "hundreds of years" might, not that we are now geared primarily for coal use or the handling of its sulphur content. Even while he is worrying over what area of our national heritage is to be ravished in its extraction, the observer will remember that by the time this harvest is being reaped, coal operation will almost certainly be controlled by the oil companies with the best political connections. *New York* Magazine mentioned Union Oil in an article by Walter Pincus, "Silent Spenders in Politics—They Really Give at the Office." The article describes the difficulty the media have in getting information that should be available under the Corrupt Practices Act about corporate financing of political campaigns, and Union's employees are described as having contributed at least $100,000 in 1970 to Senate and House candidates through Union's Good Citizen Fund. Its Employees Bi-Partisan Political Fund permits deductions from paychecks, Pincus writes, making the workers see their contributions almost as one with other deductions to support the functions of government. The recipients may see it that way too—after all, to serve the taxpayer, they have to get elected.

The cheief concern of Long Island conservationists about their shores had been beach erosion, until rumors of oil interest in offshore areas about 30 miles at sea began to circulate. Exploration was said in mid-1971 to have been confined to seismographic tests and the findings to indicate the possibility of a major source of crude, similar to that found off Nova Scotia. Reaction was swift and as strong as it could be over what was still an undefined threat, and the rallying cry became "No Santa Barbara for us." Most Long Island antioilers were familiar with the battle put up by conservationists in Maine against the proposed Machiasport oil terminal, and they were aware of the contribution made by the press in alerting the area to the environmental hazards involved. Notable among these voices was that of a weekly, *The Main Times*, edited by a former Long Islander, John N. Cole, who did something in the way of preservation of Penobscot Bay as the *News-Press* tried to do for the Santa Barbara Channel. The victory at Machiasport, managed largely by putting such restrictions in the way of a terminal that the proposers were finally aghast at the problems to be solved, was not an easy one. The area is economically depressed, its main revenue being from a tourism that is seasonal, with fishing and a declining lobster industry making a contribution. How much influence was brought to bear by affluent summer residents on the bay's islands, such as Dark Harbor, is still unknown—they certainly had reason to feel threatened and some were in a position to do something about it behind the scenes. Among this select company are Rockefellers, whose advanced environmental thinking is said to have had its part in Standard Oil of New Jersey's early clean seas program, and the Dillons, of Dillon, Read. It is here that Union's cover operation, the Barracuda Corporation, owner of the *Torrey Canyon* and her sisters, was dreamed up by a partner, Peter Flanigan. He is described by *Time* Magazine as "thoroughly hard-nosed, very much Richard Nixon's no-nonsense subaltern."

"We learned a lot from Machiasport's struggle," says one Long Island conservationist, whose concern is primarily for the area's wetlands. "But whether we know enough yet to be able to pull off what Santa Barbara hasn't—determining the future of our enevironment—time will tell. If we don't make it, it won't be for want of trying or lack of clout—there's more oil money on our beachfronts than on those Penobscot islands."

Long Islanders are in a stronger position than the antioilers at Santa Barbara in that oil hasn't come yet, and unlike Maine, it is not suffering privation, economic or otherwise. Its economy on the eastern half, the area most threatened, is based largely on residential and recreational income with some commercial and shellfish operations. The majority view is that while oil is recognized as a necessary evil, the only amount welcome is that actually consumed. East Enders are content to let Nova Scotia produce it, saying "If that's what they want, they're welcome to it. Let them pump it, and we'll use it."

Nova Scotians do want to pump it, and it's easy to see why if one talks to the young at Sydney—there is such unemployment that the armed forces are looked upon as the way to live and the U.S. draft is regarded enviously.

"There's a hitch with our forces," explains a would-be recruit, who has twice failed to get into the army. "With us, a fellow has to be an effing genius to make it!"

The oil finds off Cape Breton Island are important ones, and while the industry is playing its cards close to its vest, the companies involved are happy. Prominent among them is Shell Canada, Ltd., currently doing exploratory drilling with the SEDCO H, an 18,000-DWT rig which with its auxiliaries cost almost $15,000,000. This semi-submersible drilling platform is a self-contained world, yet can be moved to the North Sea and be in operation in forty-five days. The thirty-five wells put down by late 1971 vary from 3,000 to 16,000 feet and the industry sees the rig as the ultimate in efficiency, flexibility and safety. Its fifty-two-man crew, who work twelve hours a day for seventeen days before being helicoptered to shore, are serious, highly professional and dedicated. They appear to take as much pride in the East Coast offshore manager, Chris Greentree, a relaxed, very able young Canadian, as he in them.

"We in the industry only want a chance to present our case," he says, with an engaging earnestness. "The record says it—one spill in 2,300 wells, and I'll stand on that."

Pollution concern is such that antispill procedures are practiced as if they were lifeboat drills, and shore facilities for control and cleanups are said to be highly organized and to provide the latest in techniques and equipment. From the standpoint of Long Islanders, however, even though the rig is as foolproof and fail-safe as the industry can make it, it is an exploratory rig and not a production unit—and it is with the latter that most spills occur. Now would any antioiler be reassured by the fact that in Nova Scotia the greatest advance in pollution control is viewed as the application of peat moss, a local product. It implies that a major spill wouldn't be handled with any more control than the *Torrey Canyon's*. Then, too, an antioiler might ask, if the rig is as safe as it appears, why are escape ladders mounted on the sides of the three enormous caissons which support the deck 145 feet above the water necessary?

"Well, we could say they're for painting and that with all our modern escape equipment we don't need them," explains a crew member. "But you might just want to haul ass faster than with the fastest gimmicks we got."

During the summer of 1971 the rumors of an offshore Long Island oil find grew, and by the time a conference at Montauk sponsored by the New York Ocean Science Laboratory was held, tensions were running high enough for that organization to be accused of fronting for the oil industry. This accusation was based on the meeting not being open to the public and its exclusion of an environmental organization, the Committee on Resource Management (CORM), the co-chairmen of which Thomas Macres, Jr., and Robert Howard, were denied admission. Ultimately, the Suffolk County legislature's chairman and now county executive, John V. N. Klein, threatened to boycott the session unless they were admitted. Both government and industry speakers, who made up the majority of the panel, employed a soft-sell approach in their efforts to reassure the public that the pollution and other hazards associated with offshore drilling and production were exaggerated. As a member of the audience observed, if the panelists didn't have identification cards in front of them, you couldn't tell one from the other. Once the meeting was opened to questions from the floor, attitudes hardened and the soft-sell approach was abandoned. Tension had risen by the time Klein said that he was more disturbed by the prospect of offshore operations now than he was before the meeting, and then he announced that he would instruct the "County Attorney to commence legal action against the Federal Government to block exploration drilling." Representative Norman F. Lent (R., N.Y.) announced his intention to introduce bills in Congress to establish marine sanctuaries in the waters over which the state of New York has jurisdiction and to increase drillers' liability in event of a spill to $100,000,000. The audience indicated a feeling that it would take more than that to stop the industry because, as one member put it, "If oil is there, that kind of money is only a drop in a bottomless bucket." As another said, on the basis of the A.P.I.'s estimate of better than 7 billion barrels of crude and 46,000,000 cubic feet of gas off the East Coast, that might well be.

A spokesman for the U.S.G.S, Robert Speer, said in mid-October that the target dates leading to leasing of offshore tracts were being "speeded up as much as possible" so that drilling could begin within five months after the issuance of an environmental impact statement. Congressman Lent reacted by calling the speedup "a blatant rush for the money" on the part of Interior.

"It now seems as if plundering the Atlantic has become a much higher priority," he said, according to the *Long Island Press*.

Secretary Morton denied that there was a speedup in progress, although in November the Newhouse News Service reported that he told the American Petroleum Institute (API) that the administration "will speed up leasing of additional acreage on the outer Continental Shelf." *The New York Times* editorialized its concern over East Coast offshore operations and Interior's dual role as promoter and regulator of oil production, saying that "the mighty oceans are in danger. . . . The seas themselves are now in need of sanctuary." East Coast antioilers began to be heartened as the list of officials on record against offshore operation grew steadily. On it were many Republicans such as New York Attorney General Lefkowitz, Senators Javits and Buckley, as well as Brooke of Massachusetts, Mathias of Maryland, in addition to numerous Democrats, including Kennedy of Massachusetts and Williams of New Jersey. Soon the backing was strong enough for Representative Lent to write Secretary Morton, supported by sixty-six members of the House, asking him to rescind the schedule change. Morton, it was said, was beginning to feel some antioil heat, as evidenced by his calling a conference with the governors of five East Coast states to reassure them on environmental issues and to bring them up to date on Interior's thinking.

"He can say it with one word," observed an antioiler familiar with the Santa Barbara blowout. "Drill."

East Coast antioilers took heart from the U.S. District Court decision granting a preliminary injunction halting the sale of leases in the Gulf of Mexico (since rescinded), and also from a suggestion by Senator Kennedy that instead of Interior undertaking the environmental impact study, it be done by the National Academy of Science (since ignored). In a meeting with Congressmen, Morton confirmed rumors that the most promising area was the Georges Bank Trough, which runs from a point about 100 miles off Cape Cod to almost 50 miles off Montauk. Reassuring the Congressmen about the consideration to be given environmental matters, Morton said, "We don't want to dirty up the East Coast. We don't want to see another Santa Barbara." Some antioilers regarded as a sop to public opinion Interior's having decided to make the impact study in conjunction with the National Oceanographic and Atmospheric Administration. In his meeting with the Eastern states governors and their representatives, Morton pledged that they would be consulted before a decision was reached permitting offshore drilling.

"We want to cooperate as closely as we can on such a sensitive issue, but there comes a point where the buck stops," he told them, according to the *Press*. "When that point comes I will take my recommendations to the President and his advisers."

The speaker of the New York Assembly, Perry B. Duryea, Jr., was so impressed by the hearings held in Boston that he decided to prepare a comprehensive plan for New York, and the possibilities of enacting legislation similar to that of Massachusetts designating waters 200 miles off its coast as state-controlled was under study. The federal government had already declared the law unconstitutional, but the commonwealth planned to fight all the way. The development was watched with interest by other states, an official of one calling the fight one "like to take a while." Attorney General Lefkowitz introduced a bill in the New York legislature which would prohibit drilling for either oil or gas in state coastal waters, and it was said to have influential backing.

The reference to Georges Bank by Morton led to new alarms, this time on the part of commercial fishermen, who were concerned about the prospect of spills killing off the marine life upon which fish feed. The industry was not inexperienced in protecting themselves, having already taken on Russian trawlers, sport fishermen and surf casters claiming a monopoly on striped bass. The Long Island Baymen's Association, strongly on record against offshore operations, had thought itself fairly well protected against its chief threat, illegal clamming and scalloping by the hordes "from away," who see no distinction between picking up an empty shell on the beach by hand or a full one from the bottom by rake.

"Some slickers got scared off by our pollution warning signs," says an East Ender, concerned for his seed oysters. "But sewage isn't going to worry fossil fuel operators."

Congressman Lester L. Wolff (D., N.Y.) in a letter to *The New York Times* wrote:

The Secretary [Morton] provided a detailed explanation of the energy crisis and did not, except for a few passing references, address the problem of environmental impact. While emphasizing the need for offshore development, Mr. Morton stated that he could not guarantee against a repeat of Santa Barbara. In fact, he stated, "We have learned from tragedies." We cannot afford to pay the price of another Santa Barbara to secure questionable added safeguards.

The sense of frustration at the lack of congressional action was reflected in the state legislature. New York's legislators felt that environmental protection was going to be up to them, and in mid-February a bill that would ban drilling within 3 miles of Long Island's shore was passed unanimously. This rare consensus was partly due, according to one Albany veteran, to the fact that no member of the Assembly wanted to be charged as a holdout in an election year—they had all registered both the popular feeling and the slurs being hurled at their congressional opposite numbers because of alleged obligations to the oil industry.

The three largest environmental groups in the United States, the Sierra Club, National Wildlife Federation and National Audubon Society, in a letter to Morton asked for postponement of Atlantic Coast leasing and for preparation of a national energy policy. The letter, no less strong for being open, stressed that while Morton had conferred with industry and political leaders, environmentalists were yet to be consulted. It went on to experss concern at the approach to the problem of supplying energy needs, to some extent echoing industry's frequent warnings of shortages.

This nation cannot continue, willy-nilly, to sell off and exploit and waste its fossil fuel and other energy resources on the basis of industrial opportunism and without an intelligent plan for the future. A national energy policy must be formulated and put into effect . . . in a manner calculated not to deprive future generations of a decent standard of living and not to leave our nation helpless to defend itself.

A couple of political leaders of New York and Connecticut, Assembly Speakers Duryea and William R. Ratchford, got together in rare state concord to propose a bistate agency to combat the possibility of offshore operations. Named to it were officeholders responsive to their constituents' environmental anxieties, who would oversee its functions of surveillance, coordination and the sponsoring and drafting of legislation. Observers predicted that with time its functions would broaden to include pollution problems common to both states, with quite possibly the addition of other state legislative bodies to form a strong coastal organization.

"What makes this possible," said a commentator, "is the recognition that when Uncle Sam and oil money get together, the environmental controls belong to the state capitols."

Congressman Lent attacked Interior for what Karl Grossman in the *Long Island Press* quotes him as calling the Department's "relegating to miniscule roles all energy sources but oil." The Congressman referred to a report by Interior's Bureau of Mines dealing with a process for converting solid waste to "low sulphur oil potentially suitable for use by power plants for conversion to use as gasoline or Diesel fuel." Interior ignored the Bureau findings, Lent charged, saying, according to Grossman, that "a billion tons of waste could yield a billion barrels of oil." At least some of those who read his statement agreed that since Long Island's beaches already suffered from city-folk pollution, it would be a nice bit of justice if they were to be saved from that of oil by the city's waste.

"Waste," pleaded one, "make haste."

That the coastal states were beginning to feel their own strength was illustrated by a proposal of New York State Senator Bernard C. Smith, who called on them to join in an embargo on any oil produced off their shorelines. Other senators agreed that if industry and Interior went ahead with their leasing program, they would "arrange to make sure that they can't bring any oil in." Interior's William Pecora, whose promotion to Under Secretary of the department from his directorship of the U.S.G.S. some said was in recognition for his firmness with the Santa "Barbarians," was quoted by Grossman as saying that talk of oil drilling "along the coast of New England is a fantasy willfully generated by some people suffering from petro-phobia." The ailment was described by wits in one state house as being not unlike "petro-fiscalisis, a contagion invariably caught by those who confuse size of money with quality of life." One who didn't pick up the sickness was Speaker Duryea. A Montauk lobster wholesaler whose father, a political power, had been a gravel-mining conservation commissioner during Prohibition's rum-running days, Duryea called for the leaders of all East Coast states to set up a coalition outlawing offshore operations, including the dumping at sea of garbage and sewage. It was thought by those East Enders familiar with the diet of lobsters to be "right self-sacrificing."

Dick Seelmeyer, of Newhouse News Service, closed out the month of February with a quotation from Gene P. Morrell, Interior's gas and oil division director and a former member of the petrochemical industry. As he addressed the International Association of Drilling Contractors, some of his lines made Seelmeyer's readers wonder if Morrell and Morton worked for the same Department of Interior. Said Morrell, "I know that we must explore the OCS (outer continental shelf) of the East Coast so that if oil or gas are there, and indications are that they may be, we can develop and produce these resources," in spite of Morton's having said there were no plans for same. According to Seelmeyer, Morrell went on to predict that oil will be outmoded as a fuel by the end of the century, adding that only 31 percent of the in-place oil has been pumped, leaving a reserve of 59 percent in already drilled wells.

At the beginning of March, the beaches of Fire Island and Westhampton, among others, were assaulted by crude oil, presumably from a tanker well out to sea. There was enough of it so that the cleanup was still being pushed two weeks later, and in time for those who had witnessed the difficulty with which it was being conducted to be greeted by a Corps of Engineers survey of possible Long Island mooring sites for supertankers of the size rightly called mammoths. One feasible location, it appeared, was near the juncture of Long Island Sound and the Atlantic off Montauk, where there is the 100 feet of water needed for the sea giants. The prospect and its implications were so startling that immediate reaction from area leaders was not forthcoming, but one can say that such a seaport is not what the late Carl Fisher had in mind when he dreamed of Montauk being the American terminus for transatlantic voyagers. His plan was for the passengers on ocean liners to go on to New York City by rail (a choice they wouldn't jump at if they had to use today's service), or even by dirigibles moored to Montauk's skyscraper, an eight-story edifice largely populated by real estate salesmen. His port was intended primarily to serve genteel people, not crude oil. Use by the latter, observes an elderly resident, would be enough to make "that old grand-manner developer turn over in his grave. But then, if he's been watching Montauk, he must be used to it."

So far had those politicos opposed to offshore operation come in their thinking that elected representatives of New York, Massachusetts, Connecticut and Rhode Island met at Albany in early March to map procedures designed to halt plans for the leasing of drilling rights, and further, for Connecticut and New York to discuss the Long Island Sound problems they have in common. This body of water, though both states front on it, has never been considered jointly before, and it marked a long step in interstate marine cooperation. The group considers themselves an extension of the newly formed bistate Committee on

Coastal Resources and will concentrate on such action matters as public hearings, antidrilling lawsuits and legislation. Planned was a visit to Washington to impress members of Congress and the White House with the coastal states' determination to defer leasing until more is known about both the environmental hazards and foolproof techniques of spill prevention and slick control. The need for an offshore sanctuary was again advanced and it was agreed that so unique is the nature of this coast with its estuaries, wetlands and fisheries which provide half the world's supply, even a small spill could be disastrous.

"Offshore drilling," said Suffolk County Executive John V. N. Klein, according to Grossman in the *Long Island Press*, "is the greatest single environmental threat in the entire history of the East Coast from Maine to Florida. Just think what a federation of all the involved states banded together could accomplish."

Although the committee stressed that time was of the essence, it began to look as if that element, at least, they would not be short on. According to *Newsday*'s Tom Incantalupo, Orme Lewis, Interior Deputy Assistant Secretary for public land management, put the leasing of drilling rights five years away. Lewis blamed the delay on the court-ordered cancellation of the sale of Louisiana drilling rights as a result of the suit brought by thirteen Atlantic states for jurisdiction in the waters off them up to 90 miles, and "opposition by politicians and conservationists, especially on Long Island and in Massachusetts." The result, Lewis explained, is that impact statements for the Gulf Coast area would be prepared first, since it has already been examined and developed, and "there is less public opposition." Antioilers' reaction to the delay was for the most part a delighted "what have we wrought?" response, but there were those ready with a fast answer. It was "only time."

An issue appeared that would make their Santa Barbara brothers feel right at home. Nassau County Executive and Environmental Council Chairman Ralph G. Caso raised the earthquake-drilling menace threat at a New York State legislative hearing at Mineola, Long Island, saying that the strain of drilling on fault lines, which are present on the continental shelf, presented a danger far more serious than spills. Interior's U.S.G.S. representatives, old hands at answering such fears with respect to the San Andreas fault, made no response this time—they were not present. Council members described Interior's refusal to be represented as "insulting," and while the oil industry was present in the form of "truth monitors," they refused to comment on the testimony. There was an industry-written statement, though, which is more than Interior offered. It said that offshore operations could be conducted in such a way that there would be "virtually no environmental disturbance," a guarantee no other group had ever made.

Rollin M. Huyler, co-chairman of the Environmental Management Council, referred to studies by the National Oceanographic and Atmosphere Administration, which have established that there has been a lowering of the Gulf of Mexico's floor due to oil extraction. He was concerned that such a condition would result from any possible East Coast operations. Such a straining of fault lines would include the one in Long Island Sound, which extends from the Atlantic to Connecticut. Those who heard this warning wore somber looks, particularly when Hulyer said that his views were supported by both geologists and marine experts. If there were any in the room equipped to comment, they were silent—they were up against quake facts, an area so little considered by Easterners, it gets a "Who, us?" reaction. Chairman Wayne Aspinwall (D., Colo.) of the House Interior and Insular Affairs Committee called for hearings to explore once and for all the total available information and points of view relative to oil operations, so that misinformation can be discarded and the facts assembled in such a way that they are intelligible to the citizen. It is a laudable ambition that, if realized, will make history on Capitol Hill, East Coast beaches, Alaskan tundra and the Channel Islands.

"Amen," said a writer, who until the *Torrey Canyon* disaster was able to keep up on the literature pertaining.

Such a study is not apt to be entirely reassuring, but an example of improvement in drilling safety controls is illustrated by a design known as a surface-controlled subsurface safety valve. While these devices are not new, the particular sophistication of this model is, as is the price. Their function is to close the well automatically when unusual pressure or heat is sensed, somewhat as do conventional storm chokes (spring-loaded valves in the well casing). The new design can be operated manually from the platform and checked periodically, and it is about as foolproof as a valve can be. Yet, a valve can and sometimes does jam, as happened during one of the Problem Platform crises. So, the art has come a long way on the safety journey, yet it is clear that there can still be detours and that the end of the trip—complete safety—by the very nature of matter is unattainable. Progress will be facilitated now that the U.S.G.S. has more inspectors and their own helicopters, and no longer alert drill rigs of imminent inspection by asking for permission and transport. A small advance, but not the less for being overdue.

The best medicine for a spill is, of course, prevention. That having failed, the best way to handle a slick is to get rid of it. Except in fairly still water, such as harbors and estuaries, oil is best collected for removal by containing or corralling it. For this purpose booms are used, although there is a new technique utilizing air bubbles, and in certain applications forced air or marine propeller wash has been employed. Containment is not a serious problem in protected waterways, even with a current up to 2 knots. There are now over forty commercial products available, varying greatly in ease of handling, effectiveness and cost (the Headrick boom used at the Problem Platform now runs $35,000 per 1,000-foot section). In principle, boom construction and operation are fairly simple—they consist of floats or air flotation devices to support secured barriers designed to prevent oil going over or under a desired line. Wave action of over 3 feet raises problems largely unsolved, and while one thinks of oil as stilling the sea, conditions at the site of most tanker strandings suggest that a major spill is one time when, paradoxically, there's never enough oil available to aid the device designed to contain it.

"It isn't that oil has a mind of its own," says an observer of many spills. "It's as mindless as those who spill it. The trouble is the stuff just won't cooperate."

Names given to commercial booms run on the cute side, though whether intended as a marketing gimmick or a symbol of desperation on the part of those who have witnessed the plight of oil-soaked wildlife is unknown—Aqua Fence, Boom Kit,

Elo-Boom, Flexy Oil Boom, Flo-Fence, Spillguard, Seawall, Sea Curtain, Sea Fence, Sea Skirt, Slickbar, and the most elegant, English China Clay. The Coast Guard's research program is particularly interested in devices that are air-transportable and easily assembled—there is a problem with designs such as the Navy-Merritt model, which is best assembled with air tools, a sizable gang and power cranes. The Coast Guard and E.P.A. are funding and testing a wide range of devices to collect the oil once it is contained, under classifications best described as scoop, suck and slurp.

While there are over 200 products designed to disperse oil, most have some undesirable side effects. Except in areas such as oil terminals already so polluted that no life remains, dispersal itself is frowned on—the wider the area oil covers, the more harm it can do and the harder it is to collect. In harbor areas care must be taken not to contaminate the water supply with dispersants, and when used on beaches, they have been found to have the same effect they do on wildlife—more harm than good. Not only are beaches turned into quicksands, erosion by wave action is encouraged and the toxicity rate rises. Oil, as has often been said, is alien to the environment, and its removal requires on its taking, not its sending.

In its uncooperative way, oil spilled on the sea is not amenable to burning except in refined states, and even then, aeration makes it lose volatility fairly rapidly. Crude needs an agent to begin and support ignition, and while many have been tried, as demonstrated in the attempts to ignite the *Torrey Canyon*'s cargo, to date no generally satisfactory agent has been found. In the case of those that do work, not the least of the problems are the hazards to those who are performing the operation. Burning oil on the sea in the vicinity of a natural gas source, such as a drilling rig, is chancy, and that applies to vapor-filled tankers also. Then there is the problem of chemical changes which take place with oxidation, and the residue is not necessarily benign to marine organisms. In a mildly successful experiment with a substance called Sea Beads, a U.S. destroyer's side was scorched, to the disgust of its skipper, who didn't fail to observe that the slick itself came through pretty well. Another product which has had considerable success on still-water spills is Cabosil.

Research is currently under way in the development of gelling agents, both to be applied to spills in order to absorb and congeal oil for easier handling, and to slow the flow from tankers with leaking tanks. A few of the problems already encountered include cost—one product runs $3 per gallon on a 1:1 spill ratio. Industry sources have even raised the question of whether crude once gelled is salvageable, a rather surprising thought in the face of the urgency of spill control and the fact that cleanups have run as high as $2.50 a gallon. Regulation suction pumps capable of handling crude are not up to the gelled substance, and as yet a portable, flexible pump that is has not appeared on the market. When it does, predicts a ship's engineer, it will probably carry a name as unseafaring as Gellopump, or as unbusinesslike as the new Mop-Cat. This is a self-propelled rig on a catamaran hull which picks up spills with a rotating drum from which the oil is squeezed, containing, it is said, less than 10 percent water. The rig can be operated by one man, its water-jet propulsion making it highly maneuverable in calm seas. In the open seas, experts assume that it would be both inefficient and unseaworthy, conditions that limit most of the collection types, including a design by an aircraft manufacturer that depends on a rotating drum with perforated vanes. These are connected to internal discs from which the oil is scraped by wiper blades. The American Petroleum Institute has funded an air-transportable barge intended for seas up to 8 feet on which is mounted equipment for centrifugally separating oil-and-water mixes. One problem, common to all vacuum equipment, is maintaining suction in a seaway, and while flotation rigs for the suction heads have been tried, success is thought to be in the quite distant future. Problems common to all oil-collection devices, both in protected areas and in the open sea, are keeping the water ratio within bounds and overcoming the menace of debris.

Sorbents are one of the greatest aids to collection of spilled oil, and a prime requisite is that they should float under all conditions. Those of natural ingredients are numerous and the choice depends on local availability and efficiency—materials tried extend from vegative products, such as ground bark, through mineral sources, including fuller's earth, to products of animal origin, such as leather by-products and feathers. While none of the available products possesses all the desired characteristics, many offer the requirement of being oleophyllic (more attractive to oil than water), high-capacity, oil-retentive and low-cost. Of the last, it can be said that the major cost lies in handling and applying, not the basic material acquisition. Manufactured sorbents, such as those made from plastic materials, are being used with increasing frequency. Generally, they are non-toxic, but as they absorb oil, their weight increases. Collection is heavy work, and those who have been so employed say that the dairyman's fork-handled product is far easier to cope with.

The Coast Guard is progressing with experimentation on various devices to facilitate the off-loading of stranded tankers based on air delivery for rapid on-site operations, known as ADAPTS (Air Delivery Anti-Pollution Transfer System). This consists of 500-ton-capacity collapsible plastic bags delivered by plane, with needed equipment, such as pumps and hose, lowered by helicopters. On being filled, the bags are towed to a receiving source. The problems unsolved include what to do about the newer mammoth tankers when the projected operational unit consists of only forty bags, being a mere 20,000 tons. It is possible, of course that even the 20,000 tons off-loaded might make it feasible to work her off the ground holding her, but most mariners are appalled at what can happen to the bottom of one of these giants in a high-energy stranding. Eventually, bigger-thinking techniques and equipment can be devised, but at the moment it looks like an awful lot of cargo to salvage by bag.

As with oil on the sea, beaches polluted by oil are best treated by its removal, unless the do-nothing-but-wait-for-time-to-do-it practice is employed. Oil, this school of thought argues, will disappear eventually (while old age overtakes those who are waiting to use the beach). It is true that blowing sand will cover the oil, but it will still be there. The chemical approach no longer has official sanction, as stated by the E.P.A.'s Howard J. Lamp'l: "We firmly believe that the use of dispersants, emulsifiers and other chemicals is entirely unjustified in the cleanup of oil-polluted beaches."

While there are various special machines being developed for beach cleanup use, much depends on both the nature of the beach and the type of oil polluting it. In general, the philosophy is to remove as little sand as possible, and for this hand labor is often desirable, however undesirable. Cold water can be applied to the oil if it is not sufficiently weathered to make it more viscous, and in cases where the spill is of a light oil, such as diesel fuel, penetration makes it difficult to collect. Here a disc-type harrow can be used to turn over the mix to promote aeration, but the evaporation takes time. For the heavier oils, motorized elevating scrapers, a member of the earthmoving family, have been used with fair success, once the operator gets used to a feather touch on the cutting controls. Motor graders have also been tried, but they require high flotation tires, and unless half-tracks are installed, must be all wheel drive. Similarly driven front-loaders could be used if snowplows were adapted to the bucket and depth of cut is controlled. Tracked machines, such as bulldozers, are not advisable since the cut tends to be too deep and their compaction factor is high. There are various designs for polluted beach sand being tried out currently, one being based on the principle of heating the oiled sands so that the oil can be drawn off. Another relies on a screening technique, and a third on boiling the sand to remove the oil. The most unlikely, and possibly hazardous, design appears to be that of employing fixed flamethrowers on a vehicle to burn off the oil.

There will be time to research a far larger number of techniques than now under consideration before we run out of oil for demonstration. Current estimates put the oil spill total at 7,100,000 tons a year, and the fact that tankers account for over one-third of this can be illustrated by the history of near disasters during a three-day seminar at the Edison Water Laboratory in January, 1972. On the first day antipollution forces were alerted that a tanker at Port Jefferson had broken in half; the second, that a pair of tankers had a light collision at Philadelphia (known as a brush); and on the third, that a Japanese tanker said to be under command of her chief officer (the master having died at sea), grounded off the Jersey coast. Undersea explorer Jacques Cousteau estimates that the vitality of the sea in terms of flora and fauna has declined as much as 50 percent in the last ten years, and another marine explorer, Jacques Piccard, warns that unless measures are taken, the oceans will be dead by the end of the century.

The United States alone is said to contribute up to one-half of all industrial pollutants to ocean waters, according to Professor Edward D. Goldberg of Scripps Institution of Oceanography, and yet federal officials in mid-March of 1972 announced that the prohibition against the dumping of sewage sludge in the Atlantic was being relaxed. The reason? As a result of the government's effort to clean up the nation's water, there are now so many sewage-treatment plants that there is no place to put the sludge except in the ocean, where in the New York Bight, off Sandy Hook, it has been dumped for years. It is known locally as the dead sea, and the product of both river and harbor maintenance dredging is fast reducing other areas to the same condition. Such a decision by the pollution watchdog, E.P.A., makes the oil industry appear almost as environmentally responsible as the antioilers.

The chief sufferers from oil pollution and the most obvious are waterfowl. It is due to the pity the deaths of thousands of them, portrayed by the media, inspired that the public first became concerned about the ecology. The prospects for oil-soaked birds are looking up, but there is a limitation. Once a bird has ingested oil, which occurs with preening in the attempt to clean its feathers, there is no antidote, or at least not one that can raise the survival rate above the present 2 percent. Hope of treatment of oiled feathers, however, has been provided by a California veterinarian, Dr. James L Naviaux, a founder and director of the National Wildlife Health Foundation. Dr. Naviaux, working under a small Standard Oil of California grant, has come up with a therapeutic approach likely, he thinks, to save 75 percent of those birds suffering from oil-saturated feather covering. Originally, he explained, in treating the victims of the San Francisco collision between two Standard tankers, care was taken to leave intact the natural oils and waxes on the feathers, so that the victims could contend with water and cold. After much experimentation and with the assistance of others, Dr. Naviaux discovered that isoparaffin 150, an agent used in lighter fluid, can be applied to remove the oil from feathers, leaving them in a condition apparently oil-free yet able to repel water. How this is accomplished is not yet understood, but out of fifty ducks recently found suffering from oil exposure in a small spill, thirty-nine of them survived after isoparaffin treatment. Two cleanings were necessary to insure that all the oil was removed, and the birds were kept under surveillance for only two days. Of the eleven fatalities, six were autopsied and found to have ingested large amounts of oil.

The problem of what is to be done with obvious cases of oil ingestion has no easy answers. Perhaps, the hardest one for the handlers may be the easiest for the birds, and it is a grim commentary on the present pollution bind. To arrive at its answer, the San Francisco ASPCA publication *Our Animals* asks if in view of the low recovery rate, it is in the interest of the birds to attempt treatment. Its answer would also apply to the victims who suffer from oil ingestion.

"At the present level of ability to treat oil-soaked birds, there might be far less suffering if all such birds were humanely euthanized at once."

This somber view notwithstanding, Interior's assistant secretary for mineral resources, Hollis M. Dole, says that environmentalists have overreacted to oil spills. He told a Senate Interior subcommittee that since "small leaks and spills offshore have been cut in half, there is no need to sacrifice environmental quality while expanding outer continental shelf explorations." He didn't explain that pollution stems not from exploration but production, but he did say that oil tankers contribute 20 percent of the world's total oil pollution, while offshore drilling's share is only 2 percent. This, to his thinking, justifies the expansion of offshore production instead of increased imports via tanker, even if it overlooks the pollution risk offered by those projected forty tankers to bring home the Prudhoe Bay crude. Interior's thinking, it has been suggested, may see Alaskan oil as less likely to spill than that from foreign sources because it's ours; you just can't trust those foreigners.

The House Interior committee heard much about the energy crisis in 1972 and, in addition, was able to get an idea of the number of interested governmental groups. Interior Secretary Morton explained that over sixty departments and agencies have provided advice, "often conflicting." A good example is that while he predicted that by 1985 we will have to import half our oil requirements, an undersecretary of State, John N. Irwin, warned that this would be the case by 1980:

"Production of oil in the U.S. will be about 12 million barrels per day," he said, "including some 2 million barrels per day from the North Slope of Alaska. Demand is projected to rise from the current level of 16 million barrels per day to 24 million by 1980."

The Atomic Energy Commission's Chairman, James R. Schlesinger, could also be counted on by Morton to provide conflicting advice and, for that matter, conflicting figures; he puts the percentage of oil imports by 1980 at 60 percent. Warning that the U.S. must abandon such dependence, he points out that a tanker will have to arrive in a U.S. port every hour of every day and says that "there is widespread agreement regarding the net environmental advantages from properly operated nuclear generating facilities in relation to fossil fuel facilities."

Use of the word fossil in connection with nuclear power does not reassure those who like to assess the horrors of nuclear spills, and who worry about thermal pollution. Philip Herrera, as knowledgeable and readable an environmental expert as there is around, points out in his book *Energy* (with John Holdren), that thermal pollution is a problem that is not unsolvable. As to the danger of radiation, he quotes nuclear power adherents with a line not apt to please another industry. "The average American is annually exposed to more radiation from sitting in front of his TV set than from a nuclear plant."

Those who were jobless in the Depression years see in Assistant Secretary Dole's dire warnings a reminder of a practice of the same name, the dole. Dole, an alert strategist, picks on the American's love affair with his car as a telling threat, saying that "there are unmistakable signs that even gasoline—which most people take for granted just as much as the air they breathe—might be in tight supply." Saying that we face "trouble, trouble, trouble" with all forms of energy, he points out that there might be 19 billion barrels of oil and almost 50 trillion cubic feet of gas along the Atlantic coastal plain, and that it "has almost no production of its own." The possibility of self production is enough to make residents on that coast reflect on a return to some alternative sources of power and locomotion—windmills and feet. Sources of heat would present a more difficult problem, but then there is a dividend in that old Vermont saying, "Cut your own wood and it will warm you twice."

There is a suspicion that the energy crisis is being used as a device by the petrochemical industry to push offshore development; both the government and utilities have been sold that the only way to be sure we don't run out of oil before alternative power sources are developed is to get at the outer continental shelf (OCS) while the getting is good. Doubt is increased by voices such as Ralph Nader's claiming that we do not face an energy crisis and that "the oil companies are misleading America." The Columbia Gas System, Inc., in a full page ad warns that "the energy crisis is threatening your way of life." Con Ed begs us "to save a watt" (less, it is said, because of an impending fuel shortage than the inability of its plants and distribution systems to meet peak demands), and Mobil advises that "Oil is precious—let's not waste it." Unlike some utilities, which advise "notifying your Congressman of your concern" (presumably to encourage him to vote for a more relaxed environmental control system on natural resources), Mobil passes along some tips on how to use petroleum products more efficiently. They tell us they are doing this on their end, concluding that "Between us, we can do our best to make the oil last longer." Indeed, the matter of an energy scarcity is taken seriously enough for the Ford Foundation to allocate a $2,000,000 fund for an "overview," a spokesman saying that present energy policies are "contradictory and outmoded." Among the more intriguing areas of investigation scheduled are whether Federal controls related to the environment, leasing and pricing combine to create a gas shortage, the effect on foreign relations of increased imports, and if the Government is getting adequate returns on the resources it leases.

Americans, according to *Time* magazine, use six times as much electric power as the world average per capita, and the demand for energy is doubling every fifteen years. It goes on to say that no one knows for sure how much time remains before we run out, but quotes M. King Hubert, of the U.S.G.S., who predicts that 90 percent of all oil and gas will be gone by the year 2035, and about 90 percent of all coal by 2300. At present, says the *Time* study, 40 percent of our power production goes to industry, 22 percent to commercial uses and 34 percent to residential uses. For the present, however, the problem is not so much running out of energy as running out of clean energy, and this is causing severe difficulties for the utilities. A Rockefeller family advisor warns that if "you sabotage power, you sabotage the future," yet to those utilities which plan on "going nuclear" to solve their supply problems, oil rich Alaska's Senator Mike Gavel says an accidental atomic explosion is "the ultimate pollutant."

One of the few Government figures who speak of approaching the energy problem by cutting consumption is that of the Chairman of the White House Council on Environmental Quality, Russell Train. He goes at some length into how to make better use of the power we have, even if he doesn't dwell on rethinking our life styles as consumers. At least he is not one of those who predict that the steadily expanding cost of power presents its own solution—the less we can afford, the less we will use. A biologist of note, Barry Commoner, rejects such thinking, saying, "Any effort to find a solution to the power crisis is certain to engage at the deepest level the nation's concept of social justice." It is also certain, as *Times* makes clear, to make demands upon those habituated to waste, adding that these are small sacrifices when, as Maurice Chevalier said of old age, "you consider the alternatives."

In his statement before the Senate Committee on Interior and Insular Affairs, the Sierra Club's Carleton E. DeTar claimed that our oil import restrictions cost us 5 billion dollars annually, obliging us to resort to environmentally hazardous sources, such as the Alaskan reserves and the OCS. He recalls that in February 1970, a cabinet-level task force appointed by President Nixon concluded that "the fixed quota limitations that have been in effect for the past 10 years bear no reasonable relation to current requirements for protection either of the national economy, or of essential oil consumption." He concluded by saying that since the report has been ignored, an alternative is to reduce our consumption and that this can be done by as much as 40 percent per capita by cutting out waste.

While this figure may seem an exaggeration, we have only to remember that electric home heating (still being promoted), uses almost twice as much fuel as oil heating. A quarter of our energy goes into transportation, with the efficiency of the Detroit product going down as those touted antipollution options are added. The aluminum industry is the largest product devourer of electricity, suggesting a return to at least some of the materials it replaced. (Tin cans are not pretty to contemplate as they rust away, but they degrade faster than their aluminum cousins.)

Natural gas, once regarded as a nuisance to be burned off, has become increasingly popular and this relatively pollutant-free and efficient energy source now supplies almost a third of our needs. As its use has grown so has its price, which is regulated by the Federal Power Commission. The FPC has been under considerable pressure to permit an increase in the rate lately, and not only from industry sources. Secretary Morton has urged an increase as a means to attract needed capital for production and distribution expansion, and also to retard the upsurge in demand.

"In terms of the entire American ethic, the price of energy has been entirely too cheap," he warned, adding that a higher fuel cost is the most effective form of conservation of our supplies.

In twenty years our gas consumption has tripled to 1970's figure of 23 trillion cubic feet, which is 5 trillion more than was discovered. The industry maintains that it can't explore for new reserves at current prices, so that we now face not only a natural shortage but a production shortage. It is hard to arrive at a relia- ble figure of how much gas is underground, since proved re- serves have a direct relation to price (as the rate goes up, so does exploration), and, as with the oil industry, the government is dependent on the producers for information. Much thought has been given to improved methods of getting at the gas, the most controversial suggestion being nuclear underground blast- ing. Gas produced by this method is slightly radioactive, but what worries environmentalists even more is the effect of seismic shock and possible contamination of ground water. A test shot is projected at a site about 50 miles north of Grand Junction, Colo., and while the few residents of the area are not too concerned about a single blast a mile or so below ground, they aren't anxious to have it become a habit. *The Wall Street Journal* quotes a rancher as saying, "I don't mind a single shot, but if they knock the house down 200 times, that gets kind of old."

Importation of natural gas currently uses an approach almost as radical as nuclear mining. The temperature of the gas is reduced until it becomes a liquid (at −259 F.), and this liquified natural gas (LNG) needs only about 1/600 of the space required in its natural state. The result is that an LNG tanker equivalent in size to a 200,000 DWT oil carrier can take on almost 4 billion cubic feet of LNG and, through the use of highly sophisticated refrigeration equipment, can keep the cargo at the required temperature until its discharge ashore. There are some unknowns, of course—steel becomes brittle at low temperatures, and for all the insulation and safeguards aboard, what will happen if the ship breaks up? At the least, the resultant fire could be catastrophic, and while there are doubts that it would necessarily be accompanied by an explosion, there is the possibility of a release of LNG forming what could become a fire cloud as vaporization takes place. The Coast Guard classifies it as a hazardous material and will regulate construction and design of LNG tankers in this country, for which invitations to bid are in preparation. The tanks require very precise welding, and our experience in aerospace programs with cryogenic equipment will give us an edge over foreign shipbuilders, notably France and Norway, which have had a near monopoly in the construction of LNG tankers. The edge will not be so great, however, that our yards can dispense with their subsidy; the builder will receive the difference between the lowest cost available abroad and the actual price here, estimated at 30 percent. As has been noted often enough, this American way of doing business, however curious, confirms that pollution is not the only cost of affluence; it's expensive to be rich.

In politics it is expedient to look ahead, and this the Nixon administration did in May, as noted by Bert Schorr in *The Wall Street Journal*: "The administration is anxious to assure plentiful heating oil supplies at the start of the winter heating season, which coincides with Election Day in Northern parts of the country." Schorr predicted an increase in oil import of as much as 30 percent, a major relazation of the oil import quota that, luckily for the consumer, will not be accompanied by projected legislation requiring that U.S. flag vessels carry half of all imported crude. The proposal, designed to alleviate the distress of our merchant marine, was rejected by the Senate in spite of intensive lobbying. At present only about 5 percent of oil imports are carried in our vessels and this figure is not apt to change unless our costs come closer to those of foreign operators. If the bill had become law, the transportation costs could have been increased by as much as 1 billion dollars, and as Schorr quotes one Congressman as saying, "Anyone who believes the oil companies wouldn't pass that on to the consumer must sure believe in Santa Claus."

Spring of 1972 found the Santa Barbara Channel with only one exploration rig at work. Union Oil drilling a 12,000 foot well from Platform B and Humble Oil had suspended exploratory drilling while it awaited approval of its production application, one so massive it weighed 55 pounds. A reminder of the Problem Platform spill turned up in the form of oil soaked spoil at the harbor entrance, where sand was being dredged. The oil was thought to be that sunk when the harbor was invaded with the stuff, and it wasn't long before some beaches took on that familiar color, consistency and smell which had so enraged Santa "Barbarians." The dredge was shut down for a couple of days, although Public Works Director W. D. Hogle saw the problem as belonging not to his department but to Union Oil, the *News-Press* quoting him as saying, "They put it there."

A delegation from Santa Barbara went to Washington in April to testify against Channel development at a Senate joint committee hearing of Interior, Public Works, Commerce and Atomic Energy committee members studying energy policy. These committees outnumbered the members, only Senator Frank Moss (D. Utah) being present to listen to the testimony. The witnesses, however disheartened (and at least one much angered), went ahead with their statements. Supervisor Clyde said, "The reason we didn't realize the threat of pollution before the blow-out is that we were reassured, time and again, by the industry and by the Interior Department that technology was such that there would be no pollution. They said they had perfected shut-off devices that were fool-proof, even in such disasters as a ship running into the platform or an earthquake. We were wrong to believe this, but those of us in decision making positions did accept these protestations of perfection."

The presence of only a single committee member and the small audience didn't deter GOO!'s energetic president, Mrs. Sidenberg, either. She stated that the consumer is now subsidizing oil companies at a rate of 4 billion dollars a year through depletion allowances, import quotas and production controls. She went on to quote the Smithsonian Institution's figure of 9,700 reported oil spills in 1971 and added that over 2,000 drilling facilities off U.S. shores routinely discharge some oil and use detergents and dispersants, many of which are thought to be toxic. Another witness, Robert C. Sharp, a retired drilling company vice-president, made the point that oil companies usually let contracts for drilling rather than doing their own, and that since human error is a greater cause of blowouts and pollution than equipment failure, the companies should be obliged to require proof of training and expertise on the part of drilling employees. He quoted the *Oil & Gas Journal* as saying that "in the 10 year period between 1960 and 1970, blowouts cost the industry over 200 million dollars." He added that since the Santa Barbara disaster, insurance coverage against the hazards of offshore drilling is unobtainable.

"If the Channel spill would happen today," he quoted the Secretary of the Union Oil Company as saying, "we would not be covered for the liability. It is not possible to buy pollution insurance for offshore operations."

Even though the Channel continued to be relatively quiet, GOO! wasn't taking it for granted that the battle was won, or even near it. Among the needles it used to keep its membership alert to the fight ahead was a reminder that even by the time the spill was 1200 days old, the Problem Platform was still leaking more than 800 gallons of crude per day; that although 70 OCS related bills were pending in Congress, in three and a half years not one had gotten out of committee; that of the 6,362 oil spills in U.S. coastal waters from September, 1970, through June, 1971, 20 percent were caused by offshore facilities; that Humble proposed production in over 800 feet of water, although 380 feet has been the production limit because of diver capability, and that operations would have to be monitored by TV and repairs made by robots.

While oil companies were able to point to the millions being spent in research for spill control and cleanup, the Coast Guard produced a discouraging report of a test with a new boom used in coralling a deliberate spill of soy bean oil. It found that as soon as a current above one knot is encountered oil slips under the barrier, and that in waves over 5 feet oil splashed over the barrier and dispersed into the water. News of the test did little to reassure Santa Barbarans, and news of projected tanker size didn't help either.

"If they keep getting bigger," says a harbor tug engineer, "something's got to give. Like the ocean rising higher."

Even without them, the ocean is rising —3 inches in 8 years— and if it continues for 30 years it will be catastrophic for the coastal areas. *The New York Times* quotes an oceanographer with the Department of Commerce, S. D. Hicks, who calls it "unprecedented." Expressing concern about unduly alarming the public, he added that "there is nothing to worry about in one man's lifetime." Among the possible causes for this rise, Hicks explained, could be a combination of the sea rising and the land sinking, due to glacier melting and the growing amount of water and petroleum being removed from below ground. The latter possibility raises a new question about development of OCS resources, and it is one in which New York Staters who live on the coast will find no comfort. Already, 47 percent of those 600-odd miles are undergoing "widespread loss of land and property," and Long Island's South Shore alone suffers more than $9,000,000 in damage yearly. These residents would take issue with the tug engineer's line, arguing that something better stop giving.

Summer justified the efforts of GOO! in trying to keep the natives restless, for the ban Secretary Morton had placed on Channel operations to give Congress time to debate bills terminating some leases with due compensation to the oil companies, was negated by a decision of a U.S. district court. It found that the Secretary had no authority to suspend operations for such a purpose and ordered that the complainants in the action—Gulf, Mobil, Texaco and Union Oil—be reissued exploratory drilling permits, extending them by 32 months. The dismay of Santa Barbarans was reflected in their demand for an appeal, supported by Senators Cranston and Tunney. They claimed that such a decision could have been avoided if the Secretary had denied permits on the basis of environmental impact.

"Congress has shirked the special environmental responsibilities it owes to residents of California," the *Los Angeles Times* quoted the Senators as saying. "And the Interior Department is not far behind . . . it has consistently been unwilling to consider environmental values when they conflict with the production of oil."

Long Island was not short on reminders of the pollution threat facing them during the winter and spring of 1972—oil kept appearing on the beaches (much of it from undetermined sources, in spite of the investigative techniques of the Coast Guard), a tanker stranded causing a major spill off New London (an improperly licensed pilot mistaking a shore light for a navigational one), and Port Jefferson not only experienced a grounded tanker blocking its harbor, another one broke in half after discharging cargo. Ironically, there were conservationists who found themselves espousing the cause of a pipeline running east and west to reduce the tank truck traffic on what is known as the world's longest parking lot, the Long Island Expressway. By early summer, offshore exploratory operations became active, paralelled by onshore politics. This was not unexpected; as one candidate said, "It's not so much that oil makes a campaign run smoother, it's that it can fuel a dead issue into a burning one."

Assembly Speaker and lobster dealer Duryea, seen by many as a 1974 front runner for governor of New York should Rockefeller not try for a fifth term (and to judge by growing press references to his family's connection with Standard Oil, there are those who are determined he won't), began developing himself as a maritime conservationist. He opposed offshore drilling and foreign over-fishing by what he calls vacuum-cleaner ships.

"Ecology used to be a hobby for many," the *Long Island*

Press quotes Duryea as saying. "To all of us now, and certainly to our children, it may mean the difference between life and death."

Long Islanders did not find the conflicting statements regarding offshore plans that came out of Washington helpful. The confusion grew with each statement, and all that seemed sure was that exploratory drilling would continue. Dr. Henry Berryhill, chief of the U.S.G.S. Office of Marine Geology, announced that core drilling would be carried on off the George's Bank area of the OCS, about 100 miles east of Cape Cod and about 200 miles off Montauk Point. In the previous summer an oil company consortium had made seismological studies over 3,000 square miles and $10,000,000 was said to have been spent. A state senator observed that "they wouldn't be throwing that kind of money into the ocean if they didn't think there was oil out there." The day after Berryhill's announcement, Nassau County Comptroller Angelo Roncallo returned from a meeting with Secretary Morton in Washington. He quoted the Secretary as saying that there will not be any drilling for oil in the Atlantic Ocean off Long Island "in the foreseeable future," adding that there would be no oil drilling in the Sound because it is under state rather than federal jurisdiction and there is no oil there anyway.

The reassurance those statements brought were dissipated in early June. Governor Rockefeller vetoed a bill introduced by Glen Cove Assemblyman Joseph Reilly that would prohibit drilling for oil or gas in state waters and in the Atlantic within three miles of Long Island. The Governor maintained that the bill could "inhibit attempts to achieve a balance between environmental interests and the need for legitimate gas and oil exploration." Environmentalist response was summed up by the president of the Suffolk Conservation Council, Charles Pulaski: "The only thing we can do now is buckle down and fight a little harder—apparently the Governor isn't running for re-election because if he were, he'd be playing a different tune as far as ecology on Long Island is concerned."

In spite of Morton's statement about oil drilling in "the foreseeable future," the Department of Interior announced on June 16 a five year program to lease offshore oil and gas rights off Long Island, in addition to areas in the Gulfs of Mexico and Alaska. Reaction was immediate and loud, and some towns changed their zoning codes to prevent either oil storage depots or supply bases for offshore operations. Karl Grossman quoted Congressman Otis Pike's chief aide, Aaron Donner, as saying that the Nixon administration planned to open the Atlantic for drilling "immediately after the election" if it is returned to office.

"The oil industry," Donner told a Montauk meeting, "is used to dealing with irate citizens' groups. They think you'll get tired. They want to wear you out, grind you down, to seduce you. They'll give you parks and marinas. They'll imply America and the Lord and oil have a lot in common. You'll be assaulted at every angle. There'll be slight amendments to local laws, constant erosions. . . . This battle will never end. If I bring you any message, it's that of stamina and vigilant."

As *Newsday* pointed out, the Democratic plank on offshore operations was more like a splinter. ("We support the monitoring and strict enforcement of all safety regulations on all offshore drilling equipment and environmentally safe construction of all tankers transporting oil"), but Senator George McGovern accused the Nixon administration of an "unconscionable sellout," calling it a rape of the environment.

"The only rational explanation," Grossman quotes McGovern as saying, "is that the oil interests have befriended through their support the Nixon administration. Secretary Morton obviously has not learned the tragic lesson of Santa Barbara."

The announcement of the oil and gas lease sale had been scheduled for December, 1971, originally, but three environmental groups—Friends of the Earth, the Sierra Club and the Natural Resources Defense Council—had obtained a court injunction claiming that the department's environmental impact statement was deficient. Observers on the side of the environment were disheartened by the news that the three groups didn't plan further legal moves. Word of it coincided with the sailing from Casco Bay, Me., of the Norwegian tanker *Tamano*, which had spilled about 100,000 gallons of Bunker C oil after striking a ledge two weeks earlier in Hussey Sound. The total claims in lawsuits brought for damages was 115 million dollars, and the ship was released after an insurance company filed a letter of assurance for 1 million dollars (a form of commitment to pay up if the ship's owners are found liable for damages). The ledge is known as a killer, and among the vessels claimed is the battleship *Iowa*, which spilled 50,000 barrels of Bunker C in World War II.

As if in support of Secretary Morton's approval of the trans-Alaska pipeline on the basis of "national interest," the Administration authorized an increase in the importation of foreign oil by a daily 230,000 barrels. A plus for conservationists came in Canadian reaction to the approval of the line, summed up by its Minister of External Affairs, Mitchell Sharp, who called it "a very, very foolish move." Among the 60 Congressmen who promised a fight all the way to the Supreme Court is Rep. Aspin, who attacked the approval as "a blatant example of the interest of the oil industry superseding that of the consumer."

Canadian objections were increased by a 12,000 gallon tanker spill of crude at Cherry Point, Wash., which resulted in the fouling of 5 miles of British Columbia beaches. To some Canadians it symbolized loss of control of their environment and U.S. dominance. The growing tension was underlined in a letter to *The New York Times* by Thornton F. Bradshaw, president of Atlantic Richfield, which is a partner in Alyeska:

"It is entirely possible that some Canadian interests would welcome a pipeline for Canadian oil built across Canadian territory and financed by American companies. But . . . can any reasonable person believe that the operation of such a pipeline, including the setting of the rates charged for its use, would not become a convenient source of friction and controversy?

"It is precisely because a trans-Canadian pipeline is so obviously a spurious rather than a serious alternative to the Alaska pipeline that it is worth discussing."

The delays caused in construction of the line by environmentalists' legal maneuvers have been expensive for Alyeska, and Arthur M. Louis reported in *Fortune* that David Brower, president of Friends of the Earth, was still optimistic about eventual victory.

"It's my kooky thought," Louis quotes Brower as saying, "that some day we're going to get a grant from the oil companies for saving them from a horrible mistake."

Such is the present economic plight of Alaskans due to the pipeline delay that it may be quite a few days before Friends of the Earth can feel wholly safe in the company of friends of the pipeline. Among the latter is Fred Hartley, president of Union Oil (a partner in Alyeska). *West* magazine quotes him in an interview:

"People oppose this pipeline because they just don't want it to be built—period. It isn't a question of being irrational. It's more sinister than that, actually. I don't know who's behind the Sierra Club, but it obviously isn't people of good will. Not sincere environmentalists. Those same people are using energy. You show me an environmentalist who walks, really walks, doesn't just put on a sweat suit on Sunday morning, and I'll recognize this man as a contributor to the elimination of pollution. But they're all hypocrites.

"What stands in the way of that pipeline now is unemployed lawyers making a living off of misled people who supply dues and fees to environmentalist groups that are perhaps led by men of ill will."

The interview was published before the death of Union's public relations manager, Fritz Springmann, in July 1971. He was said to have collapsed at his desk from exhaustion during the Problem Platform disaster, and almost exactly a year later another figure in that crisis died. Dr. William T. Pecora, an outstanding geologist, was respected by many on both sides of the environmental struggle. His candor led him to tell a Santa Barbara meeting, in the midst of the spill furor, "You will have pollution here. Face it. Get used to it. The oil rigs are here to stay."

Such advice might be reflected on by the House Public Works Committee in light of its having reported out a water pollution bill considerably diluted by what observers see as the demands of special interests. Passed unanimously in stronger form by the Senate, the Committee's action brought forth sharp comments from a coalition of labor and environmentalists. "It is evidence," said a spokesman, "that the Committee has caved in to Administration and industy pressure."

At least some of the environmental bills stuck in committee may one day reduce the amount of plastic residue encountered by Woods Hole Oceanographic scientists in their nets while sampling marine life in the Sargasso Sea. Many pieces were intact enough to be recognized as cigar holders, needle shields for syringes and jewelry fasteners, and the find spread over an area of more than 1,000 square miles. Minute organisms had attached themselves to many of the objects, raising the possibility that an increase in population of certain species might occur with unknown results on the balance of life in the area. Another unknown and a more disturbing possibility is that a plasticizer (polychlorinated biphenyl), which has much in common with the properties of DDT, is being released as the plastic materials break down. As to degradable plastics, the problem is how to avoid having them degrade too soon.

"Hard to get ahead, isn't it?" says a worrier, convinced that we will be buried in our garbage. "We used to complain that plastic gadgets didn't hold up long enough, now they hold up too long."

Another industrial product, even more indestructible, is finding its last resting place in the ocean, too. Old tires have been found to make fine artificial reefs, to the delight of anglers; but those who hope to alter our view of the ocean as a convenient dump are not sanguine. One estimate sees tires in the billions going down to the ocean floor, and the industry claims that it is by far the most pollution free means of getting rid of them, even if the handling cost runs as high as 40 cents each. Says a marine biologist, "We don't know that they won't break down in sea water eventually. We do know, though, what tires are made of. When they start returning to their elements, those happy fishermen are going to be taking home pretty sick catches."

Half truths have a way of behaving like boomerangs claim some environmentalists. They point to a Mobil ad downplaying the Problem Platform spill:

"Santa Barbara was a bad accident but no disaster. . . . The channel has long since been clean and so have the beaches. . . . Dr. Dale Straughan, a marine biologist at the University of Southern California, recently led a team of 40 scientists in a biological examination of the affected area. Conclusion: environmental damage was minor and temporary, and is well on the mend. . . . Within three months the bird population in the area had not only returned to normal, but had actually increased. . . . The need to find new oil is as urgent as the need to protect our environment."

To them, Mobil goes along with Union's Fred Hartley calling a disaster an event in which a death takes place, and they take issue with the channel and beaches being clean one month after the ad appeared. They feel that a fair appraisal of the Straughan study should mention its financing (the oil industry) and that respected scientists take issue with both its approach and its findings. As to the increase in the bird population, they insist that whole truth would demand that the migratory stage at the time be examined.

These critics were amused by a company not unknown to Mobil, Esso, coming up in an 8 page spread in *Harper's* magazine in June 1972, with truth so whole that one wonders which cause the copywriter thought he was working for. Writing of research on oil spill cleanups, he says, "Surprisingly, most authorities agree ordinary, plentiful straw is still one of the most effective ways to absorb oil." This example of reseach progress confirms the thinking which would postpone offshore production until efficient spill control and cleanup techniques are available. It may even make David Brower wonder if the oil companies aren't about to make him a grant, after all. They are not encouraged by a recent discovery by a microbiologist, Robert Nuzzi, at the New York Ocean Science Laboratory in Montauk, however. He has found in experiments that domestic heating oil leaves an unidentified toxic substance on being removed from water, even after the water is distilled and filtered. This discovery tends to confirm the conclusions of Dr. Blumer, who had stated on the basis of his observations that "oil is much more persistent and destructive to marine organisms and man's marine food resources than scientists had thought."

The deputy head of the E.P.A., Robert W. Fri, says that it is cheaper to spend 100 billion dollars plus to clean up the environment than to continue present pollution. It is costing us 25 billion dollars a year to live with pollution, he claims, and puts cleanup costs at 38 billion dollars for water, 23 billion for air and around 43 billion for garbage. In some cases, Fri feels, pollution controls can mean greater production efficiency.

What the future will bring in terms of a clean environment

time will tell. There will be many clockwatchers and there should be, but short of a major nuclear catastrophe, neither fossil fuels nor the hours will run out before we can have the kind of air, water and land we want. As with oil production, however, there has to be demand. And that is up to us.

Our voyage has yet to begin, but we are standing by. Our cargo consists of man's responsibility to himself and his environment. After a few more pollution disasters the order will come to let go the lines. Then the course will be entered in the log, the helmsman will steer steady as she goes, the engine room telegraph will ring down Full Ahead and our ship will be outward bound with a bone in her teeth.

With good seamanship, determined watch-keeping and fair winds, we will make port safe at last. Its name is Future.